MONEY
FOR
NOTHING

Stories of Michigan's Million-Dollar Lottery Winners

by

JERRY DENNIS

Friede Publications

Money For Nothing:

Stories of Michigan's Million-Dollar Lottery Winners

Copyright, 1988, by Jerry Dennis

Friede Publications
2339 Venezia Drive
Davison, Michigan 48423

Printed in the United States of America
First printing, September 1988

ISBN 0-9608588-8-1

For my son Aaron.
A winner if I've ever seen one.

Acknowledgments

I owe thanks to many people who have been helpful in the research and writing of this book. First, of course, are the lottery winners themselves, many of whom are trying very hard to live normal lives and would rather not be bothered by writers and reporters. That they opened their doors to me is not a tribute to my powers of persuasion—it is a tribute to their generosity and open-heartedness.

Thanks also to Paul Maurer for support that helped make the early stages of my research possible, and for his continued friendship and encouragement.

Special thanks to my lovely and talented wife, Gail, for inspiration, assistance, and for her ruthless and always on-the-mark criticisms of my work.

I am grateful to my parents, Gerald and Eva Dennis, for the unflagging, unconditional, and sometimes unearned belief they have in their children and for their suggestions and criticisms of the manuscript.

Thanks are due to Nancy Quick and Laurie Kipp-Klecha of the Michigan Bureau of State Lottery for their patience with my persistent and sometimes nagging questions. Although they were glad to help when they could, it should be made clear that this book does not represent the aims or views of the Michigan Bureau of State Lottery and is not in any way associated with, underwritten by, or endorsed by that bureau.

And last, but not least, thanks to my editor at Friede Publications, Gary Barfknecht, who conceived the idea of this book, suggested I write it, then stepped graciously aside and served as outstanding editor, advisor and friend.

Contents

Introduction

There is no such thing as a free lunch, the saying goes . . . unless you're born rich or win the lottery.

For millions of people in Michigan, the lottery is considered, at least occasionally, as hope for an unconditional, no-strings-attached free lunch. Or, to be more accurate, it's hope for a lifetime of free lunches, because most people are determined if they win to invest wisely and control their spending so that 20 years' worth of annual lottery checks will grow into a nest egg so large the nest will need additions and renovations. They'll live on the interest it earns. They'll have accountants automatically pay bills and taxes and send modest, but adequate, allowance checks every month for fun money. And because they've invested wisely and used uncommonly good judgment, those allowance checks will keep coming—to their children, their children's children—forever.

Dreams? Maybe. But what's the lottery about if not dreaming? It's the great dream machine. It's the incredible long shot with the incredible payoff. The chance of hitting it big—really big—is so slim as to be virtually nonexistent. Yet this country's 24 lottery states are creating new millionaires nearly every day. In Michigan alone at the beginning of 1988, 280 people had won million-dollar or larger jackpots, with new millionaires being created at the rate of nearly six a month. At that pace, by the year 2000 there will be more than 1,100 big winners, enough to populate a fair-size city of their own. Call it Big Bucks, Michigan—pave the streets with gold, then line them with banks.

But are we really talking "big bucks" when we talk about most lottery winners? Is winning everything it's cut out to be? Are there really any free lunches? Every million-dollar (or more) winner—from Hermus Millsaps, Michigan's first, to whoever redeems the next winning Super

Lotto ticket at the Lansing office of the lottery bureau—has a unique story to tell and an entire set of hard-earned opinions about what it means to have large sums of money dumped into one's lap.

The stories of some of the big-bucks winners are in this book, but it is not a complete account, by any means. Many winners prefer to live quietly and anonymously, and have shielded themselves so completely from strangers that even intrepid journalists can't always break through to them. Most make the switch to unlisted telephone numbers. Some treat all requests, even harmless ones, with caution or outright suspicion and mistrust, and have made it abundantly clear that the last thing they want is more publicity.

Also, this book does not pretend to be a complete study of the lottery in Michigan. If its scope were that broad it would have to include several early lotteries, beginning with the 1808 effort to raise $6,000 for a road from Detroit to near Toledo and ending in 1829 with the Michigan Lottery, which was initiated to raise $10,000 to eliminate toll bridges on the road between Detroit and Monroe. During that period, other local lotteries attempted to raise money for a variety of projects: a new fire engine and the first city library for Detroit, for example.

Such lotteries were common in the United States in the early 19th century, when—according to John Samuel Ezell's exhaustive study of early lotteries in America, *Fortune's Merry Wheel*, (Harvard University Press, Cambridge, 1960)—as many as 24 of the 33 states held "internal improvement" lotteries. All those early efforts in Detroit, by the way, apparently failed. And as far as I have been able to learn, there are no records that tell what the lives of Michigan's very first lottery winners were like or, in fact, whether there even *were* any winners.

Michigan's modern lottery winners, on the other hand, are a matter of clear record. Most are still living; most remain residents of Michigan; and some, when approached with courtesy and consideration, are more than willing to talk about their experiences.

Who are these people? They're anybody. The nature of lotteries assures that. They are a representative cross section of all the people who play the lottery. They are factory workers and bank managers, housewives and businesswomen. They are young and old, white and black. They are common people with common (believe it or not) problems who have been struck by uncommon fortune. They have been singled out and branded as extraordinary by that mysterious, elusive, capricious thing we call luck.

The Fortune Machine

It has been a long time since Hermus Millsaps had his moment of glory. Fifteen years in fact. Not that he's counting. His life is much quieter now, but not so quiet that he has nothing more to do than look back over 68 years of highs and lows. As we talk this January 1988 evening, he is just one of the hopefuls who have put up money for a chance at the Michigan lottery's largest prize ever, a $28.9 million Super Lotto jackpot. And, like all but five of the millions who played, he is a loser. His $20 wager has gained him nothing, and another week's dream is now obsolete.

"Who needs that much money, anyway?" he asks. "A person couldn't spend 22 million dollars." When he talks it is with the drawling, long vowels of the Tennessee hill country he left when he was a young man, 40 years ago. "Besides," he goes on, "I don't mind losin'. I consider it my little donation to help support the lottery, which is only fair. After all, the lottery's been supportin' me for 15 years."

Ask Hermus Millsaps what he remembers best about the night 15 years ago when he became the first million-dollar winner of Michigan's new lottery, and some of the old glory comes back to him. You can hear it in his voice when he tells about the rabbit's foot he carried onto the stage that day and how the other finalists stepped down, one after another, and left him standing alone.

"I've still got the old rabbit's foot," he says. "But the hair's about all worn off it now."

He has always contended that it was that rabbit's foot, dyed chartreuse and mounted on a brass key chain, that brought him his moment of good fortune. When he put it into

1

his pocket that February 1973 morning after paying 59 cents for it in a Lansing dimestore, he was an ordinary working man, a $176-a-week laborer at a Detroit automobile plant. When he pulled it out later that evening, he was a celebrity. He squeezed it in his hand when he became the last finalist and stood alone at the center of the stage surrounded by blaring music, popping flashbulbs, and a shouting, applauding audience. And he held it in the air as reporters rushed at him and one shouted above the others:

"Hermus Millsaps! How does it feel to be a millionaire?"

His answer came from a place far beyond words. It came from somewhere in the foothills of the east Tennessee mountains, a land of small farms sliced neatly by railroad tracks, a place only a barefoot boy in dungarees would remember.

Hermus Millsaps closed his eyes, raised his arms high in triumph and roared like a Santa Fe freight train.

◆

It was Monday, November 13, 1972, and the start of an ordinary week in America. The Paris Peace Talks were about to stall amid disagreements over a proposed cease-fire in Vietnam. A Southern Airways DC-9, with a total of 31 crew members and passengers aboard, would be hijacked to Cuba, where the hijackers, after failing to collect a $10 million ransom, would be taken into custody by Cuban police. A storm would strike portions of the Midwest, and high winds and flooding would cause extensive property damage. The Dow Jones Industrial Average would close, for the first time in its history, above the

2

1,000-point mark—an economic high that some forecasters would claim was a harbinger of good times to come.

In Michigan, meanwhile, the week promised to be anything but ordinary. By 8 o'clock Monday morning, thousands of customers had lined up outside grocery, liquor and department stores, banks, pharmacies and other outlets to legally purchase—for the first time in Michigan since 1829—lottery tickets. Six months earlier, the citizens of the state had voted, 2-1, to establish a Michigan Bureau of State Lottery, and interest had steadily grown since. Now, with tickets finally on sale, that interest exploded into a frenzy.

Even before the day was over, sales at almost all 7,000 licensed lottery outlets had surpassed even the most optimistic expectations. A Port Austin liquor-store owner, for example, reported that in the first six hours of business, all but one of his customers had bought tickets. The lottery bureau's manager of the Upper Peninsula announced in amazement that that region's entire allotment of 370,000 tickets was in danger of disappearing. When Hudson's in downtown Detroit opened that morning, customers were lined up 20 deep. By closing time that store and several other Hudson's had sold nearly half of their week's allotment of 100,000 tickets. Many outlets around the state sold out completely. A Detroit cafeteria's 2,000-ticket supply, for instance, ran out within hours. The lottery's first day left officials reeling.

By the end of the week, they were staggering. Nearly six million tickets had been sold. The state of Michigan had netted a profit of $1,510,189, thousands of vendors had earned commissions, and several million people owned small, green slips of paper potentially worth $25 to $1 million. At the very least, those slips of paper, at a cost of 50 cents each, were good for a week's worth of dreaming.

One of the dreamers was Marilyn Moore, a 48-year-old homemaker from St. Clair Shores. Early in the week her husband, William, a steamfitter for Chrysler, stopped for lunch at a Detroit pizza parlor and purchased six tickets. That same evening, he offered three to Marilyn. She chose one with a 544 on it, because four had always been her lucky number, then waited until the end of the week for the announcement of the winning numbers.

◆

3

The players of Michigan's first lottery game had no role in the selection of the numbers they bet on. Tickets came preprinted with two sets of three-digit numbers, such as 123 and 456, and the buyer had no choice but to take them in the order they came, then wait until the end of the week for the selection of the winning numbers.

The first winning numbers were drawn November 24, 1972, in Cobo Arena at Detroit. Not surprisingly, the event was decked out in all the gala trappings of a circus. Clowns and a joking, taunting master of ceremonies entertained the crowd of 4,000 spectators, and the Detroit Police Band played tunes such as "The Best Things in Life are Free" and "We're in the Money."

Placed in full view in the middle of the arena's stage was the center of attention—a contraption suitably dubbed the Fortune Machine. At its heart was a large, transparent-plastic drum. Behind it were high racks lined with rows of small colored balls, each painted with a number from 000 to 999. The thousand balls were arranged in sequence with the numbers facing outward so that any skeptical ticket holders could see if, indeed, the numbers printed on their lottery tickets were represented. Though designed to select random numbers as efficiently and flawlessly as possible, the Fortune Machine was also as garishly decorated as a fortune-teller's booth at a carnival. It seemed to suggest a link between pure chance and prophecy, between science and superstition.

At 11 a.m. the crowd quieted, and the balls began to roll to the ends of the racks, where they then funneled down a tube into the plastic drum. For a moment they stopped, bottled up in the neck of the drum until a human arm poked through the curtains at the back of the stage and shook the rack. The balls broke free and began rolling again.

When the last of the balls had dropped into the drum, it began to rotate, tumbling and mixing the colorful numbered spheres. An attendant then stopped it and tipped it up on end. From a hole in the bottom, 10 balls dribbled out, one at a time, and settled into a row of 10 numbered cups.

Then, also on stage, Governor William Milliken stood beside a small rotating plastic globe which contained 10 unmarked envelopes. When it stopped, he paused in indecision for a moment, then reached inside, pulled out an envelope and unsealed it. The slip of paper he then removed was printed with the name of a racehorse (Big Red Hog) and the number 3, the horse's post position when it had won at the Detroit

4

Race Course on July 19, 1971. The name of the horse and the race date had absolutely nothing to do with the selection of the winning lottery numbers.* What mattered was the number beside it. That number—in this case, 3—determined which of the numbered cups beneath the large drum held a ball with a winning number. Cup 3 contained a ball with the number 130 on it. The governor chose another envelope—horse Kenavo, number 6—and the process was repeated. A ball with the number 544 was plucked from cup 6, and Michigan had its first set of winning lottery numbers.

Those first two numbers—130 and 544—created over 24,000 winning tickets from the Michigan lottery's first week of sales. They also prepared the way for two important events. The first was the Super Prize Drawing, in which nine people with tickets matching both 130 and 544 would compete for prizes of $10,000, $50,000 and $200,000. The second event was the Million Dollar Drawing, in which 120 semifinalists would be chosen from the thousands of people whose tickets matched only one of the numbers, either 130 or 544. Those tickets won $25 and were automatically entered into a drawing for further prizes of $1,000 to $1 million.

That such large amounts of money were about to be handed out, no strings attached, caught at the imaginations of nearly everyone. Only six states—New Hampshire, New York, New Jersey, Connecticut, Massachusetts and Pennsylvania—had begun lotteries before Michigan, and of them, only New York and New Jersey had given away jackpots of $1 million or more. Six- and seven-figure prizes attracted nationwide attention, excited people, stirred imaginations. "What would you do if you won a million dollars?" became one of the most frequently asked questions of the decade. And nearly everyone had a ready answer for it. So when the first Michigan residents were about to be given the opportunity to demonstrate what they would do

---

*The racehorse connection was nothing more than a method, modeled after one first used in New Hampshire in 1963, to circumvent federal excise taxes on lotteries. Tying the game, even superficially, to racetrack parimutuel betting made it, by Internal Revenue Service definition, a sweepstakes, not a lottery, and exempted the state from paying a 10 percent federal tax on ticket sales. In early 1975 a new law exempted state-run lotteries from federal taxes, and the racehorse connection was no longer necessary.

with that kind of money, not just talk about it, there is little wonder that the rest of us sat up and took notice.

On Thursday, November 30, nine people whose tickets had matched both 130 and 544 took the stage at the Lansing National Guard Armory for the first Super Prize Drawing. Like the drawing a week earlier at Cobo Arena, this event took place in a carnival-like atmosphere and was officiated by luminaries, including Lt. Governor James Brickley. In what would become standard practice at Michigan lottery drawings, the people whose names were selected first were awarded the smallest prizes. Three winners' names were drawn, and each was presented with a $10,000 check. Then five more names were matched to $50,000 prizes.

The survivor of that elimination process and the winner of the Michigan lottery's first six-figure jackpot, $200,000, was Marilyn Moore, the St. Clair Shores woman whose husband had purchased her winning ticket at a Detroit pizza parlor. "Nothing good has happened to me in my whole life," she told reporters after the drawing. "The only good thing that's ever happened to me," she then added, "is when I married my husband." She also said that the only prize she had ever won before was a dozen doughnuts.

Though Marilyn Moore's story made headlines in most Michigan newspapers the next day, bigger news was yet to come. Each week, thousands of people whose tickets matched one of the two winning numbers held to the hope that they would become finalists in the first Million Dollar Drawing. After redeeming their winning ticket at a lottery office, each of the winners had received a $25 check by mail. Printed on each check stub was a six-digit number. When ticket sales totaled 30 million, those six-digit numbers would be entered in a drawing. From that pool, 120 semifinalists would be selected and would automatically win $1,000. Ten of the 120 would, in turn, be chosen for a final drawing. Nine of them would then be awarded prizes of $5,000, $50,000 or $100,000.

One would become the Michigan lottery's first million-dollar winner.

The First Millionaire

"Buy a ticket and you buy a dream."
—Mary O'Dell, Michigan lottery winner

F ebruary 22, 1973, promised to be a very long day for Hermus and Ann Millsaps. Well before daylight after a night of little sleep, they dressed in their best clothes. For Hermus that meant putting on a freshly ironed shirt, a sports jacket, and a clean pair of the ordinary work trousers he wore every day to his job as a sawman for Chrysler. It occurred to him that by the end of the day he might be able to afford a new suit.

Born in 1920 and raised on a farm in the eastern Tennessee hamlet of Emory Gap, Hermus Millsaps was one of nine children. Like his brothers and sisters and many of his friends, he did not attend much school, quitting after the sixth grade to help on the farm. Then, like many others in the South of that era, he was lured north to Detroit by employment opportunities in the auto plants. He hired on at Chrysler in 1947, when he was 27 years old. Twenty-six years later, after marrying and raising three sons, he earned $4.57 an hour cutting up scrap wood and pallets. Money was so scarce at times that Hermus often had to take a second job to make ends meet.

Adding to those hard times, in 1969, after two of his sons were grown and on their own, Hermus' first marriage ended in divorce.

A few years later, at Julia's Bar in Dearborn, he met Ann, a widow with two grown sons. That night at Julia's, where she often went to attend polka dances, Ann was so distressed to see "the hillbilly who just ran around on the dance floor" that, she later jokingly explained, she wanted to marry Hermus so she could teach him to dance a proper polka.

They were married March 1, 1972, and bought a small one-bedroom house in Taylor. Ann spent her time gardening, sewing and taking care of the household. Hermus worked, listened to country music and enjoyed a cold beer now and then in the evenings. Occasionally they went with friends to a movie or dance.

They had very little extra money, but each week Hermus managed to buy four or five of the new 50-cent lottery tickets. He liked the idea of the lottery and enjoyed spending lunch hours at the plant talking with his friends about what they would do if they won. Hermus' ideas about the subject were not grandiose, but neither were they terribly modest. They definitely did not include staying on at Chrysler.

One day in mid-December he bought tickets at the Vermont Drug Store in Taylor. That week one of the winning numbers, 792, matched the number on one of his tickets. He redeemed it and, a few weeks later, received a check in the mail for $25. The six-digit number on his check stub automatically went into a pool with about 120,000 others.

Two months later, Hermus had been selected as one of the 120 semifinalists in the first Million Dollar Drawing, and he and Ann rushed around the house getting ready for the trip to Lansing. The 80-mile-plus drive from Taylor was too far to risk on the bald tires of their 1961 Chrysler, they decided. So instead, they packed sack lunches and caught the 7:10 a.m. Greyhound.

They were at the Lansing Civic Center by 10 that morning and sat in the audience to watch the drawing of the latest weekly winning numbers. Hermus pulled that week's tickets from his pockets and checked them. One was a $25 winner. It seemed like a good omen. Then to kill time until the Grand Drawing, he and Ann wandered through stores in downtown Lansing. At a dimestore Hermus bought a chartreuse rabbit's foot mounted on a key chain and put it in his pocket for luck.

That evening, Hermus Millsaps and the other 119 semifinalists converged upon the Civic Center. As they registered in the lottery arena, 110 who had failed to be selected in a preliminary drawing were handed a check for $1,000, congratulated, and instructed to join the audience. The remaining 10 finalists, dazed and shaken, were led to the stage and seated in front of several thousand spectators. In a few moments, nine of those finalists would pocket checks ranging from $5,000 to $100,000.

And one would become a millionaire.

Or would he? Michigan, following the lead of New York and New Jersey, had implemented a plan to award major prizes in installments rather than in lump sums. The plan was met with a good deal of suspicion and skepticism. The lottery bureau probably invested the million-dollar prize, people groused, and paid the winner out of the interest it earned. That way, at the end of 20 years when the winner was paid off, the lottery bureau would still have the $1 million principal.

But in fact the lottery bureau is left with nothing at the end of those 20 years. The bureau retains none of the principal, and the earned interest is used, in effect, to create lesser prizes. (See Appendix VI, p. 202.)

There are other advantages to the installment plan, the lottery bureau is quick to point out. One, spreading the money out over a number of years reduces the federal income-tax bite (Michigan lottery winnings, as of 1988, are exempt from Michigan state income tax). Also, the annual payments lower the chances of a winner being wiped out by poor investments or unchecked spending.

In spite of such good arguments, the fact remains that receiving $1 million in installments over a period of 20 years does not automatically make a winner a millionaire. That is a point that most million-dollar winners will argue, sometimes bitterly. Fifty-grand a year, they say, doesn't even lift them out of the middle class, and it certainly doesn't free them from such middle-class concerns as taxes, house payments, medical bills and retirement plans.

If they received their million in a lump sum, they wouldn't have to worry about such mundane matters. They would invest the principal and live off the interest. Their $1 million would earn $100,000-$150,000 a year, forever, and they'd never have to touch the principal. They would cruise the Caribbean on their yachts, buy a new Mercedes every couple of years, and take month-long shopping trips to Europe.

On the other hand, theoretically it shouldn't be hard to turn an extra $50,000 a year for 20 years into $1 million. If it is invested into a safe account earning 7.4 percent interest, $50,000 a year plus accumulated interest would add up to over $1 million in about 12 years.

By the end of 20 years the total would swell to over $2 million. But, of course, that is only if the winner has another source of income that covers living expenses and income taxes—taxes that will increase dramatically as the worth of the investment increases—and if the winner can resist the considerable temptation to spend some of that money.

As the 10 finalists for the first Michigan Million Dollar Drawing stood on stage in Lansing, such subtleties were far from their minds. One of them was about to become a millionaire, pure and simple. Everyone said so. Reporters assumed it. Headlines blared it.

One of those finalists was 23-year-old Roy Arthur Renner of Montrose, who at the time was employed as a shop worker at Fisher Body in Flint. Because of his age and because he carried his 7-week-old daughter on the stage with him, he became the crowd's favorite to win the grand prize. When he was interviewed briefly on stage by master-of-ceremonies John Quinn, deputy director of the lottery, he explained that he had learned he was a semifinalist the same day his daughter, Mickie Lynn, was born. He carried her now, he said, because "if she brought me that much luck, I'd better have her with me all the way."

Then, officials reached into a tumbler and, one by one, pulled out envelopes containing the finalists' names and placed them in slots designated by prize amounts. Seven envelopes went into $5,000 slots, and one each went into a $50,000, $100,000, and $1,000,000 slot. The $5,000 awards were presented first and went to: Robert W. Cunningham, a 32-year-old mechanical-engineering student living in Lincoln Park; Alberta M. Haag, 52, a public-school teacher from Breckenridge; John Moriarty, a 55-year-old father of seven from Detroit who worked as a security guard at Chrysler; Frank N. Palazzol of Sterling Heights; Kenneth J. Stillson, 39, of Grand Haven, a tool and die maker and the father of five teen-age children; Theodore Weatherly Jr. of Detroit. When the name was pulled from the seventh envelope and the final $5,000 prize was presented to Roy Renner, the crowd groaned in disappointment.

But 15 years later Renner recalls that, because of his infant daughter, he had already convinced himself that not winning the million dollars might be a blessing in disguise. "The night before the drawing, my wife and I stayed up real late talking about it. We don't pray much, but that night we prayed and said that if winning a million dollars was going to bring hardship and suffering to our children in any way, then we didn't want it. So when we didn't win the big prize, we

10

weren't disappointed. We figured it was God's blessing."

What Renner *did* win was enough money to buy a parcel of land — the same land near Montrose, north of Flint, where he lives today — and to take a vacation to Florida. Now he is literally living on his lottery winnings. "Every day I can look outside my house and think, 'I won this.' I can't complain a bit. I'm not rich, but I've got a family I'm real proud of. Maybe that's my million dollars."

The $50,000 prize was awarded next. It went to Marion Poblock, 57, of Detroit, who was unable to attend because she had been injured in an automobile accident earlier in the week. She was represented by her daughter, Carol Golpe, who stepped forward to accept the check.

Now it was down to only two finalists: Hermus Millsaps and Mary Virginia McCrumb, a 50-year-old homemaker from the town of Eagle, near Lansing. She had purchased her winning ticket in Petoskey, where she and her husband, Ronald, had temporarily lived while he worked a construction job.

Lengthening the suspense, John Quinn asked the two finalists how they felt. Mrs. McCrumb, who had earlier insisted that she would be happy winning only a $1,000 consolation prize, said, "I feel pretty good. I believe in prayer."

Millsaps' answer was more succinct. "I feel lucky," he said.

Teri Cousino, Miss Michigan, drew the envelope from the $100,000 slot. She opened it and read aloud Mary McCrumb's name.

The realization of what that meant came slowly to Hermus Millsaps. He was the only remaining finalist. The only remaining prize was a million dollars. Yet he stood for a few seconds, waiting patiently for the last envelope to be drawn. Photographers asked him to move over a few steps, and as he obliged, it finally struck him. A grin spread across his face, and he raised his arms in a Richard Nixon-style victory gesture. The crowd cheered. Reporters rushed the stage. Hermus performed his rendition of a Santa Fe freight train whistle.

It's safe to say that for the next few hours, at least, Hermus Millsaps did, indeed, feel like a millionaire. Ann ran to him and kissed him, saying, "That's my jewel." Together they answered reporters' questions.

When someone asked if Hermus would return to work at Chrysler the next day, Ann answered for him. "Are you kidding?"

"I've had three bosses riding my back," Hermus added. "They've been pulling for me, but they want the job done. So, I'll ask them, 'You want to work for me?' "

Ann said: "It's not going to change my life at all. I like to sew, cook, and work in the garden. We've always been kind of poor, and this isn't going to change things that much."

"I'm pretty shook right now," Hermus said. "God bless everybody. God bless you."

"Been married a year on March first, and now I bet we'll take a honeymoon," Ann said.

"I'm going to pay off my house, get the bill collectors off my back and get straight for a change," Hermus said. "I'm in debt about $24,000. Just might be a little left over, eh? . . . This will be headlines? I've never been in a newspaper before. Never gave a speech either. . . . I'm thinking about taking a little trip to Lookout Mountain in Chattanooga. . . . Think I'll buy the Greyhound we rode here in this morning. . . . I might even go to "Hawaiiee' tonight. . . . Guess maybe I'll get myself some Edison stock. . . ."

Ann said, "I never thought things like this happened to people like us."

Hermus said, "I sure do appreciate this here lottery. It's a fine thing. . . . It probably won't change me a bit."

Later the Millsaps led a group of reporters outside and across the street to the Filibuster Bar at the Lansing Olds Plaza Hotel, where Hermus offered to buy a round of drinks. But after Hermus had finished his bottle of beer and Ann her vodka screwdriver, the bartender informed Millsaps that he could not cash the $50,000 check, and a reporter had to pick up the tab. Later that night, Hermus and Ann returned home in a car driven by a lottery official.

The next day they went shopping. But they only purchased a $240 television set (the $500 models were "too expensive"), looked over a few other things, then went to the bank and added their $50,000 check to the $5 balance in their savings account.

That same day they also began to see the other side of the celebrity coin. Carloads of people pulled up to the curb in front and stared at their house. The phone rang constantly. At first they didn't mind, because as Ann explained to one caller, "It's a beautiful new world for us."

But the calls didn't stop, and the ringing phone quickly became an annoyance. A florist called to ask for $10,000 to save his floundering business. Insurance salesmen called. And at least one got his foot in the door — Hermus later went to court to ask for the return of a $5,342 premium on a $100,000 life-insurance policy he claimed he was pressured into buying. Hermus' first wife called, too, and not to offer her congratulations. She informed him she was going to file to have his child-support payments increased. (She eventually settled for an increase from $18 to $50 a week). By 1977 the Millsaps had had their phone number changed four times. About the same time, Hermus stopped granting interviews, telling reporters that he was tired of the publicity, tired of being recognized in supermarkets, and tired of being hit up for handouts from strangers. And he had an elaborate burglar alarm system installed at their home, with contacts to every door and window and a direct line to the local police station.

He and Ann made positive adjustments to their status as lottery millionaires, as well. They set out, for instance, to spend some money on the things they had never been able to afford. Hermus had never owned a new car; now he would buy a new Chrysler New Yorker every two years. They put a new roof and new aluminum siding on the house, carpeted the floors, added a sunroom and a patio, and had their driveway surfaced. They bought four new television sets and two new stereo systems, and filled their little house with more furniture than it could comfortably hold.

Now, a decade and a half after a moment of extraordinary fortune changed his life forever, Hermus Millsaps lives a life of quiet ease, sleeping until midafternoon when he feels like it, tinkering around the house, working in the garden or polishing his car. He and Ann travel often — Florida and Las Vegas are favorite destinations — and have plans to take a Caribbean cruise.

When asked how it feels to be a lottery winner, Hermus thinks first in terms of security. "It's good to know you got the money to pay the bills," he says. "It's not like it was, when if I got laid off I didn't know if I was going to lose my house. Now I can take it easy and know that I've got enough to pay the bills every month and there's nothing to worry about."

There is also a certain amount of concern for the future. He's well aware that his lottery checks will come only until 1993. In preparation for the day he picks up the last installment of his lottery prize, he's made a number of investments, including the purchase of Detroit Edison stock and two lots on "alligator land" in Florida. He bought that property soon after winning his jackpot in 1973 and has since paid

$14,000 to have water and sewer lines put in. He plans to build a retirement home there, even though he has never seen the land. "I seen pictures of it," he says. "Looks like a lot of weeds and gravel. But they've put some roads in there now — I seen pictures of that, too — and there's seven or eight houses built up 'round it now. The place is only 10 minutes from Disneyland. I figure a few more years, when it gets all built up, it's gonna be a gold mine."

He has invested in less speculative ventures as well. Says Millsaps: "I've been putting about $10,000 a year lately into them Ginny Maes — you know what they are? — and I'm lettin' my money work for me now. My Social Security is about $800 a month, and nobody can live on that these days. So, with that money invested at 9.1% — earning me $91 a month for every $10,000 invested — plus my pension from Chrysler, plus the Social Security, well, we'll be sittin' pretty comfortable when the checks quit comin' in. I been thinkin', too, about puttin' some in municipal bonds, tax-free investments."

Hermus Millsaps also recognizes that there are many things more important in his life than possessions and money. In 1977, when he won $1,000 with an instant lottery ticket and was once again the focus of newspaper and television attention, he told reporters that he had learned that money isn't worth anything if you don't have friends. Given a choice between the two, he would always choose friends, he said. Years later he still feels the same way, still works hard to "keep straight, on the level," as he puts it.

"I pretty much stay to myself, now," Hermus says. "I watch what I do, where I go, and I tend to my own business. There's a lot of crazy people out there. I've never had any trouble, but I figure why put myself out there where I might find it?"

He remains the easy-going, guileless, self-proclaimed hillbilly who *Detroit News* columnist Pete Waldmeir once said was so perfect for a first-time million-dollar winner that he must have been invented by the lottery bureau. "My friends say they like me because I don't let the money go to my head," he says. "I don't let it swell me all up."

He still has the chartreuse rabbit's foot he bought the day he won the lottery, though all the hair has worn off and it's become difficult to tell what it is anymore. He spends a lot of time listening to country music — playing along sometimes on his electric guitar — and still enjoys going out with Ann for a night of dancing.

But, no, he never did learn to polka.

Early Winners

"Then you feel it. You just get this chill running up your spine."

—Ron Northey, Michigan lottery winner

When Christeen and Elias Ferizis left their home in Greece in 1965 and came to America, they had a dream. Jobs and money were scarce in their native country, and Elias, the son of a farmer who had been killed by the Nazis in 1944, was tired of being poor. His and Christeen's dream was to come to America and get rich.

Eight years later, when Elias was 42 and Christeen 46, they were well on the way to realizing that dream. They lived with their two teen-age sons in a $100-a-month rented house in Detroit and, from the $595 a month Elias earned as a tool-and-die maker with Quality Control Company in Taylor, had managed to put $25,000 into a savings account. In April 1973 that savings account received a major boost.

Elias was a regular player of the new lottery and usually bought four tickets each week. One March day while Elias was buying his weekly allotment at a Detroit drugstore, Christeen dug into her purse for 50 cents and bought a ticket for herself. The night before, she explained to Elias, she had dreamed that she would be a lottery winner.

Her dream proved prophetic. At the end of that week, the ticket won $25 and, a few weeks later on April 5, made Christeen Ferizis Michigan's second million-dollar lottery winner.

Mrs. Ferizis spoke very little English, but she understood perfectly what was happening as she stood on the stage with nine other finalists in the Million Dollar Drawing that day. Accompanied by family friend Sam Memos, who served as interpreter, she lasted through each step of the elimination process. When she had survived the final drawing to become the grand-prize winner, she jumped up and down and began to weep with joy. Elias, weeping also, joined her on stage. Reporters asked her, through Memos, what she wanted to do now. "I just want to go home to the kids," she said.

Later, they celebrated at Bernie's Bar in Detroit, a neighborhood tavern owned by Sam Memos. Mrs. Ferizis posed for home movies with her sons and made plans for a family visit to Greece. Elias, while sipping a glass of the Greek liquor ouzo, presented Memos' wife, Niki, with the title and keys to his 1970 Pontiac, as he had once promised to do if he ever won the million-dollar prize. He announced he would also give $1,000 to his church. After some calculating, he told reporters that his wife's lottery prize was equivalent to 30 million Greek drachmas.

The next day Christeen Ferizis began packing for the trip home to Greece. Elias went to work and fulfilled his usual 11-hour shift. Much of the work he did at Quality Control Company, he explained, was for government contracts, and he had too much to be grateful for to simply abandon that responsibility. "I like America," he said. "You make me a very rich man."

◆

When Michigan began its lottery in 1972, it was only the seventh state-run lottery in the country and the first in the Midwest. Not surprisingly then, interest in bordering states was intense.

Michigan ticket sellers located near the borders reported that thousands of Ohio, Indiana, Illinois, and Wisconsin residents regularly crossed state lines to buy chances at the Michigan lottery prizes.

In 1973, one out-of-stater, Frank Kaminski of Toledo, Ohio, had his Michigan lottery luck delivered directly to him. Fifty-seven-year-old Kaminski, who had lost his career job and pension a few years earlier, worked as a water reclamation engineer for the city of Toledo.

But there was very little security in his new position. He was near the bottom of the seniority list, and even if he worked until retirement age, he couldn't put in enough years to expect much of a pension.

One of Kaminski's co-workers was a Michigan resident who commuted to Toledo each day. When the Michigan lottery began, that co-worker would occasionally stop on his way to work in the morning and buy tickets, then offer them to his friends in Ohio. One day he asked Frank Kaminski if he wanted to invest in any. Frank thought it sounded like a good idea and bought one ticket.

That single ticket won $25 and earned Kaminski the chance to become a finalist in Michigan's fifth Million Dollar Drawing. A few weeks later, on August 2, 1973, he stood on a stage in Ionia, pulled an unmarked envelope out of a tumbler and placed it in a slot for the $1 million grand prize. That envelope, it turned out, had his own name in it, and Frank Kaminski became the first out-of-state million-dollar jackpot winner.

Although he no longer needed to worry about a pension, Kaminski continued to work until he retired at age 63. He and his wife bought a new house and spent some time traveling, to South America once on a cruise, but primarily in the United States. Otherwise, their life continued much as it always had.

"There's nothing exciting in my life, except I'm enjoying it more," he says, "—not necessarily enjoying it more because I won the lottery, but just enjoying my free time."

Like many lottery winners, he has found that some people have unrealistic attitudes about his good fortune. Soon after he won he received a number of phone calls and letters from people requesting loans and handouts. "There was one party in Michigan (who) wanted me to invest in oil they thought they had on their property," he recalls. "And there were a few others that were sort of heartbreaking. But like I say, you've got forty-thousand dollars, you can't give thirty-thousand away. I'm 71 now; I could live to be 90 or 100, who knows? I got to save for the future. . . . You've got to keep your feet on the ground. You can't go throwing money away, because you don't know what's going to happen the next day or the following year. Anybody who thinks you're loaded to the gills, they've got another thought coming. I'm only getting forty thousand a year, and that's nothing. People nowadays are used to making more than that. But right away they think, 'Gee whiz, you've got the million and twice as much salted away.' You can put it away to draw interest, sure, but don't forget Uncle Sam is there, the state's there, you've got living expenses . . . ."

When his checks stop coming, after 1993, Kaminski hopes that the investments he has made over the years will maintain his income at the level he is accustomed to. But he's aware of the uncertainty of the future. "You can't foresee what's going to be in five years," he says. "Everything might be so sky-high that people in the factory might be making $100,000 a year. Who knows what will happen?"

◆

A "first" of another kind occurred on November 12, 1973, when the seventh million-dollar jackpot was won not by an individual, but by a number of people who had joined together as a club. Lottery clubs — formed by players who recognized the long odds against winning and decided they would rather win a share of a prize than no prize at all — had sprung up almost as soon as the lottery began.

It is not difficult to form a club. Friends, family or co-workers decide to band together, choose a name, then register for a Federal Tax Identification Number using Form SS-4 from an office of the U.S. Treasury or Internal Revenue Service. Once that tax number is assigned, a process that usually takes about two weeks, any winnings the group claims are registered using that number and go to the club, rather than individual members.

There are several advantages to forming a club, especially, in certain cases, regarding income and estate taxes. But for most people, no doubt, the attraction is the communal approach to betting. Ten people in a club betting two dollars each have a better chance of winning a lottery game than one person betting two dollars. And lottery clubs *do* win. In the first 15 years of the Michigan lottery they claimed a total of 26 jackpots of $1 million or more.

That first million-dollar-winning lottery club was called Lotta Four Lottery Club. Its members, all friends and co-workers, were: Carl Giuseppe, 59, of Mount Clemens; Michael Parda, 50, also of Mount Clemens; Thomas McClure, 29, of Fraser; and Philip Malo, 42, of St. Clair Shores. Dividing the jackpot four ways, each of them would receive $12,500 a year for 20 years.

Lotta Four stayed intact — and lucky — for a number of years. In

April 1974 they won again, that time a new car awarded in a bonus drawing for an instant-ticket game.

◆

The drawing for the eighth million-dollar prize — held December 18, 1973, at the Detroit Light Guard Armory — was attended by several dignitaries, including Detroit Tiger Willie Horton and Michigan's first lottery millionaire, Hermus Millsaps. Millsaps performed his freight-train whistle for the benefit of the audience, then turned to the 10 finalists on stage and said, "I wish all of you here tonight the same luck I had. God bless everybody."

The surviving finalist that day became the Upper Peninsula's first million-dollar prize winner—Paul Wedell, a 34-year-old furnace and appliance installer from Gladstone. Like many other winners in both earlier and later drawings, Wedell broke into tears when he was declared the grand-prize winner. "It's unbelievable," he said. "It's once in a lifetime . . . ."

Though Wedell was not a man to let money go to his head, he abandoned his furnace and appliance business (because it was "just a hell of a lot of paperwork"), then spent a couple of years fixing up his own house. But he could not stay idle. When there was not enough to do to keep busy at home, he went to work for someone else as an hourly employee.

Today, when he looks back, he says that the best thing about winning the lottery is that it gives him a feeling of comfort, a sense that "there's no problems, only opportunities." He works as a union plumber on construction sites. He goes where the work is, and as most residents of the Upper Peninsula are painfully aware, that is often far away. It is not unusual for him to commute hundreds of miles a week to and from a job site, or to stay — sometimes for months at a time — in motels in places as distant as Detroit.

Why would a man who has won $50,000 a year for 20 years choose to spend his time like that? When his wife is asked that question, she sounds perplexed. "What else would he do?" she answers. "Paul likes his job. He likes to work. He's not the kind of man who could just sit around doing nothing, no matter how much he won in the lottery."

◆

19

By 1974 the Michigan lottery was really hitting its stride. Revenue for the state's general fund reached $64,828,003, exceeding the predictions of even the most optimistic lottery supporters. More important, perhaps, the lottery was becoming firmly entrenched as a way of life in Michigan.

Ironically, the first million-dollar prize of 1974 did not stay in Michigan, but found its way to West Unity, Ohio, a town of 1,600 inhabitants located about 15 miles south of the (Hillsdale County) Michigan border. A small factory in town employed a number of Michigan residents, one of whom was in the habit of bringing lottery tickets each week to distribute to his co-workers. One of those co-workers, in turn, would stop on his way home from work and give one ticket to Ruth Cotter, a 54-year-old mother of six who worked as a bus driver for the local school. The man would give Mrs. Cotter a ticket of his own choice, and she would reimburse him the 50-cent purchase price.

One of those tickets earned her a $25 prize. When the number on her check stub was selected to enter her in the next Million Dollar Drawing, Ruth Cotter found herself pulled headlong into the Michigan lottery world.

The drawing was held in Saginaw on February 5, 1974. Mrs. Cotter and 119 other semifinalists were ushered into a reception and registration line and were given a packet from the Internal Revenue Service describing tax obligations. They also received a rabbit's foot from the Michigan Bureau of the Lottery and were then directed to a bin where they drew out plastic balls numbered from 1 to 120. The number that each finalist picked was written on a badge which each then wore.

When Mrs. Cotter drew number 111, a lottery official who was standing nearby commented that it looked like a lucky number. So did the photographer assigned to take pictures of the winners. And as Cotter walked toward her seat, a number of other people took the trouble to stop her to say the same thing. But she thought little of it. She was sure they would make the same comments about 001, or 100, or 077, or any other conspicuous number.

She sat down, and as she listened to the final instructions, she gradually became aware of a conversation behind her. A man repeatedly asked the young woman beside him if she was going to "tell her."

"I don't know," the woman kept replying.

"I think you should tell her," he insisted.

"I don't know," she said again.

It was obvious to Mrs. Cotter that the couple was talking about her, so she turned around to face them. "Tell me what?" she asked.

The young woman looked at her and, obviously embarrassed, shrugged. She hesitated, then softly said, "I dreamed last night that your number — 111 — would win the million-dollar prize."

A few minutes later, the number 111 was announced, and Ruth Cotter was one of the 10 finalists. She climbed the stairs to the stage, then immediately began looking for the young woman. She saw her get up from her chair and leave, perhaps in disappointment because she herself had not been chosen one of the finalists. Mrs. Cotter never saw her again.

Mrs. Cotter was now guaranteed a minimum prize of $5,000, already five times more than she had expected. "I went to that drawing to get a thousand dollars," she recalls. "That's all I had any hopes of getting. I never dreamed that I would get any more than that."

But she did. She survived the eliminations until only she and one other person, a young man from Indiana, remained on the stage. The master of ceremonies asked, jokingly, if the two wanted to split the prizes.

"I said I'd be willing," Mrs. Cotter remembers. "But the other fellow, he said, 'no,' because he'd come after the Big One. Then his name was drawn, and mine was last and I was the winner of the Big One."

When her husband, Vincent, rushed up on the stage to celebrate with her, Mrs. Cotter thought she might have to perform first aid on him. A month or so earlier he had passed out while watching a ball game on a hot afternoon, so she carried a bottle of smelling salts in her purse just in case it should happen again. When she put her arms around him that day on the stage, he was shaking violently.

"All I could think of was, 'Where is that smelling salts?' and was I going to have to dump my purse in front of all these people to get at it? He was more shook up than I was."

The Cotters returned home that day with a check for $50,000 and absolutely no idea how it would affect their lives. They bought a new house, which had an indoor swimming pool and, of more importance to the Cotters, enough space for friends to hold rehearsal dinners, birthday parties, anniversary celebrations, and other functions too large to fit into their own homes. Vincent stayed on as street superintendent of West Unity until his retirement at age 65, and for a short time Mrs. Cotter also continued at her job as school-bus driver. But when the local sheriff suggested that if she had even one minor accident, "everyone would want to sue for sure," she gave it up and instead devoted herself to volunteer work. She and Vincent became very active in the American Legion and American Legion Auxiliary, as well as a number of charitable organizations that they had not had time for before winning the lottery money.

Mrs. Cotter admits that $50,000 a year does not make her a millionaire. "A lot of people think you can just do anything just because you won the lottery. They don't stop to realize that there's lots of people that make that much money a year." Also, taxes take a larger chunk out of her prize than that of a Michigan resident. Michigan winners don't pay state income tax on their prizes; Mrs. Cotter pays Ohio state income tax as well as federal income tax on her annual $50,000.

But the money seems to have brought at least a fair amount of happiness and security to their lives, she says. And when someone in the community is in need, she is able to help now, and that is something that pleases her. And, according to Mrs. Cotter, when the checks stop coming, investments should continue to keep them comfortable and still able to share their good fortune in every way they can.

◆

When 75-year-old Felix Cayemberg won $1 million on June 11, 1974, he became the Michigan lottery's oldest million-dollar winner, a "title" he held for 8 1/2 years. But the retired commercial fisherman from the Upper Peninsula town of Isabella, near Rapid River, was too ill from a recent heart attack to attend the drawing in Jackson and was represented by his son Laverne Cayemberg of Kalamazoo.

The elder Cayemberg, in fact, was so ill that there was some question as to how the news of his good fortune might further affect his health. Laverne and Robert, another son who attended the drawing, called the family doctor for advice. Ultimately it was decided that it would be best if Laverne, Robert and their wives drove to Isabella and broke the news to their father and mother gently, in person.

The news seems not to have harmed Felix Cayemberg. In fact, in a short time he was on his feet again, intent on enjoying his new wealth. The father of eight and grandfather of 32 lived another 10 years. He and his wife, Meta, stayed in the same house they had lived in for years, but also spent a good deal of time traveling, often on chartered senior-citizen tours.

And Laverne recalls that his father was far from stingy with his money. "He gave most of it away, to the kids and relatives," he said. "He enjoyed giving it away. He also liked to give parties. Up there in the U.P., life is altogether different. They hang together and have community parties. Every time a party would come up, my father would want to buy the beer. Yea, he enjoyed himself."

◆

When Norman Fletcher won a $1 million jackpot in a drawing at Kalamazoo on September 17, 1974, he surprised lottery officials by announcing that he wanted to split the winnings with his best friend.

When asked to elaborate, he said that he and his friend had long ago decided to split all their lottery winnings 50-50, something they had done a number of times with $25 prizes. "We promised each other," he said. "Some people will say I'm crazy, but I figure when you make a deal you should hold on to it."

It wasn't that Fletcher, a 44-year-old mechanic for the Wayne County Road Commission, didn't need the money. For years he and his wife, Jeanette, had used all their spare cash to make payments on an 80-acre farm — their future retirement home — in Deckerville, a town of 600 north of Port Huron. Money was so tight that Fletcher had earned a reputation at work for wearing his boots until the soles flopped.

Winning the lottery turned their dream of owning the farm, free and clear, into reality. Jeanette, who was employed at Powertran Company in Oak Park, was delighted that they could pay off the farm and that she would no longer have to work. "But we'll still be the same people," she insisted.

Norman was not only happy that they could pay off the farm, but also that they could help out his friend Jim Lewis. When he was reminded that, since his name was the only one on the winning ticket, he was under no obligation to split the money with anyone, he said, "Would you do that to a buddy?"

Jim Lewis could not have been more pleased. At the time of the lottery win, the 31-year-old former Detroit resident worked in Deckerville as both a bartender and a hair stylist. And even though he, his wife and their two children lived rent-free on the Fletchers' farm, they still had trouble making ends meet. His bank balance stood, Lewis admitted, at $30. "Now I'm going to buy the bar I work at," he said the day he and Fletcher picked up the first installment of the lottery money.

For the first three years, the arrangement between the best friends, drinking buddies, worked out wonderfully. The two men became fixtures in Deckerville taverns, where they sat together at the bar toasting their good fortune. They went into business, investing $17,000 in a bulldozer and other equipment to begin a landscaping company for Lewis to operate. And each year — in 1974, 1975 and 1976 — Lewis accompanied Fletcher to the bank to cash the lottery check and split it up, $25,000 each.

Then, somehow, things went sour. For reasons that he never made absolutely clear, Fletcher had a change of heart. He did say that Lewis, who had lived rent-free on his farm for several years in exchange for mowing the lawn and other household chores, had neglected to perform those duties, thereby negating any personal agreements they might have had, including, not incidentally, any they had about splitting lottery winnings.

Lewis, who had left the farm some time earlier to move into his own newly purchased home a mile down the road, said that he had not neglected chores on the farm and that the agreement was never negated.

Fletcher claimed that since the ticket was his alone and he had no legal obligation to share it with Lewis, the $75,000 he had already given him was a gift, nothing more. "Just like welfare," he said.

Lewis filed a lawsuit in Sanilac County Circuit Court, in an unsuccessful attempt to collect half of the money.

Fletcher said that Lewis cheated him out of money from the landscaping business by writing checks for personal use out of the company account. In the meantime, the company failed, forcing them to sell their equipment for a major financial loss.

Lewis denied writing company checks for his own use and claimed that the real reason for the collapse of their friendship began when he cut down on his drinking after a February 1977 heart attack. "We were drinking buddies, and I don't drink that much anymore," he said. "You know money talks and beer talks, but I haven't talked to him in months."

Fletcher claimed that since it was his wife, Jeanette, who actually had purchased the winning lottery ticket, that particular ticket was exempt from their oral agreement to split winnings.

Lewis said that Jeanette had agreed to honor the oral agreement, even though it was she who bought the ticket.

Fletcher claimed Jeanette had said no such thing.

Lewis said, "I trusted that man more than any other person in my life. I would have bet my life on him."

Fletcher said he didn't want to talk about it any more.

Deckerville, as the saying goes, wasn't big enough for the two men, but for a time, both lived there. When they bumped into each other on the street or in the grocery store, they would turn, without speaking, and go in opposite directions. When they both were invited, by some oversight, to the same party or wedding reception, they would leave, one out one door, one out another.

Finally, Jim Lewis sold his house and moved away, but no one seems to know where. There were reports that he had divorced his wife and was living in Brown City, 35 miles southwest of Deckerville, but he could not be traced there. Neither could he be traced to Marlette, Sandusky, or any of the other towns that dot the farmlands of Sanilac County.

Norman Fletcher remained and, after 10 years of full-time farming on his 80 acres, is now fully retired. He sold his 60 head of cattle and three tractors, and the two barns he built a few years ago sit nearly empty. The land is his — he and Jeanette paid off the last of what they owed on it the day they received their first lottery installment in 1974 — and he leases much of it to neighboring farmers.

After so many years, he says he holds no ill will toward his ex-friend Jim Lewis. "I'm not really sore," he says. "I just want to leave it alone."

But for all Norman Fletcher knows, his old friend could have dropped off the face of the earth. He has not seen him or heard from him in over a dozen years, and whatever it was that once bound them in friendship has long since slipped out of memory. He seldom even thinks of him, not even when the check arrives in September — as it will every year through 1994 — and he takes it to the bank and cashes it, alone.

The Games

"Some lucky sonofabitch hit. . . . I never thought it was me."

—Paul Otto, Michigan lottery winner

On January 12, 1976, a 35-year-old Chrysler employee from Detroit named Carolyn Jones became the Michigan lottery's 21st millionaire. Ms. Jones stood apart from the 20 previous winners, however, because she did not win her jackpot in the 50-cent Weekly Game. Carolyn Jones was the first winner of a million-dollar drawing in Play Today, Win Today, an instant game which used tickets with a metallic foil "rub-off."

The introduction of instant tickets began a new era in lotteries in America. When Michigan began selling the Play Today, Win Today tickets on October 7, 1975, it was following the very inviting lead of Massachusetts, New Hampshire, Pennsylvania and a number of other Eastern states. Similar instant tickets had created a sensation nearly everywhere they appeared. They offered immediate gratification, the chance to win large sums of money on the spot without having to wait a week or more for a drawing. Massachusetts, which in the summer of 1974 became the first state to sell instant tickets, sold five million of their $1 tickets the first week they were offered and a total of 17 million over the first 10 weeks.

Michigan sales a year later were even more impressive. At the end of the first week, nine million of the instant tickets had sold, prompting lottery-director Gus Harrison to state optimistically that Play Today, Win Today might be "far and away the most popular lottery game ever offered in the country." His optimism turned out to be well-founded. By the end of only six weeks the entire printing of tickets, an astonishing 50 million of them, had been sold, with players clamoring for more. In just six weeks the lottery had earned the general fund about $20 million, almost one-third of the previous *year's* total. By the end of 1975 the net amount that went to the general fund had topped $106 million, $42 million more than the previous year.

Clearly the lottery bureau was on to something. The solution to a problem that plagued all lotteries—what to do when people simply got bored with the same games—had been solved, at least temporarily.

Carolyn Jones became a finalist in the first instant game's millionaire drawing when she purchased one of 55 tickets that had been marked with the word "Finalist" in place of the usual sets of dollar amounts, which ranged from $2 to $10,000. Each of the 55 finalists was guaranteed at least $10,000. In a drawing held with the customary fanfare, Carolyn Jones—clutching a rabbit's foot and dressed in the "lucky" skirt she had been wearing when she bought her winning ticket—ended up in the familiar position of million-dollar winners, alone on the stage. She decided she would take a few days off from her job as a universal-joint grinder at Chrysler and "really celebrate."

Once it was recognized that the lottery-playing public would respond—and respond heartily—to new, unusual and titillating lottery variations, the call went out for more of them. A second instant game was begun the day after Carolyn Jones won her million dollars. Like the first, 55 tickets printed with the word "Finalist" were scattered throughout the state. In addition, 110 tickets were printed with the word "Auto," and holders of those special tickets could redeem them for any American-made car selling for under $5,000.

But that was only the start. The lottery commissions of Michigan and every other lottery state found that as the novelty of games wore off, ticket sales leveled or declined. As a result, there was—and is—a constant search for new games and variations of games, a search that led eventually to the highly successful Daily and Lotto games.

Following is a chronological list and brief descriptions of the Michigan lottery's games through 1987.

The Weekly Game. Commonly known as the "green ticket," this game — the Michigan lottery's first — was begun November 13, 1972. Tickets sold for 50 cents each and could be purchased at any of about 7,000 lottery outlets in the state. Each green ticket was preprinted with a pair of three-digit numbers — digits randomly arranged — and winning numbers were determined by weekly drawings. Tickets matching one set of three-digit numbers won $25, redeemable at lottery offices, and also made their holders eligible to be among 120 semifinalists who were awarded prizes of $1,000 to $1 million in drawings held after the sale of every 30 million tickets. Ticket holders who matched both sets of three-digit numbers on a single ticket were entered in weekly Super Prize drawings for prizes of $10,000 to $200,000. The game created a total of 26 millionaires and ran until the fall of 1978, when it was discontinued because of lagging sales.

Instant Tickets. This new concept was introduced on October 7, 1975, when the $1 tickets went on sale at the same outlets where 50-cent weekly tickets were sold. The first game — Play Today, Win Today — was typical of the many similar games which followed. The player rubbed off metallic foil (later, latex plastic) to reveal six separate dollar amounts. If three of the amounts on one ticket matched, the player won that amount — which ranged from small sums such as $2, $5, $10, and $50 to $1,000 and even $10,000 — immediately (though large prizes had to be redeemed at lottery offices and payment was then mailed from Lansing). In addition, a set number of tickets were printed with the word "Finalist," which guaranteed the holder $10,000 and qualified him or her for a $1 million drawing.

Later instant games were created around various themes. Popular ones included: Surprise Package, Tic-Tac-Two, Michigan Baseball, Horoscope, Loose Change, Cash for Life, Joker Plus, 7-11-21, 3 for the Money, Holiday Bonus, Lifetime Deal, Michigan Fortune, Celebration, and Michigan Summer. Many were played using a variation of the first Play Today, Win Today tickets, with winners determined by matching three like-dollar amounts. Other variations included adding numbers to exceed a certain sum for each prize, and tic-tac-toe games with X's and O's lined up diagonally or in columns and rows. Others made use of detachable stubs that could be rubbed off to reveal letters that if collected until a word or slogan was spelled out (such as "JOKERS PLUS"), qualified the winner for additional prizes.

Prizes varied almost as much as the games and included automobiles, a $500,000 house, a variety of Michigan vacations, grand-prize amounts of $1,000 a month for life, a $2 million jackpot, and, once, an amount determined by the total number of Michigan votes cast for Michiganian Gerald Ford in the presidential election of 1976 (it totaled $1,893,742). The million-dollar (or more) jackpots created a total of 44 lottery millionaires (usually determined by special drawings) through 1987, including several who won $1,000 a week for life with a guaranteed minimum of $1 million. There was also a significant number of winners who received prizes such as $500,000 in a lump sum or $1,000 a month for life.

By 1984, market research showed that players preferred many small prizes to the chance of winning a few large ones.

So instead of jackpot amounts that could go as high as $1 million or $2 million, instant-ticket games were designed to limit top prizes — at first to $10,000, then $1,000 — which made it possible to create many more small and middle-range prizes of $2 to $100.

Michigame. This variation of the Weekly Game began October 7, 1975, and continued until May 7, 1981. It, too, featured 50-cent tickets, weekly drawings to determine winning numbers, and large prizes distributed in special or bonus drawings. The most obvious departure from the original 50-cent game was that each ticket came printed with one two-digit and one three-digit number, rather than the two three-digit numbers of the earlier game.

Prizes were awarded as follows:

—A ticket matching the week's winning two-digit number could be redeemed for a $5 prize.

—A ticket matching the three-digit number could be redeemed for a $50 prize. Payment came by mail in the form of a check with a detachable stub printed with numbers which were automatically entered in one of two special drawings. If the stub was printed with a four-digit, or "entry," number it was entered into the next Monthly Jackpot Drawing, with prizes determined by a percentage of total ticket sales. If a check stub came back with a five-digit, or "elimination," number it was automatically entered into a much-less-frequent Million Dollar Elimination Drawing.

In the four and a half years that Michigame was played, only three million-dollar drawings were held. In each, prizes were awarded to the

10 finalists as follows: Seven received $10,000, and one each received $25,000, $50,000, and $1 million.

—If a ticket in the regular weekly drawing matched both the two-digit and three-digit numbers, it qualified for yet a third drawing, the Super Play, held whenever six contestants came forward with their winning tickets. In this elimination drawing, the finalists were awarded either $4,000, $5,000, $6,000, $7,000, $8,000, or became what was known as the Grand Winner. The Grand Winner was given the choice of three unmarked envelopes to determine whether his or her prize would be $30,000, $40,000 or $50,000. If the Grand Winner selected either of the two smaller prizes, the difference between it and $50,000 was distributed equally among the other five contestants.

Daily 3. The use of computer terminals at lottery outlets made it possible, for the first time, for lottery players to have a hand in their own destiny by choosing the numbers they wanted to bet on. The Daily 3 game, begun on June 6, 1977, is based on the illegal numbers games that have flourished in large cities for decades. Players place 50-cent or $1 bets on a three-digit number of their choice between 000 and 999, and the winning numbers are chosen in a televised drawing held each evening, Monday through Friday. (Later, Saturday evening drawings were added).

Players can bet three different ways:

—Straight. In a straight bet, the player must match all three digits of the winning number in sequence. For example, a straight bet on the number 321 pays off only on 321. The odds of winning are 1 in 1,000, with a payoff of $250 for a 50-cent bet and $500 for a $1 bet.

—Boxed. Players who "box" their numbers win if any combination of their three digits comes up. Using the same example, a "boxed" 321 pays off on either 321, 312, 213, 231, 123 or 132. Odds are 1 in 166, with payoffs of $41 on a 50-cent bet and $83 on a $1 bet.

—Two-Way. A player also has the option of betting on a combination of straight and boxed, in which one $1 ticket automatically includes a 50-cent straight and 50-cent boxed wager. If the number bet—in our example, 321—matches the winning number exactly, the payoff is $291 ($250 for the straight bet plus $41 for the boxed bet). If the winning digits match but in a different order—say 123—then the payoff is $41, the amount of only the boxed portion of the two-way ticket.

31

Quickly after its introduction, the Daily 3 became the best-selling game in Michigan, a position it still held in 1987, even after the introduction of Super Lotto.

Superplay. Superplay, a third variation of the original Weekly Game, began May 14, 1981, one week after Michigame ended. Each of the $1 tickets was printed with a six-digit lottery number and a five-digit bonus number. Bonus numbers were automatically entered into occasional "Bonus Drawings." The six-digit number—composed of one digit in a red-shaded area, two digits in a white area, and three digits in a blue-shaded area—was good, during the week purchased, for a drawing held each Monday, with prizes awarded as follows:

—Tickets matching the one-digit number (red area) won a free ticket.

—Tickets matching the two-digit number (white area) in sequence won $10.

—Tickets matching the three-digit number (blue area) in sequence won $100.

—Tickets matching both the one-digit (red) and three-digit (blue) numbers in sequence won $500.

—Tickets matching both the two-digit (white) and three-digit (blue) numbers in sequence won $5,000.

—Tickets that matched all six digits in sequence were entered in a Superplay Grand Drawing, held whenever 10 winning tickets had been validated. At those drawings, prizes were awarded by the usual elimination process. The first five finalists, in the order their names were drawn, received $10,000, $15,000, $20,000, $25,000 and $30,000. The five remaining finalists entered a second stage of the drawing, and four were given, again in the order their names were drawn, $35,000, $40,000, $45,000 and $50,000.

The lone remaining finalist then picked one of three unmarked envelopes to determine whether his grand prize would be $550,000, $775,000 or $1 million. As in Michigame, if the grand-prize winner drew either of the lesser amounts, the difference between it and the million-dollar prize was divided among the other finalists. For example, if the $550,000 envelope was drawn, $450,000 was distributed equally among the other nine finalists, in this example adding $50,000 to what each had already won.

In the three years that Superplay was in operation, only one million-dollar jackpot was awarded—to Louis Morgando of Giles, Wisconsin, on June 27, 1983.

On June 28, 1983, over-the-counter sales of Superplay were halted, and the game became available only by subscription. A year later, on June 21, 1984, Superplay was discontinued altogether, and players who still held valid subscriptions were given the choice of a refund or conversion to a subscription to the new Lotto game. Over three-quarters of the subscribers, according to lottery-bureau reports, chose to switch to Lotto.

Daily 4. Following the success of Daily 3, the Daily 4 was introduced on October 4, 1981, as a nearly identical game, but one that offers considerably larger prizes. All tickets cost $1, and as in Daily 3, players can bet straight or boxed. For a straight bet, the player chooses a four-digit number between 0000 and 9999. If the winning digits match in sequence (odds 1-10,000), the payoff is $5,000.

Boxing with four digits, becomes somewhat more complicated than with three. Bettors can box a four-digit number in a variety of ways, depending on how many *different* digits they use. A number with four different digits—4567, for example—can be bet Boxed 24 Way since there are 24 possible combinations of the digits. The number 4456, on the other hand, with three different digits, creates only 12 possible combinations and becomes a Boxed 12 Way wager. The following chart illustrates all possible winning combinations and corresponding prizes:

Type Bet	Example	Odds of Winning	Amount Won on $1 Bet
Straight	4321	1:10,000	$5,000
4-Way Box	4333	1:2,500	$1,250
6-Way Box	4455	1:1,666	$833
12-Way Box	4456	1:833	$416
24-Way Box	4567	1:416	$208

Card Game. This game of lottery "poker" began August 28, 1982. Each of the $1 tickets was preprinted with symbols representing three of the cards in an ordinary five-card poker hand. A ticket, for example, might contain symbols for the 5 of hearts, the queen of clubs, and the 8 of diamonds. In the same televised daily drawing that determined winners in the Daily 3 and Daily 4 games, two playing cards were also drawn. Those cards, added to each ticket's three symbols, completed the poker hand. Using the same example, if the cards drawn were a 5 of diamonds and an 8 of spades, the 5 and 8 would combine with the 5 and 8 on the ticket to create a poker hand of two pair, redeemable for a prize of one free ticket. As another example, a ticket that contained symbols for a 4 of any suit, a 6 of any suit, and a 7 of any suit, when combined with the drawn cards, became a straight—4, 5, 6, 7, 8—and could be redeemed for a prize of $10. Prize amounts increased with the rank of poker hands as follows:

Hand	Prize	Approx. Odds of Winning
Two pair	Free ticket	1:16.5
Three of a kind	$3	1:28.1
Straight	$10	1:287.4
Flush	$15	1:330
Full house	$20	1:340.1
Four of a kind	$50	1:900.9
Straight flush	$4,000	1:81,301
Five of a kind	$5,000	1:94,340
Royal flush	$50,000	1:735,294

An actual deck of 52 playing cards was used in the drawings, held every day except Sunday. The cards were placed in 52 identical unmarked envelopes, which were tumbled in a clear plastic drum for a minimum of two minutes. A lottery official then pulled out an envelope, opened it, read the rank and suit of the card, and displayed it. The procedure was then repeated with a second envelope.

For the first few months of the Card Game—from August 28, 1982, to January 1, 1983—preprinted tickets were sold over-the-counter as they came off sheets. After a six-month hiatus, the game resumed on June 7, 1983, and until it was discontinued on August 12, 1985, tickets were available "on line" from the same computer terminals that dispensed Daily 3 and Daily 4 tickets.

Lotto. The "lotto" game popular in Italy for centuries served as the inspiration for the American version, first introduced in Massachusetts and New York in 1978. Michigan followed with its own Lotto in 1984—tickets went on sale August 13 and the first drawing was held August 25.

In Michigan's Lotto, bettors chose six numbers between 1 and 40 for each $1 ticket they purchased. They could pick their numbers in one of three ways. Similar to the daily games, players could fill out an application form with numbers of their choice. (Because of that self-determining aspect, Lotto and the Daily 3 and Daily 4 are termed "active" games, as opposed to the "passive" weekly and instant games which used tickets preprinted with numbers.) Or, they could use Easy Pick and let one of the system's "on-line" computer terminals select six numbers randomly. A surprising number of Lotto players preferred not to take an active role in choosing their numbers; as many as 45 percent in some weeks used Easy Pick, according to lottery-bureau personnel. The third option—one used by 150,000 players the first year—was to buy a one-year subscription that automatically entered the same six digits of the player's choice into each week's drawing.

Tickets were winners if four, five or six of the numbers matched those drawn during a televised broadcast every Saturday evening. The total prize money awarded was determined by the "pool," or the amount wagered in any one betting period. The largest prize, awarded to the ticket holder (or ticket holders) who matched all six winning numbers, began at $1 million and was increased if ticket sales were unusually high or if the pool "rolled (carried) over" during weeks when there was no six-digit winner. If more than one player matched six numbers, the jackpot was divided equally between or among them. Winners who matched four or five of the six winning numbers won a share of the pool determined by the amount bet that week.

For example, in a typical week when the jackpot stood at $1 million, two winners might match all six numbers, 209 match five of six, and 8,688 match four of six. The two 6-of-40 winners would split the $1 million, each receiving $25,000 a year for 20 years; the 209 5-of-6 winners would typically share $280,896 in a lump sum of $1,344 each; the 8,688 holders of tickets matching four of six would divide $338,832, taking home $39 each.

The Michigan Lotto quickly broke all existing North American records for similar games. In its first 10 days of operation, $3,156,634 worth of tickets were sold, four times more than the previous record, set by Illinois. In August 1985, Lotto began offering a second drawing, on Wednesdays, partly in an effort to reduce the long lines that had formed outside the limited number of available terminals.

However, shortly after the introduction of Super Lotto, the original Lotto was terminated on May 6, 1987.

Super Lotto. When the original Lotto game failed to create many rolled-over jackpots and the resulting enormous multi-million-dollar prizes that were attracting so much attention in other states, Michigan countered with Super Lotto. It was exactly the same game as Lotto, with one significant difference: Players had to correctly match six of 44, rather than 40, numbers.

The difference may seem inconsequential until you realize that the addition of four numbers lowers the odds of winning from 1 in 3,838,380 to 1 in 7,059,052. With the odds cut nearly in half it was fair to guess that there would be fewer jackpot winners and, thus, more rollovers and large jackpots.

Initially, Supper Lotto and Lotto ran simultaneously. Betting forms were color-coded, and Super Lotto drawings were held on Saturdays, Lotto drawings on Wednesdays. However, confusion between the two games, plus the fact that Super Lotto ticket sales quickly eclipsed those of Lotto, resulted in the termination of Lotto on May 6, 1987. From then until this writing, Super Lotto—with a 6-of-44 drawing held each Wednesday and Saturday evening—remains the only game of its kind in Michigan.

◆

Largely as a result of new games—especially instant games, Lotto, and Super Lotto—but also because of new marketing techniques and a very successful advertising campaign, Michigan saw its lottery revenues grow at a rate that few people could have anticipated. In 1972, lawmakers who suggested that the Michigan lottery could add as much as $60 million a year to the state's coffers admitted that they were being rampant optimists. But their predictions turned out to be grossly conservative. By 1986 the lottery was contributing more than $415 million a year to the state's school-aid budget.

Such growth also resulted in dramatic increases in the numbers of winners of million- and multi-million-dollar jackpots. From 1973 to 1984, jackpots of $1 million or more were awarded in the Weekly Game, Michigame, Superplay, and instant-ticket drawings a total of 60 times, creating an average of about 5 1/2 lottery millionaires a year. In 1984, when Lotto jackpots were awarded only in the final four months of the year, that average jumped to 14 a year. In 1986, with twice-weekly Lotto and Super Lotto drawings, 88 people—more than the combined total for the first 12 years of the Michigan lottery—won $1 million or more. (For a comparison of million-dollar jackpots created by each of the Michigan lottery games, see Appendix V, p. 201.)

Lottery millionaires had become, as one winner said in 1987, "a dime a dozen." Winning $1 million had become so commonplace that the announcement of million-dollar winners had gone from front-page headlines to a passing mention in "News in Brief." The chance to win $1 million no longer created the lottery frenzy that it had in 1973. It would take something stronger. It would take large jackpots, very large jackpots.

Megabucks

"It just keeps growing . . ."
—Michigan lottery bureau television commercial

In the history of lotteries in America there had never been a year like 1984. It was the year of megabucks, the year lotteries went crazy.

It started early in the year, on January 14, when a Canadian truck driver named Stuart Kelly stepped forward to claim a $13,890,589 prize in the Canadian Interprovincial Lottery Corporation's 6-49 game. The prize, equivalent to more than 11 million U.S. dollars, was far and away the largest unshared jackpot in North American history. The previous year, in July, Nicholas Jorich had won $8.8 million in the Pennsylvania Lotto, and in 1982 an $11 million jackpot had been shared by four ticket holders in New Jersey. But Stuart Kelly's prize was a landmark; it was the first time more than $10 million had been awarded to a single winner. Kelly received his jackpot in a lump sum that, if invested conservatively, would earn him nearly $21,000 interest every week—more than he and his wife, Lillian, had earned in a year before they won.

But that was just the beginning of the megabucks madness. On March 19—after a week of frantic lottery fever in New York, during which ticket sales had reached a peak of 1,000 per minute—Lula Aaron, a 54-year-old grandmother, won $10 million, the largest unshared prize in U.S. history.

On May 15 another record was set in New York, this time for the largest North American lottery prize, a $22.1 million jackpot, which was shared by four winners.

Then, on July 15, a 45-year-old secretary from Westfield, Massachusetts, claimed a $15,619,880 prize in the Massachusetts Megabucks. When Marcia Sanford won that jackpot, with only the second lottery ticket she had ever purchased, she became the largest single jackpot winner in North America, perhaps the world.

Her record didn't stand for long. Eleven days later, Venero Pagano, a 63-year-old retired carpenter from New York City, won $20 million in the New York Lotto.

A week later, the record for the largest jackpot in North American history was again eclipsed when, in Ohio, eight ticket holders split $24.6 million.

On September 3, a 28-year-old printer from Chicago shattered every record, everywhere. Michael E. Wittkowski that day claimed an Illinois Lotto jackpot of $40 million, the largest unshared prize and the largest single jackpot in the history of lotteries in North America and probably the world.

It was the climax of a remarkable year, but the excitement wasn't over yet. On December 6, five winners shared a $13 million prize in New Jersey, and 10 days later in New York, 11 ticket holders split a $20 million jackpot. But after Michael Wittkowski's $40 million, everything else was mere anticlimax. His jackpot would stand as the largest and most famous in America until October 19, 1987, when Don Woomer and his fiancee, Linda Despot, won $46 million in the Pennsylvania lottery.

And where was Michigan during all the activity of 1984? While other lotteries were exploding, Michigan's made some quiet noises of its own. It was, in fact, a Michigan lottery winner who lit the fuse to all the fireworks by winning the nation's first million-dollar-plus jackpot. On January 17, 1977, David Shepherd made national news when he won the grand drawing in the President's instant-ticket game. The amount of the jackpot: $1 for every Michigan vote cast for the presidential candidate who carried Michigan in the previous November's election. Thanks to the campaign efforts of Gerald Ford—who lost the election to Jimmy Carter, but carried his home state—Shepherd won $1,893,742, the largest lottery jackpot in U.S. history at the time. (Shepherd, it turned out, won both ways; he voted for Carter.)

The evening he won that prize, Shepherd, a self-employed carpenter, said, "This may be my year to retire. In fact, this may be my *night* to retire." Reason apparently prevailed, however, because the 23-year-old man did not retire, but rather combined his $75,750 annual checks ($94,687 less an initial 20 percent federal tax deduction) and his carpentry skills to open a building-supplies store in his hometown of Onsted, south of Jackson.

Shepherd's jackpot remained the largest in Michigan (though not in the U.S.) until June 3, 1983, when Millicent Gallup, 58, of Traverse City stood as the last of six finalists in a Detroit grand-prize drawing of losing tickets from the Tic-Tac-Two instant game. Mrs. Gallup—who had been a widow for 17 years and had worked as a Michigan Bell Telephone directory-assistance operator for 14 years—was given the opportunity to choose one of three envelopes that would determine whether her prize would be $1 million, $1.5 million or $2 million. She chose the blue envelope, the fattest one, and won an even $2 million. On March 9, 1984, Douglas Simpson, an unemployed part-time student at Northern Michigan University in Marquette, won the grand drawing of the Instant Lotto—an instant-ticket game that preceded the 6-of-40 Lotto by several months—and walked away with $100,000 a year toward a $2 million payoff. That jackpot equalled Millicent Gallup's as the largest in Michigan history, but was overshadowed nationally by the announcement, just 10 days later, that New York Lula Aaron had won $10 million.

So in 1984, Michigan's lottery still seemed like the poor kid on the block. It was there, but hurrying to catch up.

The one common denominator in all those huge jackpots in Canada, New York, Pennsylvania, Massachusetts, Ohio and Illinois was that they were generated by "rollovers" in lotto games. The long odds of one-in-three, -four, -six, or -eight million ensured that there would occasionally be consecutive weeks when no one won the jackpot. It would grow then, throbbing and monstrous, like the bank vault in one of the Michigan lottery's memorable television commercials. And as it grew, it would attract attention, spurring more ticket sales and adding even more to the jackpot and the resulting excitement.

When Michigan finally got in on the tail-end of that excitement with its own lotto game—the Lotto 6-of-40, which began August 13, 1984—the publicity surrounding the huge prizes in other states contributed to getting Michigan's game off to a fast start. More than three million tickets sold that first week, establishing a national record for a game's first seven days of sales. It was still far short, however, of the $18.56 million in sales in New York the week in July that Venero Pagano won his $20 million, or the $24.6 million in sales in Ohio the week before their $24.5 million jackpot was awarded in August, a fact that Michigan lottery officials must certainly have been aware of.

What Michigan needed, if it hoped to compete for the attention the other states were getting, was a big jackpot, a spectacular jackpot of $10 million or more to a single winner. It wouldn't be long in coming.

Michigan's first Lotto jackpot was a "mere" $2,950,059, and its winner, banking-executive Thomas LaPenna of Marquette, came close to losing his fortune before he even claimed it. On September 1, 1984, as LaPenna, 45, and his wife, Carol, browsed through a Houghton gift shop, they heard an announcer on a radio that played in the background read the numbers that had just been selected in the state's first Lotto drawing. They knew their ticket matched four of the numbers, but they weren't able to hear the other two. During the drive home with the window down, LaPenna's ticket slipped out of his grasp, blew around the inside of the car and was nearly sucked out the window. He finally got a firm grip on it and, the next morning, discovered that it matched not just four numbers, but all six. LaPenna had become the first Michigan Lotto winner, and his jackpot became, briefly, the state's largest lottery award.

Six weeks later, on October 13, the Lotto jackpot stood at $7,795,896, and Michigan finally began to enter the big leagues of lottery prizes. The jackpot was especially noteworthy because—unlike any before or since—it wasn't split equally between the winners. Monroe resident Thomas Horney received one-third, and Steve Glesner of Midland won two-thirds of the prize. Glesner won his $5,197,264 share because he had two tickets—one a subscription ticket that automatically entered him in each week's drawing, the other a regular over-the-counter ticket he had purchased—each with the same set of winning numbers.

On November 17, a Michigan lottery jackpot finally broke the $10 million barrier. It came following three weeks during which nobody matched all six winning numbers, creating the same rollover effect that was building such spectacular jackpots elsewhere in North America. It had reached $10,397,771 when Patricia Parker of Kalamazoo matched the winning numbers with her Lotto subscription ticket. Mrs. Parker, an accounting clerk, and her husband, William, a private nurse's aid, did not come forward to collect their prize for two days, until after they had hired a lawyer and discussed what to do with checks of nearly half a million dollars a year for 20 years.

During a press conference after she had picked up her first check, Mrs. Parker refused to give her exact age—"over 40"—and wouldn't say whether or not she and her husband had children. She did remark, however, that even after two days to get used to the idea, she was still "numb," and that she was not really much of a gambler. "I don't even win at bingo," she said. "I was playing the lottery for the fun of it and the fact that the money goes for education." Asked what she would do with the money—$417,257 initially, followed by 19 checks for $415,840—she said she wanted to buy a new car. She then held up a photograph of television-actor Tom Selleck and announced that she also hoped to be able to buy *him*.

◆

Patricia Parker's $10 million dwarfed the Michigan Lotto jackpots that followed in 1984, and it wasn't until January 19, 1985, that a jackpot swelled so full, again following three drawings in which no tickets had matched all six numbers. The jackpot that day—$13,300,931—was shared by six ticket holders, the most lottery millionaires produced in a single day in the Michigan lottery through 1987.

◆

Almost exactly three months later, on April 20, 1985, a single winner, Richard Berdeski of Utica, won a Lotto jackpot worth $9,194,911. The 41-year-old machinist at a Sterling Heights manufacturing plant told lottery officials that he had always believed he would be one of the early Lotto jackpot winners. That conviction was strong enough to keep him buying $10 worth of tickets every week during the first eight months of the Lotto game.

But when, in his words, he "wasn't getting anywhere," he took a more radical approach to choosing his numbers. After stripping a deck of cards of its face cards, he improvised a game of solitaire, in which he dealt cards into stacks, then used the cards on the top of each pile to compose a set of six numbers with them—numbers, it turned out, worth $9.2 million. "I turned absolutely purple when I found out," he said. "I just couldn't believe it. . . . The whole idea is just too unreal. I just want to get some sleep."

Berdeski had once told his fellow workers that if he ever missed work on a Monday it would be because he had gone to Lansing to collect his first Lotto payment. That Monday, he not only missed work as promised, but also went into immediate retirement.

Berdeski then spent the next few days in motels with his wife and children while they tried to decide what to do with their sudden fortune. Richard had investments in mind, but only after the turmoil had diminished. His wife said that she would like to buy a nice home and a new car and do some traveling. But, she added, "I don't want our attitudes to change toward anything."

◆

Another large jackpot—the largest until January 1988—was created July 13, 1985, after three weeks without a Lotto winner. Three ticket holders shared the $15,167,989 prize: Harry Fryckland Sr. from Detroit, Gerald Rickrode Sr. of Wyandotte, and Terry Showalter from East Detroit.

◆

Almost a year later, on June 29, 1986, Rose Marie Lajoie, a 42-year-old Chrysler office worker from Livonia, sat down at her kitchen table with the Sunday paper and performed what had become a little ritual. She turned to the page where the winning lottery numbers were listed and began checking them off against those on her usual four tickets. On one ticket, six numbers matched. The jackpot that day stood at a cool, round $10 million.

"I screamed," Ms. Lajoie said a year later in an interview in *Metropolitan Detroit* magazine, "I jumped back from the table like it was a hot potato, and I just said, 'Oh my Lord, what did you do now?' " The first thing she did was hide the winning ticket in a box of catfood until she could deliver it to the Lansing claim center the next day.

Lajoie had two immediate plans: to take a year's leave from her $38,000-a-year job at Chrysler's Outer Drive Manufacturing Tech Center, and to share the wealth with her mother. The year's leave from work turned into early retirement, and during her first year as a lottery millionaire, she gave her mother a Chrysler New Yorker, a new wardrobe, and a pair of diamond earrings. For herself she purchased a customized van with which to visit relatives in West Virginia and travel some of the rest of the country. She also began donating a great deal of time to charitable organizations such as Children's Hospital of Michigan and the Humane Society. Thirteen months after winning, she moved out of the small house in Livonia where she had lived for 16 years and into a newly purchased $200,000 home in Northville.

Did winning $500,000 a year for 20 years change Rose Lajoie? A year and a half after her lottery win she told the *Detroit Free Press* that it had, and it hadn't. It had, she admitted, because her life was now considerably more complicated. "I can't do anything without my lawyers," she said. She had been involved in two lawsuits, one with a builder she had paid $9,000 to construct a garage that was never built, the other with a former friend—"a co-worker, a so-called 'Christian' "—who had reneged on a $3,500 personal loan, stating flatly that he would not pay it back because Lajoie did not need the money. Lajoie, who was single—and "loving it"—also found it sometimes difficult to date. Men seemed intimidated by her money, or overly conscious of it, and admitted that they did not know how to "approach" her.

But Lajoie also let her real friends know that she was still the same girl they'd always known, still the fun-loving former high-school drum majorette who liked to shop sales, party, and attend sporting events. Her friends' worries were put to rest, she told the *Free Press*, when they saw that she was "still crazy."

"Fancy cars, great clothes—all of that is surface," she said. "Friends who call you a dummy and go to a hockey game and get rowdy—that's real."

Lajoie selected her winning ticket using Easy Pick, the random choice of the lottery computer. It was a departure from her usual method of choosing numbers—combining variations of her lucky numbers, threes and sevens. The winning numbers included neither of those digits.

◆

Another $10 million jackpot made big news on January 10, 1987, when it, too, went to a single winner, 59-year-old Fred Goodson of Pontiac. Goodson, who had retired in 1980 after 30 years as a sheet-metal worker for General Motors, expressed doubt that the $400,000 checks he would receive each year for the next 20 years would have much effect on his lifestyle. "I like cornbread and beans," the Arkansas native drawled during the press conference announcing his win. "I want to be myself. . . . I'll get a little inebriated here and there. I'm going to get a customized van and remodel my home the way I want it." His wife, Dorothy, also insisted that the money would not change them and that she would remain at her job as a teacher's aid in the Pontiac school district.

That determination to remain unchanged apparently paid off. Although at first the Goodsons reported that many people requested loans and gifts, within a few months life had settled pretty much back to normal. They paid off their house mortgage, bought the customized van, and installed some much-needed appliances—refrigerator, washer and dryer. There was also time for the nearly obligatory vacation to Hawaii.

Goodson selected his numbers by combining his and his relatives' birthdates. Like Rose Lajoie, with whom he had tied as winner of the second-largest individual prize in Michigan lottery history, he saw his winning numbers in the paper the morning after the Saturday night drawing. "I must have looked at it a hundred times," he said later. When his wife came into the room he told her she was "looking at a millionaire." Later that day he took his ticket to his favorite tavern and gave it to the owner to lock in the bar safe. Asked afterwards if he had ever worried that the ticket—and the bar owner—might disappear, Goodson said, "No. If you don't have anyone you can trust, you don't have anything."

By Saturday, August 15, 1987, the Super Lotto jackpot had not been claimed for four consecutive weeks and had grown to $13 million, making it the third-largest jackpot in Michigan lottery history. On Sunday, Clifford Nutto, a 48-year-old sheet-metal worker from St. Joseph learned that he had the winning numbers, or rather that he *might* have the winning numbers. He was skeptical—actually, *worried*—enough that the newspaper where he saw the numbers might have printed them wrong, that he tucked the ticket away in an envelope and told no one about it, not even his wife.

Nutto had purchased the ticket at a local mini-mart, where he often picked up his usual allotment of five instant tickets and five Easy Pick Super Lotto tickets. That day, however, the store had sold out of instant tickets, so Nutto bought an additional five Super Lotto tickets instead. One of those extra tickets turned out to be the winner, which he finally confirmed Monday morning, when he went to a local store and bought another newspaper. He then suggested to his wife that they take the day off to visit Lansing because, as he said, "I think we have something that's going to change our lives."

The next order of business was to learn whether or not he was the *only* winner. Thirteen million dollars split two ways, or four ways, or even 13 ways would be easy to take, of course, but to win it all, that would really be something. He got the news over the radio while riding in his car. The announcer said: "Lottery officials report that a computer check showed that one ticket matched all six numbers in Saturday's Lotto drawing, making it the largest single jackpot in Michigan lottery history. . . ."

Clifford Nutto had just become the winner of the largest unshared jackpot in the state, replacing Patricia Parker and her $10.4 million. "I just went crazy," he said later. "People ask me all the time, 'What did it feel like to win all that money?' What a question. How do they think it felt? It felt wonderful. But riding in the car then, realizing I had won *all* that money . . . I couldn't even imagine how much it was."

A few days later, he found out exactly how much it was when he picked up his first of 20 installments, a check for $520,000.

As of June 1988, the largest jackpot ever created in the Michigan lottery was $28,914,801 on January 20, 1988. It came in the Super Lotto game just two weeks after a lotto prize in Ohio had reached $32 million. That one-two combination created a lottery frenzy of a scale never before seen in Michigan. If there is any doubt that large prizes increase ticket sales, consider that in the week before Michigan's $28.9 million was won, $35,684,339 was spent on Super Lotto tickets. The day of the drawing alone, 10.2 million of the tickets were sold.

Within a day of that January 20th drawing, the news was out that Michigan's largest lottery jackpot had been won by five people, each of whom would receive $5.7 million. One of those winners was William Colbeck, a 44-year-old self-employed machine repairman from Novi, who claimed that he had been struck by actual lightning twice in his life—and by lottery lightning just once. He also asserted that he intended to stay a bachelor, regardless of any marriage proposals that might be forthcoming.

The other four winners were:

—Albert Peel, a 31-year-old truck-tire changer from Byron, who insisted that changing tires was his life and not something he would give up.

—Raymond Winiarski, also 31, a plant superintendent from Farmington Hills, whose wife was eight months pregnant with their first child.

—Charles Towne, a 40-year-old manufacturing representative from Medina, Ohio, who had been in Michigan on business the day he spent $10 on lottery tickets at a drugstore in Dearborn.

—D. Jay Sommers, who, at 20 years of age, became the youngest winner ever of a Michigan Lotto or Super Lotto jackpot over $1 million. Sommers, a boat mechanic and race-car driver from Sterling Heights, said he had had premonitions he would win and so had spent $150 on tickets for the drawing.

Two weeks after his lottery win, Sommers—a three-year veteran of short-track races in the Detroit and Toledo areas—was in the news again when he stunned auto-racing veterans by taking fourth place in the ARCA 200 at Daytona International Speedway in a car he had purchased and with a crew he had hastily assembled after his lottery win.

But Sommers had even bigger plans. He wanted to devote one year to "sheer indulgence and generosity," which would include winning enough races to be considered for NASCAR's Rookie of the Year honors; buying a second race car, a van, a Corvette, a car for his mother, and condominiums in Hawaii and Colorado; and taking a Hawaiian vacation with 10 of his buddies. After that he would settle down, he said, and buy a marina or boat-repair business like his father's.

The Reunion

"(Million-dollar winners) are normal people; they just get extra money."

—Joe Swierczynski, Michigan lottery winner

I t's a Saturday night in November 1987 and party time at the Amway Grand Plaza Hotel in Grand Rapids. But this is no ordinary party. Wandering the lobbies, broad stairways, restaurants, bars, and gift shops of the huge hotel complex are 111 Michigan lottery millionaires. They're here as guests of the Michigan Bureau of State Lottery in celebration of its 15th anniversary, and they're intent on enjoying a free weekend of wining and dining, tax and investment seminars, and casual elbow-rubbing with members of their own rather unique class.

The Grand Plaza is an elegant hotel, ornate and spacious, with enough wings, lobbies, corridors, and conference rooms to become happily lost in. Domed ceilings sprout enormous chandeliers, and gushing fountains support miniature ecosystems of exotic plant life. Baroque paintings, elaborate woodwork, plush carpeting, and bellhops in traditional monkey suits create an atmosphere of Old World refinement and sophistication. It is a fitting place to throw a party for 111 guests who pack a combined lottery worth of more than $286 million.

It is also a perfect setting and opportunity to observe what a mixed-bag of people lottery winners are. In a reception room, one winner, a woman dressed in an evening gown accented with jewels, drinks from a champagne glass with the perfect gesture of nonchalant aplomb. A man in a business suit earnestly talks taxes to another man who is rocking on his heels, his hands jangling keys and change deep in his pockets. Perched rigidly in chairs against one wall are a woman and her husband, both staring straight ahead, saying nothing. A young man in tight jeans and cowboy boots eats from a plate of cake. A small middle-age man in a plaid flannel shirt buttoned to the neck has been cornered by a television crew and is pressed against a wall, where he answers questions like a suspect in a police line-up.

And you can't help noticing that not all the guests are at ease in the Grand's opulence. Some stand staring in awe at the chandeliers; others sit huddled in small groups in corners of the lobbies. In one of the hotel's more expensive restaurants, a place flashing with brass and crystal and attended by waiters in white coats, one group of lottery winners orders in French and knows what wine they want while, a few tables away, another group seems baffled by the menu and would much prefer—you can't help thinking—an all-you-can-eat buffet at Big Boy, where there's no question about which fork to use for the salad.

At the far end of one of the hotel's numerous wings is a cheerful, lively, brightly lit bar designed to appeal to the less formal of the Grand Plaza's guests. Called "Tootsies," it apparently aims to snare the peanuts-and-beer crowd, or at least the wine-and-cheese crowd in a casual mood. The walls are crowded with mounted animal heads, fake-antique beverage signs, old tools and weapons, and a smattering of university emblems. The place is packed. It seems to be a crowd composed primarily of businessmen and businesswomen and Michigan State alumni buzzing about the upcoming football game with Indiana.

The bartender, a robust, bearded young man in a striped barber's shirt, is a little confused about the lottery convention. "Yea, what's going on?" he asks. "Some guy comes in here a little while ago and wants to know how much a shot of whiskey is. I say, '$2.75.' He says, 'How much if I'm in the Millionaire's Club?' I say, '$2.75.' So he leaves. Hey, if he's a millionaire, why is he asking? I should have said, 'Five bucks, plus tips,' you know what I mean?"

It's a common-enough story. There are similar contradictions in the lives of many lottery winners. On one hand, they have more money than they might ever have earned—enough to afford exotic vacations to Hawaii or Europe, enough to buy luxury automobiles and new houses, and enough to hire accountants to advise them about their investments. On the other hand, they are stuck with a lifetime's worth of habits, habits learned in the days when they lived from one paycheck to another, when it was necessary to neglect the phone bill to pay the gas bill, when $2.75 seemed an exhorbitant price to pay for a one-ounce shot of house whiskey. The result is that many lottery winners are caught in a kind of limbo, well-off but not wealthy, unable to go back to the old way of life, unable to break free of it and emerge into an entirely new one.

But just a few minutes of people-watching here is enough to convince even the staunchest skeptic that, overall, lotteries dispense prizes with a totally unbiased hand. This is democracy in action. Every level of social class, education, manners, and grace is represented. There are whites, blacks, and browns; young and old; thin and heavy; male and female. There are Catholics, Protestants, Jews, and atheists. There are the formerly well-to-do and the formerly destitute; those who have been changed drastically by the strange fact that a number of colored balls happened to fall in a certain order, and those who have been changed very little by it. If there is one constant, it is only that these people, like all people, cannot be conveniently categorized.

They have come to the reunion in Grand Rapids to learn about taxes, to eat expensive food, and to sleep in $130-a-day rooms that they won't have to pay for. But they have come primarily, as several make clear, to see other winners and to learn how winning has affected other lives.

Following, are a few of their stories.

◆

It looked as if Ron Northey was out of work. Butler Computer Graphics, where he worked as a production supervisor, was about to close its Detroit and Atlanta branch offices and consolidate its entire operation at its Denver headquarters. The company, which made computer-enhanced maps for utility companies, was doing well enough to offer Northey and many of his co-workers positions with the firm in Denver.

But Ron Northey wasn't willing to relocate. He'd lived in Detroit and Madison Heights all his life, and his family and friends were all there. Besides, he figured, he wouldn't have too much trouble finding another job. He was single, only 32 years old, and well-educated, with a track record and a resume impressive enough to be taken seriously by any number of potential employers. He turned Butler's offer down.

The office building where Butler Computer Graphics was located was quite self-contained and included a small branch bank on the ground floor and, next to it, a smoke and gift shop. Every Thursday, payday for Northey and his fellow workers, they would go down to the bank after work, cash their checks, then stop at the gift shop and buy lottery tickets. Northey bought between $5 and $10 worth each week, "like clockwork." Some of his friends spent considerably more, sometimes $50 or even $100 a week. None had ever won a prize worth mentioning.

On a Saturday night two days after turning down the offer to move to Denver and two weeks before he would have to take his place in an unemployment line, Ron Northey sat down with his tickets to watch the televised drawing of the Lotto numbers. It was December 21, 1985, four days before Christmas.

"I had a friend over," he recalls. "He was in the kitchen and I was sitting right in front of the TV with my two tickets, and they picked the numbers. I wrote them down on a sheet of paper as they picked them, then I put them in order and started comparing my tickets. I would always underline a number if I had it. So I got this one particular line of numbers and I started underlining one, two, three, four.

"Then you feel it. You just get this chill running up your spine, you know, and oh God, I looked at the fifth and it's the same, and oh man, it's like I'm almost afraid to look at the sixth number. I looked over there and it was 32, and oh God, you know, I won. And I couldn't write. I underlined the first four, but the last two I couldn't underline. You just get like a chill, you can't believe it. My friend walked into the room and asked if something was wrong, because I was all white. I said, 'No, nothing's wrong. I think I just won the lottery.' I handed him the ticket and he looked at it and he says, 'Yea, it looks good to me, you won.' I was just speechless. My heart was beating so hard I thought it was going to come out of my chest. I could actually hear it; it was just 'boom-boom, boom-boom.' We waited a couple of minutes and called the hotline to make sure we had the right numbers. We did."

Northey was the sole winner of a $1 million jackpot. On Monday morning he drove to Lansing to redeem his ticket, then returned home and went to work as if nothing had happened.

"I didn't tell people right away; I waited a few days. It's funny, but when it happens you're really kind of speechless. People get the impression, you know, that you jump up and down and scream, but really it's like you've been hit by lightning and you don't know what to say. The first thing I thought of was, there's got to be a mistake. Either the ticket was printed wrong, or I'm not reading it right, or I heard the wrong number, or something. (But) I figured at the very worst I had five numbers."

One of the first things he did was call a friend, a financial advisor, and ask what to do about taxes. He wondered, for example, if there would be tax advantages in waiting until after the end of the year to cash in the ticket. The friend advised him to cash the ticket immediately. In retrospect, Northey sees that as a mistake. He had no major deductions, did not own a house, and had not had time to prepare for a $50,000-a-year increase in his income. He was "hit pretty hard"—for about $20,000—when tax time rolled around in April. He was better prepared the next year.

In the meantime, he moved out of his small one-bedroom apartment and bought a nice house on the shores of a lake north of Pontiac. He planned to take the summer of 1986 off, then find a job. But as it turned out, his vacation stretched out to more than a year.

"I've been job hunting," he says. "It's kind of funny, because everybody assumes I'm not going to work anymore or don't want to work. But I do want to work. When I won the thing, I said I was going to take the summer off, and then when I moved into the new house it was easy to do because I was living on the water and there was lots of things to do outside. I was up at 8:30 or 9 every morning, I did a lot of yard work, planted a lot of flowers, things I didn't have time to do before. I played a lot of golf. It was kind of neat for awhile. But I would like to find something more constructive to do with my time this year. A lot of people seem to have the attitude that I'm retired or that I don't want to work, but that's not true.

"In the last couple of months I've started to look for a regular job. I've had a few interviews and actually turned a couple of jobs down." The problem is, he explains, that he isn't looking for a job just for something to do or just for the money. He wants to find employment he can apply himself to, be committed to. "I don't tell them, when I'm applying for a job, that I'm a lottery winner. The kind of jobs I'm looking for, to be good at them, you have to be kind of hungry and a go-getter. I don't think they would think I have that kind of attitude. But I do.

The longer I wait to get a job, the harder it will be to account for all this time off. I haven't had to do it yet, but I'll just say I inherited some money. I really want to be just one of the regular workers. I don't want to be a guy that is just doing this for fun. I want to do a good job, be able to get raises, bonuses—things like that—to have incentives."

When Northey's good fortune was announced in the papers, he came across as something of a playboy, a big spender. It was reported, for instance, that one of the first things he wanted to do was sail around the Caribbean on a 50-foot sailboat with seven of his friends. "That thing about the sailboat was kind of elaborated on a little bit," he says. "The whole story behind it is that my financial advisor, *he* said that *he* was going to the Caribbean and maybe I would want to come with him and his friends. I said maybe, but it never panned out and that whole story got told wrong."

Nothing that extravagant was in Northey's mind. He bought his house and made a few investments but says there really have not been major changes in his life. (He does admit, however, that he was "stretched a little thin" by the end of the first year and was waiting for his next lottery check.)

"People don't change that much. You get the impression that everything is going to be 100 percent different. Well, they aren't that much different. You hear stories about people who can't handle it, it goes to their heads, they start blowing it. Even when you go up there to Lansing to cash the ticket in, you hear stories that long-lost relatives are going to call you, that people are going to want to borrow money, that there's going to be newspaper reporters and TV cameras, and women are going to be throwing themselves at your feet. But it hasn't been like that for me. It's been pretty quiet, pretty normal.

"I won on a Saturday night, and I went in on Monday to work just like normal. It was kind of funny, because whenever we'd cash our checks and buy tickets—and there were usually a few of us there together doing it—somebody'd always say, 'If I win, I'm never coming into this damned place again; you'll never see me here again.' Now I'm looking for a job I like, with working conditions I like. You can't always pick and choose like that, but I'm looking at it from a different angle now."

◆

If you're looking for normalcy, for a normal person who accepted his lottery win without excitement and never let it keep him from living a normal life, look no further than at Jay Hite. The 57-year-old registered pharmacist, who owned a drugstore in East Jordan, made it clear from the very moment he won a $1 million jackpot in a Michigame drawing on June 13, 1978, that he wouldn't be changed by it. He told reporters at the Port Huron park where the drawing was held that he planned to be behind the counter of his pharmacy when it opened the next morning. The retired Air Force pilot did concede, however, that he was nervous. "I sort of have butterflies in my stomach," he said. "I had the same feeling once when I crashed with a B-52."

Six months after winning, an interview with a *Detroit News* reporter revealed that Hite's relaxed attitude about his lottery money had not altered. "I told my wife we were going to sit on the situation and not make many big decisions for at least a year," he said. "We have to know what Uncle Sam will take out in income taxes, and I've got some certified public accountants working on that." He had no plans for early retirement, major vacations or big spending. He did buy a new hot-water heater, a washer, a dryer, a delivery truck for his pharmacy, and a car for his 18-year-old daughter, but put most of the money away safe in the bank.

Ten years later, Jay Hite's strategy is still the same. He no longer works—having sold his drugstore in 1983—although he has let it be known to his friends in the business that if they need someone to fill in for them in emergencies he might be available. "*Might* be available," he says, laughing. "It hasn't happened yet, which suits me fine." Now he spends his time "planning for the future" while relaxing in his house, which overlooks Lake Charlevoix. Those plans may include some traveling, he admits. His wife, a former reporter for the Lansing *State Journal*, would like to write a book, an idea that pleases Jay Hite. "Mostly though, we're just going to enjoy ourselves," he says.

◆

A few days before the September 5, 1987, Super Lotto drawing for a jackpot worth $12 million, 69-year-old Anna Michalski shopped for groceries at Giantway Plaza in her hometown, Traverse City. Mrs.

Michalski played the Super Lotto regularly and usually bought three tickets for each drawing. That day, however, she noticed the large jackpot and decided to buy 20 tickets instead.

It proved to be a profitable decision. While watching the Saturday drawing on television she learned that her fourth ticket was a winner. When she realized she had all six numbers she "kind of went numb. I checked, double checked, triple checked, then I gave the ticket to my husband for him to check," she said.

As one of two winners, Mrs. Michalski received $6 million. She picked up her initial check for $240,000 at the spot where she bought the winning ticket, the Giant supermarket, then drove to her home half a mile away and—determined not to let a little thing like winning the lottery change her—tried to return to life as normal.

Her plans for the money? Mrs. Michalski and her husband, Charles, 72, a semi-retired consulting engineer for Reid, Cool and Michalski of Southfield, contemplated travel, perhaps to North Carolina and, later, Spain. They also planned to provide for the college education of their 9-year-old granddaughter. First, however, they consulted with their daughter Joanne, an accountant in Bellaire, about how best to handle their windfall.

Mrs. Michalski was very clear about one thing: The money would not change their lives much. At a press conference after picking up the initial check, she said, "We're pretty comfortable right now. I wouldn't say we need anything. I'm not interested in mink coats or diamonds. We have a comfortable home already. I guess I'm just happy knowing that this money will be passed on to my children someday."

◆

Fred Molitor, a 66-year-old retired plumbing-supply salesman from Royal Oak, was on vacation in Colorado in May 1976 when members of his family frantically tried to locate him. They finally contacted a park ranger at a campground where he was staying, and the ranger left a message on Molitor's windshield that read, "Contact me immediately. I have wonderful news."

Wonderful news indeed. Molitor was one of 50 finalists who had been chosen from an enormous pool of losing Michigan Landmarks instant-game tickets that had been mailed in to the lottery bureau. Molitor left his camper where it sat and flew home. A few days later, richer by $1 million, he returned to Colorado to claim his camper and continue his interrupted vacation.

Two years later, in June 1978, Fred Molitor again made news when, six days after receiving his annual check, he filed a formal, legal complaint against the lottery bureau. According to the attorney who represented him, Molitor had requested that lottery payments be made not to him personally, but rather to him as trustee of a fund he had established the previous month. The idea of the trust fund, the lawyer said, was to prevent future lottery money from being tied up in probate court in the event of Mr. Molitor's death. "We're just trying to keep the thing out of probate court when I die," Molitor said. "I'm doing it for the kids." Another benefit, incidentally, would be to reduce inheritance taxes.

The lottery bureau claimed that it could not assign checks to anyone but the winner personally, unless they first received a court order. That was the only difficulty. When the appropriate court order arrived, the problem was resolved, and subsequent checks went to the trust fund, as Mr. Molitor had requested.

◆

Mark Gieseking was 27 years old and living with his parents in Grosse Pointe Park when he won $2,259,592 in the June 15, 1985, Lotto drawing.

There have been some changes in his life since then, but mainly superficial ones—like a $155,000 colonial-style house in Grosse Pointe Woods; and like two cars, a 1985 Toyota Supra and a 1986 Toyota 4 x 4. He still works at his $11,000-a-year job in the service department of an electronics store on the east side of Detroit, a job he has held since he was 17. His parents don't seem to consider his lottery win significant enough to change anything either—when he wrote them a check for $500 as a combined Father's Day, Mother's Day, and anniversary present, for example, his mother worried that it was too much money and waited six weeks to cash it. He still has the same friends, still likes to bowl, and neither dresses, acts, nor talks like a young man who collects a $90,320 check from the lottery bureau each year.

He admits, however, that though he has not changed, his altered financial status sometimes affects the way people react to him. His friends seldom let an opportunity pass to mention to strangers that he is a lottery winner, and they like to kid with him about picking up the check at restaurants. From friends, that's acceptable. When it comes from strangers, as it sometimes does, Gieseking is quick to set them straight.

Still, he's determined to go on with life as usual. As he told a *Detroit Free Press* reporter in November 1987, "I'm too young to retire. You've got to keep busy. Otherwise you sit all day in front of the TV set. You get bored with it too quickly."

◆

Will and Lillian Keinath left their Frankenmuth home on a cold Friday night in January to spend a couple of days at their cottage near AuGres, a frequent getaway that they liked to share with their friends. But all of their friends had previous engagements this weekend, so Will and Lil went alone.

In AuGres they pulled their car into the parking lot of the Town and Country Bar—the only place in town to buy Lotto tickets then, in 1986—and discussed how much they should spend on tickets. Lil suggested $10, slightly more than they usually spent. A few days earlier, at her job as a food-service worker at the elementary school in Frankenmuth, a co-worker had paid a debt to Lil with a dollar that she said was lucky. Lil said if it was lucky she was going to spend it on the lottery, and the woman said that if Lil won she owed her a lobster dinner. So Lil was feeling lucky. But Will wasn't. "Ten dollars is too much," he said. "Heck, you won't win anyway."

Lil said nothing. She got out of the car, went into the bar and bought $10 worth of Lotto tickets for the January 19 drawing.

In their 36 years of marriage, the Keinaths had worked hard, had raised a family, and had built solid friendships in their community. They were active people, who enjoyed traveling, cross-country skiing, and hunting and fishing, but their jobs took too much of their time to really enjoy those pastimes. Will owned a real-estate agency in Frankenmuth, an occupation that gave him the freedom to choose his own hours, but also demanded a lot of time, often in the evenings and on weekends. Lil had worked at the hospital in Frankenmuth as a dietician for 13 years, then in the cafeteria at the elementary school for another 12.

If they had a regret it was that their lifestyle did not leave enough time, day to day, to be together. It seemed as though whenever Lil wasn't working, Will was; and when Will had time off, Lil had to work. They took an annual trip to South Dakota together to hunt pheasants, and they got away for shorter periods of time at the cottage. But day in and day out it seemed like they only saw each other in passing.

When they began playing the lottery they recognized it as a possible way to get more time together. So they wrote up and signed a pact, a belated nuptial agreement, promising each other that if they ever won big in the lottery they would quit their jobs and spend more time together.

That wasn't the only plan they made. They also had told their children that if they ever won the lottery they would take them and their families on a vacation to Europe, including a visit to their daughter-in-law's 83-year-old grandmother, who lived in Norway. The children thought they were kidding.

That Saturday night, alone in the cottage at AuGres, Will and Lil sat down to watch the televised lottery drawing. As the six plastic balls rolled out of the drum, Lil wrote the winning numbers down on a scrap of paper. Then she went to her purse and got the tickets she had purchased earlier in town. She read the numbers off, one line at a time. It wasn't until she reached the 10th line—the last one, the one that Will would not have purchased because he was sure they would not win anyway—that she began to ring up matches.

"I was looking at that last line," Lil recalls, "and I said, 'Oh gee, I guess I've got four right. No, I guess I have five. No! I have six!' You know how it is, the numbers are mixed up, and I was going through and getting them straightened out. We couldn't believe it. Will turned to me and said that I must have made a mistake. So we turned on the radio and listened until they announced the winning numbers. Every time they repeated those numbers we copied them down, and they were right. It was just nerve-wracking."

Lil's first impulse was to sign the back of the winning ticket, as she'd heard repeatedly a winner should do to be protected in case of loss or theft.

But she decided to wait until they got some advice. They stayed at the cottage that night, went home the next day, then consulted their accountant on Monday morning. He advised them to form a lottery club in order to protect their children from estate taxes in the event of their death. According to him, claiming the ticket in a corporation's name would save over $300,000 in estate taxes. Fine, said Will and Lil, they would do that.

But there was a catch. Forming a corporation meant that they could not redeem their ticket until they had received an IRS number, a procedure that would take 10 days to two weeks. Looking back on those two weeks, Will and Lil laugh now, but at the time, they say, those were among the strangest 14 days of their lives. They vowed to keep the news to themselves until they had the IRS number and could safely redeem their ticket. The only people they told were their accountant and their children, whom they had called the night they won.

Lil carried the ticket in her wallet from Saturday until Tuesday morning, then Will took it to the bank and placed it in a safe-deposit box. While he was there he bumped into a friend, a fellow realtor from the office. The friend, who always kidded Will about having lots of money, saw him leaving the safe-deposit box area and asked, "How much did you put in this time, Will? A million?" Will looked him square in the eye and said, "No. Two million."

Meanwhile, Lil was having some unusual experiences of her own at work. She found it very difficult to behave as if nothing was out of the ordinary. Every day, she had to work with the woman who had given her the "lucky" dollar, knowing that she was going to be buying her a lobster dinner. She was barely able to keep the news to herself. Then, to make matters worse, another co-worker came to work one day excited because he had hit five numbers in the Lotto and won $2,000. "I'm telling him that it's great," she recalls, "and you know, he's really excited, and here I am trying to keep from bubbling right over with my own news. Everyone was talking about Lotto this and Lotto that, and I wanted to say something but I couldn't. It was fun."

And the fun was just beginning. Frankenmuth is a small city, population about 4,500, and almost from the minute the Keinaths finally received their IRS number, redeemed their ticket, and released the news, the town was buzzing about their $2,173,504 prize. The next few weeks were, in Lil's words, "a little hectic." The phone rang constantly, and cars stopped in front of the house to look and take photos. Will and Lil felt slightly invaded.

"When we went to the store it took twice as long as it should have," Will says.

"Everyone wanted to know where we bought the ticket, what time we bought it, how we chose our numbers, whether we bought it the day of the drawing or earlier," Lil says, laughing.

As for the pacts and promises they had made, the Keinaths proved true to their word. It took about a year for Will to wrap up his affairs at the real-estate office and for Lil to finish her obligations at the school, but they both did quit their jobs. They then spent the following year doing what they had always dreamed of: traveling and keeping busy *together*. As promised, they took their children and grandchildren to Europe—including a visit to the 83-year-old grandmother in Norway—and took a cruise through the Inside Passage to Alaska. In 12 months they logged about 25,000 travel miles, enough to circumnavigate the earth. And that's only the beginning, according to Will. He and Lil, he says, have become "travel-holics" who have many more miles ahead of them.

But, Lil is quick to add, the money isn't *everything* to them. "We've given away more to charity and to our friends than we've kept for ourselves, almost," she says. "I guess we're the same people we've always been, and it's not changed our lifestyle at all. In fact, a lot of people have told us that. Our friends are still our friends. They realize that we haven't changed a bit, that we're the same as we always were. That's the fun of it."

Young Winners

"What the hell am I going to do if I retire?"

—Paul Otto, Michigan lottery winner

T here is a real temptation to draw general, sweeping conclusions about certain types of lottery winners, especially a minority group like young people. They stand out—a scant 5 percent of Michigan's lottery millionaires have been less than 25 years old when they won—and are undoubtedly ripe for generalizing.

The young are the ones who go wild when they win and squander their fortunes on foolishness, right? They have all those years ahead of them to make good, sensible use of their money. But instead, they prove to be so impetuous, whimsical, unreliable and immature that they go out and buy fancy cars, big houses, televisions, stereos, VCRs, and other things they really don't need until they wake up one morning flat-out broke.

It ain't necessarily so.

◆

Joe Swierczynski was a young man with plans. Even before he graduated from high school he knew he wanted to be independent—to work for himself and build a solid, successful company that would earn him respect and a good living. While most of his classmates were packing grocery bags or slinging Big Macs for minimum wage, Joe bought a lawn mower and went into the yard-maintenance business. And he was good at it. He was an honest, hard-working young man, and his customers liked him, trusted him, and recommended him to their neighbors. It didn't take long before he had all the work he wanted, mostly in a few subdivisions near his parents' home in Roseville. He was able to buy a pickup truck, a trailer, and a supply of good tools. The future was definitely looking bright.

His success confirmed something he had always known about himself. Even when he was just a kid he knew that someday, somehow, he was going to make it big at something. When he told that to people they laughed. But that didn't bother Joe much. Why shouldn't they laugh? After all, he wasn't even sure himself what he meant by it. All he had was confidence and ambition. All he knew for sure was that someday he would have the last laugh.

That day came sooner than even Joe expected.

Since the day he had turned 18 and could legally buy tickets, Joe had regularly played the lottery, as did his parents and five brothers and sisters. All of them had personal sets of Lotto numbers that they played week after week. Once, Joe missed buying a ticket, and that week four of his usual numbers came up. He vowed never to let it happen again.

The routine was for someone at home to watch the televised Wednesday and Saturday drawings, then check the winning numbers against those on the tickets the family kept on the kitchen counter.

But Wednesday, July 9, 1986, was a busy day at the Swierczynski household, and nobody was free to watch the drawing. Joe worked late, and when he finally arrived home at 9 o'clock, he didn't think to check the numbers. Nobody did. The next morning Joe went to work as usual, his father left for the construction site where he worked as a carpenter, and his brothers and sisters also left for their jobs.

Joe's mother, alone in the house, sat down with the morning newspaper and began checking off numbers. One set required double checking.

Mrs. Swierczynski had difficulty finding Joe that morning. He was not at the subdivision where he had said he was going to work. He was running errands, she would later learn, and didn't get to the job as early as he had planned. She drove the streets looking for Joe, then stopped at a friend's house in the same subdivision to ask if anyone had seen him. It was the friend, later, who spotted Joe mowing a nearby lawn and brought him back to his house, where his mother was waiting.

At first he thought something was terribly wrong. His mother looked grief-stricken.

"You didn't check the lottery numbers last night, did you?" she asked.

"No, why?"

"You hit six numbers in the Lotto."

A year later, Joe tells that story while sitting in the dining room of his new house, on the banks of a canal a few hundred yards from the lakeshore in a very desirable St. Clair Shores neighborhood. His neighbors are, for the most part, late-middle-age couples or retirees with grandchildren who visit them on weekends. It is a neighborhood where the residents take a great deal of pride in their automobiles, houses, yards and rose gardens. Vines cover fireplace chimneys, and short sections of weathered split-rail fence are very popular. Many of the houses, like Joe's, back up to canals, where new powerboats are moored or suspended in lifts above the water.

Joe's house was built in 1926, he says, and is a ponderous, two-story affair previously owned by someone with a clear preference for stucco. There is wood-trimmed stucco on the outside, and inside, it's a complete job. Stucco covers everything but the floor—a total white-plaster coating over the walls, ceiling, and even all the ornate pilasters, crown moldings, and wainscoting the house was originally trimmed with.

"I got a deal on it, I think," he says. "When I moved in, it looked like Sanford and Son, it was so full of junk. You wouldn't recognize it now, and all I've done is clean it up. Come back in six months and you won't recognize it again."

We are sitting in a large dining room dominated by a new table and new chairs, which Joe bought, along with a new bed, shortly after moving in, four months earlier. Another small room, the "TV room," is furnished with a couch, a chair, a stereo system, and a television set. But every other room in the house is noticeably bare—empty enough to echo—and very, very white. Joe explains that he has not had time to shop for furniture and is putting it off until someone can give him a hand with the chore.

He gets up and paces. The compact, solidly built young man walks with an energetic, bounding step. One moment he seems older than his 22 years; a moment later he seems younger. "I'm a smartass by trade," he says, admitting that he likes to "mess with people's minds" and not tell them he is a lottery winner. Then, offering me a beer: "I'm something of a connoisseur of beers." He has Bass Ale, Molson and Miller. After awhile he admits that he doesn't care much for the taste of the ale.

While we talk there is a knock on the front door, and Joe gets up to let in a friend. His name is Ken, a 20-year-old neighbor who lives with his parents and has become Joe's friend in the past few months. In a few days he and Joe will be driving in Joe's car to Florida for a week's vacation. It will be spring break for many colleges, and they are looking forward, primarily, to a few intense days of parties and girls.

Joe introduces me as a guy who is writing a book about lottery winners. Ken is confused. He shakes my hand, looks at Joe, looks at me, and looks at Joe again. He seems embarrassed. "Are you a lottery winner?" he asks Joe, tentatively.

"Yea, I won a million and a half in Lotto last summer."

"Wow," Ken says. "Oh wow. That explains some things."

I want to know if I'm being kidded. This could have been pre-arranged. But Ken is either very sincere or a very good actor.

"I don't make it a practice to tell people about it," Joe says. "I mean, it's no big secret or anything, but I don't tell people unless they ask." He's got a definite twinkle in his eyes. He's enjoying this very much.

Ken is still slightly shaken. "This explains a lot," he says again. "I mean, I had to wonder, Joe being only 22, what did he do to be able to afford living over here, because everyone here, like my parents, are 50, 60, with families, kids. It falls in place now, though, why you're living here."

Joe just nods and shrugs. He goes on with the story of his lottery win with a little more animation now—his audience having doubled—and tells how he and his mother, after she had told him the good news, jumped around and hugged and called a "bunch of people" on the telephone.

Joe spent about 20 minutes celebrating, then went back and finished mowing the lawn he had been working on. "What would you do?" he asks when I show surprise. The job wasn't finished, it had to be done. He found it very hard to do, but he stuck with it to the end. Then he went home, called the Lansing office of the lottery bureau and made an appointment to validate his ticket on Monday. "I had a lot of work to do, and at the time, that was more important to me. I had to get that work done. Then I couldn't work the next day because it rained, so I went back to work Saturday."

That Saturday night, he also went to the part-time bartending job he had held for over three years. "I went to work that night like normal, and nobody could understand it. They said, 'What are you doing here?' Even my boss, everybody, they couldn't believe that I was still working. You know, it's one of those deals. What do they want me to do? I want to work. I can't go to Hawaii or nothing right now, it's not convenient."

Even after he had picked up the first installment of his $1,476,650 prize—a check for about $59,000 afer taxes—he continued with his lawn work for several weeks. Eventually he handed his accounts over to his brother-in-law—"just temporarily"—so that he could concentrate on buying a house and straightening out his new financial situation. But he continued to work at the part-time bartending job.

Joe was 21 years, 11 months old when he won his lottery jackpot, a fact he is acutely aware of. He hopes he is the youngest million-dollar lottery winner in Michigan, and when I show him the names of a winner who is younger, he is slightly upset.

Joe is well aware of the risks involved in winning so much money at such a young age. He plans to continue working part-time as a bartender, a job he enjoys, and eventually to continue with the lawn-maintenance business, perhaps expanding it and hiring employees.

"I would much rather say I got where I am now because I worked hard, invested right, did this and that. Now people might look at me and say, 'Oh yea, he's got that because he won the lottery, not because he worked hard.' Well, yea, I know they'll look at it that way, especially if I don't do nothing with the money, go blow it, make stupid investments. But if I do good with the money—double it, triple it—then people will respect me."

And already he has learned that unexpected riches aren't an automatic ticket to Easy Street. "Everybody says, 'Boy, if I won I'd do this, I'd do that.' And I tell people it's a lot different when you actually do win. I used to say the same things, that I'd do this, do that. Then I won. And I haven't actually done what I said I was going to do. One thing I said, the first thing that's going to happen, I'm going to retire my Dad. He's 50 and has worked hard all his life. But what I won isn't enough. I could retire him, but it wouldn't leave me any money. I'm not saying I'm going to take all the money for myself, but it won't be for another five or six years until I can really help out my family. My dad will retire earlier, before his time, I'm sure of that. When I first won, I thought, 'Man, I'm going to buy a Corvette.' Then I started looking at the prices of them. I figured the insurance for them—I'd have to win again just to pay the insurance. . . .

"I'm just slowly but surely going to make the money work for me, because when I get my last check I'll still be young. So I have to make it work for me so I don't *have* to work, but I can if I want to. My family understands. I mean, they don't expect nothing. They'll get nice gifts. I tell them that if they need money, for any reason, don't hesitate to come to me. But they don't need it. They don't expect nothing from me, so whatever they get they'll be happy.

"I get $74,000 and something a year, and I get a take-home of $59,000. They take 20 percent right off the top. Fifty-nine thousand is a good living for anyone, but it's not a millionaire's living. People think I'm a millionaire, but I'm not.

"All the attention I got after winning was positive—nobody really looking for a dime, nothing like that. I expected the worst. I thought I was going to get calls from somebody who said they needed an operation, their husband had died, but I didn't get anything like that—because, obviously, lottery winners are a dime a dozen. They are. I'm not embarrassed or ashamed I won. I just don't want to make a big deal about it."

Outside, in the driveway, is the new Ford Escort Joe bought instead of a cherry-red Corvette. Fastened to the back window is a yellow diamond-shaped plastic sign proclaiming, "Future Millionaire on Board." Joe laughs about that, admitting he had the same message printed on a T-shirt that he enjoys wearing around people who have no idea he's a lottery winner.

"If someone came up to me and asked, yea, I'd tell 'em," he says. "But I'm a smartass by trade. I'd give 'em a line or whatever—I'd tell the truth eventually—I'd just have a little fun messing with their minds first. People have all these myths about lottery winners. They think they're filthy rich and drive Cadillacs everywhere. But they're normal people; they just get extra money."

Joe still plays the lottery "all the time." He has no secret technique and doesn't believe that such a thing exists. He makes it clear that there is no skill involved in winning the lottery, just plain old "dumb luck." The numbers he won with were chosen because they "just looked good on the card."

"I proved to a lot of people that, I guess it is true, you *can* win. You got to play to win, that's what people don't understand. I play $5 every drawing. I don't consider myself a gambler, but believe me, you gotta play if you want to win, especially if you want to win big."

For Joe Swierczynski, hitting it big came sooner than he ever dreamed it would. "I always thought I would have to wait until I was 40 or so to get where I'm at now," he says. But, he admits, life isn't much different than it was before—"You have the same problems, just with bigger numbers"—although there are certain advantages besides the obvious financial ones. "I'm getting more respect now, the respect I deserve, I should say. People talk to me on more of an adult level. When I talk they listen now."

There has also been a certain satisfaction in knowing that he was right about the special destiny he suspected for himself all along. "What I used to say was, to friends and relatives, 'Yea, 'I'm gonna hit it big.' And just jokingly I'd say, 'And I'm gonna win the lottery just to get it over with.' Jokingly. But now I'm telling people I'll be the first to win it twice. Nobody has won it twice. Let me tell you, I will be the first to win it twice."

Remember, you read it here first.

◆

Sometimes the road to riches is paved with misadventures. That was certainly the case with 21-year-old Paul Otto of Dexter. On April 23, 1986, he won a $2 million Lotto jackpot because somebody tried to bust him in the nose with a thermos full of coffee.

He worked as a heating-and-cooling installer and, in 1986, wasn't far from completing the three-year requirement to become a journeyman. Other aspects of his job, however, weren't working out as well. He and his boss weren't seeing eye-to-eye, and the union was getting on his back because he'd had the audacity to speak out against certain policies he wasn't fond of. That was the way Paul was. He'd been raised to speak up when something bothered him, not just meekly accept what he considered to be unjust and unfair. He figured the union existed to serve its members, and when he felt that wasn't happening, he didn't hesitate to make his opinion known. His stance earned him a few enemies. One, in particular.

But the job wasn't unbearable. The best part of it was his friendship with his partner, an older journeyman with many years in the business. Together they were usually able to salvage the best out of any situation. At the very least they were always able to find something to laugh about, to find little ways to make work more enjoyable. One way, which had become a little ritual, was to come to work early every morning and sit down for a cup of coffee together before beginning the day's work.

Paul still isn't sure what got into his Enemy that morning, Wednesday, April 24, 1986. "I'd had previous problems with him," he recalls. "But this morning, with no warning, he busts in on my partner and me when we're having our coffee and starts screaming that he's gonna kill me. The next thing I know, he takes a swing at me. I couldn't believe it, he actually took a swing at me. So I blasted him. I hurt him, I know that. I didn't know it at the time, but I do now. The guy picked up my thermos, my own thermos filled with *my* coffee, and he says that was it, he'd had it, he didn't like me and never had and now he was going to kill me. He's coming at me with my own thermos, ready to hit me with it. I wasn't going to take that sitting down. How could I? I was ready to blast him again, but my partner, he grabs me around the back and holds me. He weighs about 100 pounds more than I do, and when I try to swing I can't even move. 'Don't do it, Paul,' he says, 'it's stupid.' Yea, right, except that the other guy's still coming at me with the thermos, and he's going to coldcock me with it while my partner's holding me. So my partner, *he* blasts the guy and puts him down. . . ."

"Well, that wasn't the end of it. I left work and went down to the police station and filed a report. Then my boss calls down there and wants to know what happened. I explained the situation. He gets mad at *me* because I went to the cops, and I ask him, 'Hey, what am I supposed to do? Go to work and get bashed by a thermos of coffee?' Well, anyway, I hang up the phone, and the cop I've been talking too—I knew him anyway—he says I should just go home and do something entirely different for the day, not go to work at all, just go take it easy."

Not bad advice. Paul went home—he lived with his parents—and told his mother what had happened. She was just getting ready to go grocery shopping and talked Paul into going with her. "It'll be good for you," she said, "get your mind off your troubles."

They went to the Dexter IGA, and while they were there Paul spotted a lottery-ticket terminal. His mother told him that the jackpot for that night's Lotto drawing was up to $10 million, and Paul, who had not purchased a lottery ticket in months—not once, in fact, in the entire year—decided to buy a few. He bought three: two Easy Picks and one with numbers he chose himself. Actually, he only deliberately picked one number, 26, which he had worn on his football jersey in high school; the others he just jotted down randomly on the card.

"We finished the shopping," Paul recalls, "went home, put away the groceries, then I just blew the rest of the day off. I took off, went here, went there, visited some friends. By the time I got home it was late, so I went to bed and put a bad day behind me."

In the morning he asked his mother if she had heard the winning Lotto numbers from the previous night's drawing. She hadn't; she'd forgotten about it entirely. He left for work and on the way, listening to the radio, heard that the lottery bureau had announced that five winning tickets had been purchased for the $10 million jackpot and that one of them had been purchased in Dexter.

"I thought to myself, 'Some lucky sonofabitch hit.' I still didn't know the numbers—they never told them—but it didn't matter because I never thought it was me."

At the shop, the company cat was hungry. Taking care of the cat was a cooperative effort; whoever noticed it was out of food went to the store and picked some up. If they brought back the receipt, the company would reimburse them. Paul went out and bought a bag of food, put the receipt in his shirt pocket with his lottery ticket, and promptly forgot about them both.

Later, while working on the roof of a building, he bent over abruptly, and the receipt and lottery ticket fell out of his pocket. It was a windy day, and a gust caught the bits of paper and blew them across the roof. Lunging, Paul managed to grab the lottery ticket, but the receipt blew off the roof and disappeared.

All day, whenever he had a chance—on break, eating lunch, driving in the truck—he listened to the radio hoping to hear what the winning numbers were. He knew somebody in Dexter had won—"Some lucky stiff," people said—and it was the talk of the town. And whenever the subject came up, Paul would remember his own ticket and ask, "Hey, what *are* the winning numbers anyway?" But nobody knew.

After work he stopped at the Eagles club. Paul had a $100 bet going with his partner to see who could last the longest without an alcoholic drink, so he drank a soda while he talked with his buddies. The subject of the lottery again came up.

"Doggone it," Paul said. "Somebody tell me what the Lotto numbers were last night."

The bartender said he knew them and recited five numbers from memory. But he went blank on the sixth.

Meanwhile, Paul was scanning his ticket. "I'm looking at it, and I say, 'Damn, I got five numbers.' I'm just happy as hell. The bartender takes my ticket and looks at it. Then he remembers that all six numbers are written on the chalkboard in the other room, so he goes in there. I'm just happy I got five numbers, that's enough for me. A couple hundred bucks or whatever. But I follow him in, and he's standing there reading the numbers on my ticket and looking at the chalkboard, and looking at the ticket, and looking at the chalkboard again. Then he says, 'Paul, you've got all six.' But by then it was too late. I'd already seen the sixth number and knew it was a winner. When he turns around he says, 'Paul?' and looks down and I'm laying flat out on the floor. I don't know what happened. I looked at that number, knew I had it, and the next thing I knew, I was on the floor."

They were the numbers he had picked himself, the ones that included his old football jersey's 26. "It was one of those deals where, hey, I just got lucky. A friend picked me up off the floor and was hugging me, slapping me on the back—I thought I was going to die he was hitting me so hard. 'This is great!' he's yelling. 'You're a millionaire. Sign it!' I had never signed the ticket. Hell, I'd never imagined even coming close to winning, so why would I sign my ticket? But I signed it then. And I said I wanted to buy a round for the bar. But they said, no way, the bar was buying a round for everybody, and they gave me a beer. That beer cost me a hundred bucks, because of the bet I had with my partner at work. I saw him about two days later, and he didn't know what had happened, that I'd had the winning ticket. I wrote him out a check for the hundred right on the spot. When I told him I'd won the lottery, he said, 'Come on, you're joking.' I don't think he ever cashed the check. I haven't gotten it back yet."

His partner wasn't the only one who had trouble believing Paul had won. He called his fiancee, Lisa, at work—they had planned to be married in a year or so, when they could afford it—and said, "Let's get married tomorrow."

"Why?" she asked.

"I just won the lottery."

"Oh you did not."

"No, really. I did. I won the lottery."

"Don't lie to me."

One of Paul's friends got on the line and told her it was true. He convinced her, finally, that she was engaged to marry a lottery millionaire.

"So she's just bouncing off the walls," Paul says. "It was great, you know? Well, then I try calling my parents. I try, I don't know how many times, but I can't get through. The line's always busy. So I call the operator and say, 'Look, I've been trying to get through to this number and I can't get any answer, the thing keeps coming back busy.' I tell her, 'You've got to break through; this is very important.' She tries and tries and finally says, 'I'm sorry, the phone must be out of order.' I say, 'But I just won the lottery and I gotta tell my mom and dad I won.' She says, 'I'm sorry—no, I'm not, congratulations—but I can't get through.' So I call the neighbor.

"Well, the neighbor's been known to be quite a practical joker to start with. He rides his three-wheeler down to my mom and dad's, and he's just shooting the breeze with them like it's no big deal. Something's finally said about the lottery, because somebody from Dexter had won. 'Well,' the neighbor says, 'you know, Paul's been trying to get ahold of you guys to tell you he's got the winning ticket.' My mom looks at him kind of funny and says, 'Oh sure, Dennis.' But then she thinks about it for a second and decides he would never make up a story like that. So she calls the Eagles club, and the bartender answers the phone and says, 'Yea, Carol, he's got the ticket, and he wants you guys to come up.'

"It was four or five miles from my mom and dad's house, and they came up. When I first see my dad I've got tears in my eyes because I'm so excited, right? And I look at him and say, 'Dad, I won,' and my dad looks at me and says, 'You lucky little sonofabitch.' My little brother's looking at me, and he's like, 'Wowww.' My mom grabs me and starts hugging me and crying. I say, 'What are you crying for Mom? Hell, I just won two million dollars.' She says, 'I'm so happy for you.' "

The next day, Paul, Lisa, Mrs. Otto, Paul's younger brother, and his brother's best friend rode to Lansing in a limousine rented for them by the owner of the IGA where Paul had purchased his winning ticket. The most remarkable thing about that trip, Paul recalls, is that, though they were happy and having fun, they weren't particularly excited.

"At the lottery commission," he says, "it was like they couldn't believe how calm we were. Laurie Kipp-Klecha, she said she never saw any winners as calm as us. We just wanted to blow off all the hype. It was like it just wasn't that big a deal. But then they brought me my check, and it was for $80,000. I took a look at it and I looked at my mom and I looked at my fiancee and I said, 'You hold it,' and I handed it to her. It was such a weird situation, holding a check for $80,000 that I knew was good."

Paul Otto insists that winning $2 million has had no major effect on his life. A few months after he won, he quit his job at the heating-and-cooling company—something he says he would have done anyway—and went back to his first love, repairing automobiles. He's now a certified state mechanic and works at a garage owned by a friend. He gave his pickup truck to another friend and bought a new one for himself. He also bought a race car, but Lisa won't let him drive it. Otherwise, there have been few changes. He lives in a rented house with two friends and plans to keep renting, at least until he and Lisa marry in March 1988. There have been few extravagances, and he is proud of the fact that he lives entirely on the money he earns. His annual lottery checks go directly into investments—"a week after I get them"—and he hardly gives the money another thought until tax time.

Paul has no plans to apply his money toward early retirement. "That's what everybody says they'd do. What the hell am I going to do if I retire? There's 24 hours in a day, and yeah, I enjoy fishing and hunting, but even that gets old. If I keep working, the only thing I can do is better myself, and that's what I want to do. I want to get better at what I do. What I do is repair cars. Everybody looks at me and says, 'God, if I had your money . . . .' I say, 'Right, if you had my money all you'd want to do is retire and spend it.' Everybody doesn't understand that. Everyone has a stereotype of someone who wins the lottery. I hear it every day. 'If I had your money I'd do this, I'd do that. But nobody understands what it's really like."

Misunderstanding and rumors started following him around almost from the day he won his jackpot. The day after, his fiancee's younger brother heard people talking about Paul, saying that he had gone out and bought a Porsche and a Lamborghini. Other stories were just as outrageous. A friend suggested that Paul begin nipping the rumors in the bud by starting his own. "Tell 'em you're going to spend the first $79,000 on wine, women and song, and you're just going to blow the last thousand," he said.

"Sometimes I've wished that they never gave me the money," Paul says. "It's brought me my share of problems. People today are sue-happy, you have to watch out for that. Also you have to put up with this attitude, 'he's a millionaire.' That was kind of fun at first, but it gets to you. I'm tired of hearing it. I've been dealing with it every day. Everyone has their opinions, they'd all do different things if they were in my shoes, and they all love to tell me about it. I've had to get rude sometimes. . . ."

But, all in all, winning has been a good experience for Paul Otto. "It has its ups and downs," he says, but admits that the ups have predominated. Asked if he thinks winning is harder for someone his age than someone older, he says it definitely is. "It's more challenging for a young person. In your 40s you probably'll already own a house and have a good-paying job, have assets. At 21 I didn't own much of anything. I had my clothes. I had a great truck. I had a few tools. But basically, I lived check to check. When you're older, with kids, you think what the money's going to mean to your kids and grandkids. At 21 you have to be more selfish. You have to think where you want to be when you get the last check. Rich? Poor? I want to be myself, and that's the hardest thing for someone my age. Try to be yourself. Don't rush into anything. If someone wants to take their money and blow it all on having a good time, well, who am I to judge them? I say, go for it, but don't come back crying when it's all gone. That's the way I am. I think I have the best parents in the world, and that's the way they raised me."

Elderly Winners

"I'm spending my kids' inheritance."

—Anonymous

O nly 15 percent of Michigan's million-dollar lottery winners have been over 65 years old when they collected the first installment of their prizes. And like the young, it is tempting and easy to imagine what the senior-citizen winners must be like. What can they do with the money? They're accustomed to their lifestyles, they're reluctant to change, and they don't have any unrealized desires. They're more interested in financing the dreams of their descendants than pursuing their own pleasures. Right?

Well, no, not necessarily.

Take George Shaffer, for instance. When he won $3,032,863 in a Super Lotto jackpot on May 27, 1987, he was 92 years old, reportedly the oldest lottery millionaire in America. He and his 85-year-old wife, Glenna, were living in a Grand Rapids veterans' facility, and you would think, at their age, that they would find very little they wanted to do differently. But almost immediately after winning, they set out to buy a house for themselves and hire someone to care for them. They wanted freedom and independence, and they wanted to spend their final years being taken care of under a roof they could call their own.

◆

When 82-year-old Harry Greene hit for a Lotto prize of $2,091,663 on February 1, 1986, his 64-year-old wife, Julia, wasn't quite sure how she felt about the win. The couple—who had three children, 12 grandchildren, and five great-grandchildren—lived in a small apartment complex in Bellaire. "High living" just wasn't her style, Julia told a reporter for the Traverse City *Record-Eagle.* "I'm just going to keep living off my Social Security," she said. "I like a quiet life. . . . I think about all these people who don't have anything to eat, no place to sleep. It gets to me. But I'm going to keep it (the money) anyhow, in case anything happens to my husband before me. It'll go to my kids. Let them have fun with it."

Harry, however, had other plans. The retired Ford Motor Company electrician set out immediately to spend his money. First he wanted two cars. "Over my dead body," Julia said. "He's only getting one. He's not allowed to drive outside Bellaire anyway, because he's blind in one eye and two-thirds blind in the other." Then he wanted a new house. "Harry says he wants a four-bedroom house," Julia said. "Why, I don't know. There are only two of us." He was spending money so fast that Julia had to plead with him to at least "leave me $5.95 for lunch."

Within six months Harry had purchased a $52,000 home and equipped it with a large-screen television and a stereo system, had traded his 1972 Pontiac for a 1986 Lincoln Continental, had helped family members pay bills, and had set aside some money for his and Julia's medical expenses. By August nearly all of their first installment check of $86,000 was spent, and they were not sure what they would live on until the second check came in February.

They also had to deal with another problem: large numbers of requests from strangers. They received numerous calls and letters, including one from a downstate woman who asked for $2,000 to stop foreclosure on her mortgage. Another caller insisted that God had given the money to the Greenes to "spread around," and she wanted some spread her way so that she could go on a cruise to Hawaii.

After the novelty wore off, Mr. Greene, who had survived a bout with cancer years earlier but was left with an artificial larynx, told the *Record-Eagle* reporter that he sometimes regretted winning the lottery money. "We were happier the way we were living before," he said. "We had a garden, and we got along with it." Given a chance, he said, he would gladly trade all that money for good health.

♦

It had been a long, dusty road for Ronnie Jonason, and he figured when he retired in 1976 that he could finally look forward to some ease and contentment. But it had never been that easy for Ronnie. There were no investments or savings to fall back on, and he found out all too soon that his Social Security check didn't stretch nearly far enough. Within a month or two he had no choice but to look for work. He finally found it as a laborer and handyman in a nearby orchard. He was still working there 10 years later when he won more than $2 million in the lottery.

His home is on an old farm outside of Bangor, a small town that straddles M-43 20 miles west of Kalamazoo. Bangor is quiet and unassuming, a tired little Midwestern town with shaded streets and a village constable who spends all day cruising from one village limit sign to the other. It's nestled in what once was farm and orchard country—a land of rolling hills, untended fields and pastures, fallen fences, and occasional unfinished houses surrounded by empty lots in struggling subdivisions.

Ronnie's place hadn't been farmed in years—until he won his Lotto jackpot. Now he has a second-hand Case tractor with some attachments, and he plans to plant corn and maybe soybeans come spring.

The evening of my visit he's eating fast-food fish-and-chips in the living room, watching Dan Rather mouth the news on television. Ronnie's slow to answer the door, admitting that he'd forgotten about the interview and was caught eating supper in his undershorts. He slips a pair of trousers on but remains bare-chested and bare-footed as we talk and as he finishes his supper. He has the physique of a man much younger than 70 years, the build of man who has earned his living through physical labor. There is also a definite air of relaxed and carefree mirth about him. He listens to questions and answers them as if they make him think of old jokes.

"You know, it's all right to just sit around or just play, but it gets old," he says, explaining why a man who is assured of receiving more than $80,000 a year for what amounts to the rest of his life would feel compelled to begin an occupation as diificult and time-consuming as farming. "You have to do something, I feel. Maybe some people don't,

I don't know. Maybe they can just lay around and relax and wait until they pass away, but not me. I got to do something."

What does he do? A lot, apparently. Besides starting the farm, Ronnie kept working for the orchardist.

"After I won, the guy (the owner of the orchard) called and asked me if I was going to come back to work for him. I said 'Yep.' I couldn't just leave the man settin'; he don't have nobody else to help."

In a case like Ronnie Jonason's it is difficult—if not downright criminal—to limit his lottery story to the events immediately before and after his win. You can't separate the life story from the lottery story; one explains the other.

Rollin Jonason, born in 1916, was raised on a farm in South Dakota, but he feels that his life didn't really begin until he was 13, when he and two older boys left home to see something of the world. Without their parents' knowledge, they hopped a freight train at the railroad siding near their homes and headed southwest, planning to make their way to Denver, where they'd heard there was money to be made working in the hayfields.

It wasn't until they were well into Wyoming that some of the enthusiasm for their journey began to wane. "We got out past Sheridan, or maybe it was Casper," Ronnie recalls, "before the other two boys started getting homesick and wanted to turn back. What sort of topped it off was one of them, when we was changing trains, waited too long to jump on and fell and skinned his face on the cinders on the ground. So I jumped off and the other guy jumped off and we found a place to stay that night. Well, the hurt boy, he got to cryin' he was so homesick, and then the other boy got it, too, and I said, 'You guys want to go back, it's all right with me.' "

But Ronnie had other plans for himself. The next morning they caught a train going east and rode it all the way to O'Neill, Nebraska, where they could jump off and catch another ride into South Dakota and home. Ronnie helped his friends prepare for the leap from the moving train. He told them that he wanted them to go first, so that if he lost his balance and fell they would be there to catch him.

First one boy, then the other jumped. When Ronnie didn't follow, they started running after the train shouting at him to jump. But he just leaned out the door of the boxcar and yelled to them to tell his parents that he couldn't get off, that the train was going too fast.

Ronnie had not eaten in a solid 24 hours and was able to ride only as far as Norfolk, Nebraska, before he was forced to leave the train in search of food. It was the end of a long day, and he had exactly one nickel in his pockets. While walking along a street, he spotted a girl scrubbing the floor of a bakery and asked her if he could take the job over in exchange for something to eat. The girl complied, gladly. Ronnie washed and scrubbed that floor until it shined, and the girl was so pleased, that she gave him a quart of milk and filled a large bag with sweet-rolls for him.

He then made his way back to the train yard and began looking for a suitable boxcar. Without warning, he bumped into a railroad dick, and for a moment—thinking of the stories he'd heard about such men beating and even shooting freeloaders and hobos—he considered making a run for it. But the dick was a lenient sort. He asked the boy what he was doing and where he was going. Ronnie told him he was trying to catch a train out so he could go down to Sioux City to visit his aunt.

The man pointed to a boxcar. "Get in there," he said. "You get in there and stay put. I don't want you running around downtown or something."

Ronnie did what he was told. But it was a long and boring wait for the train to start, and there was nothing to do. So "I started eating them sweet-rolls," he says. "I just sat in that boxcar in the corner by myself eatin' all them sweet-rolls and drinkin' all that milk. Then the train started up finally and started rollin' along, and I just kept eatin' them sweet-rolls and, oh lordy, about one o'clock in the morning I got so sick. I'm a hangin' my head out the boxcar, and the train is jumpin' and swayin' and everything, and it's a wonder the boxcar door didn't fly shut and cut my head right off."

At six the next morning, the train came to a stop in the yards at Sioux City, Iowa. Ronnie had visited the area once before, but that was long ago, and he only had a vague idea where his aunt's house was. He did remember that he had to cross a toll bridge, so he made his way down to the river and walked along it until he spotted the bridge. The fare took his nickel, but he now remembered where he was going and went almost directly to his aunt's house.

She wasn't exactly expecting him.

"By God, I like to scared her to death. She says, 'Where's the rest of them? Where's your ma? Where's your pa?' I told her I was all alone, that I'd been ridin' the rails. That rattled her some. She said, 'Oh my God, get in here, you're gonna get cleaned up, get something to eat, then you're getting a train right back home.' I told her that sounded good to me, but first I wanted to see my cousins, long as I was there anyway. Well, she went along with that.

"My cousins was up, just gettin' ready to head out to sell newspapers, so they asked me to go along and I did. I meet their bossman, and he looks at me and asks if I'd like to sell newspapers. He said he'd pay me two cents for every paper I sold, plus give me a hotel room, a room to myself. I had to furnish my own food and clothes and things, but that still sounded like a pretty good deal to me, so I took it and didn't go back to my aunt's house, and told my cousins to tell her I left for home."

So Ronnie had himself a job selling newspapers. And he prospered at it.

"I'd go out in the afternoon for awhile, then I'd go out at night from nine until early in the morning. I had a spot at Sixth and Pierce, right in front of the Orpheum Theatre. It was a good spot because there was a streetcar stop in front of the theatre and people would stand there with nothing to do, waiting for their cars to come. Well, in the winter I'd stand out there freezing my butt off in the cold, and I'd tell everybody to go inside the drugstore next door to the theatre and I'd come and get them when their streetcar came. It didn't take long for the druggist to come out and tell me that any time I want hot chocolate or anything, it wouldn't cost me nothing because these people were going into the drugstore to wait and they was buying stuff. And anytime I wanted to go to the Orpheum Theatre, he told me, I could go and it wouldn't cost me a thing.

"At night, after I left the corner when things slowed down, from one o'clock until almost two-thirty in the morning I would go around to all the bars, and on Broadway they had all these whorehouses, you know. I'd go in there to sell papers, and the customers would say, 'Hey, you ain't got no business in here.' Well, I'd say, 'What's the matter? Don't anybody in here read?' and they'd all buy a paper to show that they did read—also, I suppose, to get rid of me. I did have more damn fun—really—I really did.

"I was there for about three months, and my mother was callin' all over to see if anybody had heard from me. My aunt told her, 'Yeah, he was here, didn't he get home yet?' When she found out I was still in Sioux City, she come flyin' down to that newspaper stand and grabbed me by the arm and said, 'You're going home! Now!'

"So I bought a new suit of clothes and stuck my money in my shoe. My aunt thought she put me on a passenger train for home, but I kept the fare money, put my old clothes on, tucked my new ones in a dirty bag with everything else I had, and hopped a freight.

"That night I was sitting on what they called an oiler on the train, and this brakeman comes down there and grabs me—I'm about half asleep, nodding—he grabs me and shakes me and stays up with me until the train stops, then puts me in a boxcar. He said if I'd fallen off'n that oiler I'd a got ground up like hamburger. So he put me in a boxcar. Only, that wasn't quite so good. Here were these other hobos in there. They takes one look at me, and one of them says, 'You got any money on you, son?' I said, 'No, I don't. I'm broke, that's the reason the man made me get up in the boxcar.' So those hobos didn't bother me after that, and it took awhile but I got home eventually, and everything was pretty good—except that I'd got a taste of the outside. I couldn't just sit around at home after that."

Soon afterwards, Ronnie lied about his age to get a job building roads with the Civilian Conservation Corps, and he left home again, this time for good. For several years he crossed and recrossed the Western states, going wherever there was work.

One day, broke and looking for work, he stepped off a freight train in Sunnyside, Washington. He made his way to the edge of town where a carnival was set up and talked his way into a job as a general helper. He stayed with the carnival—helping to set up at each new location, then cleaning up afterwards—as it traveled from town to town. In time he proved himself to be an able performer and became a trapeze artist. It was on the high wire that he met the first of his three wives, his partner in the act.

Shortly after their marriage, they left the carnival and settled down to a more ordinary life in San Diego. But then World War II came, and Ronnie joined the Navy and went overseas. Evidently he was gone too long, because he returned home to find that his wife had fallen in love with another man. Ronnie got a divorce; bought a taxi; met, married and divorced another woman; and went to work for 18 years in an aircraft plant in San Diego.

But the lure of the road always tugged at Ronnie Jonason, and he left his factory job to become a long-haul trucker. That job led eventually to a long sojourn in Tennessee—"I was driving truck and I stopped in Memphis one day and I didn't have enough money to leave so I just stayed there"—where he met his third wife. They stuck it out through some lean years in Memphis, raising two sons and a daughter while Ronnie worked as a truck mechanic.

In 1976 they took advantage of an opportunity to move north to Michigan, where Ronnie had accepted a job maintaining a fleet of trucks for a manufacturing plant near Kalamazoo. It was a job that paid more than he had ever earned in his life: up to $418 a week take-home.

But by then he was 62 years old and figured he'd struggled long enough. He worked just a year, until he could take early retirement and begin collecting Social Security payments. "I thought, 'man, I'm really cuttin' a fat hog. This is gonna be nice. I can go do as I want to, anything I want.' But I had four kids to support, three by that last wife, one by an earlier one. That first Social Security check was all right, then the next one didn't go quite as far, and then it just got rougher and rougher until I knew I just had to go back to work and earn some money. So a month or two later I went out and found me the job in the orchard."

He managed to get by; to see his kids finish high school, marry and go off to begin their own lives; and to see his third, and perhaps final, marriage sputter to an end after 26 years. He lived alone on a combination of Social Security and income from his job at the orchard, where he spent his days. He thought about reviving his farm, which he owned. And every week he bought $4 or $5 worth of Lotto tickets, all for the Saturday drawing at first, then dividing it when Wednesday Lotto drawings were added.

"Then, this one Saturday the jackpot was up to six million, so I figured I'd just try for $3. So I went over to my kitchen counter there, and I had several old betting slips there that some people that had been visiting had left layin' around. Those people was always braggin' about how they'd win four numbers but never won anything big. So I figured I'd play their tickets in case they was lucky, but I didn't know which tickets was their's and which was old ones of mine, so I just picked up the first three I came to and went down to the store in town and played them. The girl at the counter wished me luck. I told her not to worry, I wouldn't win, I'd be lucky to get four numbers.

"That night I watched the drawing on TV. I was just sittin' there in my shorts readin' off the numbers and writing 'em down, and I seen right off I had a 40 and I thought, 'Land, I hope I've got three more that'll go with it.' So I came back over and sat down and 'Lord,' I said, 'land, I've got five of them.' So I run to the phone and called my neighbor lady, and I'm thinkin', 'Why didn't I play a 12 instead of that 15, then I'd a had all six numbers.' I called her and I said 'Carol, I got five of them.' Well, she said, 'Ronnie, you're kidding, you're always sayin' that. If you don't quit hollerin' wolf, you're gonna get hurt one of these days.' I said, 'Honest to God, I got five. I really do.' I'm really happy, thinking that it means $2,000 for me, and I read off the five numbers to my neighbor and she checks them, and about then I see that what I thought was a 15 was a 12—I'd been looking at it wrong—and I said, 'Oh my God, I don't have five. I have six!' Now she thinks she better come right down here. But I don't have no clothes on, so I tell her I'll go down there instead. And sure enough, the numbers matched, I had all six."

Ronnie is laughing as he tells that part of the story. It has been over a year since that night, and still the memory is so fresh that some of the original excitement comes back. He puts on a video cassette showing the newscast a Kalamazoo station made that featured him as the area's most-recent lottery millionaire.

The tape shows a much older Ronnie Jonason, one with missing teeth and wearing old glasses with the bows taped to the frame. Now, sitting in his living room sipping a can of beer and laughing about the telecast, he points it out: "See my teeth missin' there?" He seems to have shed 10 years since winning the lottery. New glasses and teeth are only part of the change. He is lighter on his feet than the man in the video, surer of himself. He does not avert his eyes when asked a question, and he looks like a man who knows how to relax and have a good time.

At first, after winning, having a good time is exactly what he was determined to do. He bought a new Lincoln Town Car ("the best you can get") and took off across the country to meet his brother in Las Vegas.

Apparently he had not yet exhausted his good luck. Almost immediately after arriving in Las Vegas he put a dollar into a slot machine and hit a jackpot for $1,100. He went into another casino, put $8 into a slot machine and hit a jackpot of $1,000. He then sat down at a black-jack table, placed a $60 bet, and played in a manner most card players would find rather unorthodox. When his hand beat the dealer's he added his $60 winnings to his original bet and let the $120 "ride" on the next hand. When his hand was equal to the dealer's—a "push," in which he neither won nor lost—he doubled the bet out of his own pocket.

In seven hands he hit three blackjacks—being dealt an ace and a jack, a hand that pays a player 150 percent of his bet—won two others, and pushed on two. He lost none. The dealer admitted that he had never seen anyone play blackjack like that. Ronnie attracted a crowd. The pit boss strolled over, congratulated him, asked where he was from and presented him with a coupon for a complimentary crab dinner. Ronnie, having watched his original $60 bet grow to more than $1,100, got up from the table and went out to enjoy that dinner.

Ronnie originally had planned to stop in Las Vegas on his way to San Diego to visit his sister and brother, but after a week and a half he cut his vacation short and turned back for home. "I knew I had work to do," he explains.

He had other responsibilities as well. Although his wife had moved out three years before and was living in the nearby town of Watervliet, they had never divorced. As far as Ronnie knew, she was entitled to a share of the prize money.

"I went to her and said, 'Well, we might as well get a divorce, because you aren't comin' back and it probably wouldn't work out if you did. This way you'll be free, I'll be free. If you want a lump sum I'll give it to you. If you want to use my lawyer you can.' Well, she said that she wanted $1,000 a month. So we went to the lawyer and he made out the papers and we signed them. That's what she gets for the next 19 years, unless she marries. Then of course it'll go to the kids. But we're good friends now. Ain't no sense bein' enemies, I guess."

Ronnie also felt he had an obligation to his church. Six months before his lottery win he had told the pastor at the Bangor Baptist Church that if he ever won the Lotto he would help build the new church that was so badly needed.

"Well, when I hit all six numbers I figured the good Lord had a hand in it, and he was checkin' to see if I would stick to my word. So when I come back I went down to the bank and I said, 'Write out a check for $8,000 for the Bangor Baptist Church.' I never missed it. I never even noticed it was gone."

So what does the future hold for lottery-millionaire Ronnie Jonason? He still buys lottery tickets—perhaps a few more each week than before he won—and says that if he wins again he will probably give most of it away. He plans to buy a new Lincoln every year—he traded in his first one after only six months—and do a little traveling, maybe to Florida in the winters. But for the most part, life will go on pretty much as it did before—work on the farm and in the orchard followed by evenings spent quietly at home watching television in his undershorts.

Ronnie shakes his head at the wonder of it. The 13-year-old kid who hopped a freight train and hustled newspapers, the young trapeze artist, the restless truck driver—a wealthy man now.

"Ain't it just the damndest thing?" he asks, laughing.

Misfortunes

"I wish I'd never won the damn thing. It ruined me."

—Charles Lynn Riddle, Michigan lottery winner

To practically no one's surprise, winning the lottery does not always bring instant ease and happiness. In Michigan, as in every other lottery state, some winners have found that their sudden wealth brought more problems than benefits, less fortune than misfortune. Many winners have been disappointed to find that, instead of a free ride on the gravy train, they've only been given a new pair of shoes for the same old dusty road or, as one winner put it, "the same problems, just with bigger numbers." Sometimes it gets more serious—occasionally very serious.

The most common misfortunes are not matters of strictly life and death. For example, one million-dollar winner, who asked to remain anonymous, states flatly that her family's standard of living has gone *down* since she won her lottery jackpot in the mid-1980s. Before she won, she and her husband lived a quiet, fairly ordinary life, she working part time as a librarian, he as a heavy-equipment operator for a construction firm. Though they worked hard and did not have as much time for fun and relaxation as they would have liked, they had built a good life for themselves. They owned a nice home that they liked and were proud of, had good friends, got along with their neighbors, and looked forward to putting their sons through college and settling into

an austere but peaceful middle age. They dreamed of eventually owning a small resort on a northern Michigan lake, a resort that could serve
double duty as retirement home and source of retirement income.

Then one day everything changed. The woman—I'll call her
"Judy"—had been a regular Lotto player since the game began and
always played the same six numbers, based on the birthdates of her
parents, brothers, sisters, and husband. The night of the drawing for
that week's winning numbers, Judy and her husband were visiting
friends. At one point in the evening the subject of the lottery came up,
and, realizing that they'd forgotten to watch the televised drawing,
Judy's friend called the lottery hotline and learned the winning Lotto
numbers. The friend repeated them aloud and declared that they were
"rotten" numbers. Judy didn't think so. She had left her ticket at home,
but the numbers sounded very familiar. On the way home she told her
husband that she thought she had all six. He waved off the possibility.

When they got home, Judy found the ticket and showed it to her
husband. Their oldest son called the grocery store where she had purchased the ticket and confirmed the numbers. Then he called again to
double-check. She had, indeed, matched all six numbers.

"My husband was just calm and relaxed," Judy says, "and I was
going crazy. My son and I were jumping around. It's quite an experience. We couldn't sleep at all that night, because we didn't know
how much we won, or if we were sharing it with 10 people, if we would
split it or what. All these thoughts go through your mind. It's crazy.

"You know, I always *knew* I was going to win. Since Lotto came
out I knew we were going to be winners. I just knew it all along. I think
my husband did too, In fact, once I heard about somebody who won a
real small amount, and I thought, 'Shoot, that wouldn't do any good,
that wouldn't be enough to make any difference. No, we better wait until we can win a bigger prize.' "

As it turned out they won half the jackpot, for a prize of well over
$1 million. Plenty, they thought.

At first, Judy's good luck brought nothing but good news. They
told one friend but made him promise to keep it a secret until they
could decide what to do. But he in turn told one friend, and that friend
told one friend, and it wasn't long before their entire town knew about
it. The phone rang constantly, but all of the calls were positive.
Nobody asked for money or voiced resentment or jealousy. Relatives
and friends—including one who said, "it couldn't have happened to a

nicer person . . . except me"—called to congratulate them and wish them well.

The media attention, however, frightened Judy, who is a very private person. She declined television and newspaper interviews and tried to keep the excitement toned down. "The attention embarrasses me," she said. "If I had done something great, you know, then it would have been all right to be a star. But all I did was pick some numbers."

She and her family tried to continue with their lives as usual, but found that they couldn't. Many changes were subtle but annoying. They noticed, for example, that people treated them differently than they had before, like the owner of the market where Judy shopped, who no longer gave her a deal on vegetables, never threw in an extra orange or two the way he used to. Other changes were very direct. One day, for instance, a woman asked Judy's husband—who, technically, was not the lottery winner—how it felt to be a gigolo.

Then taxes hit them. They had won at the very end of the year and did not have time to arrange any additional deductions. That year they paid taxes equal to triple the income Judy had earned during the same year as a librarian. Something had to be done. They consulted a tax accountant and in the course of the conversation mentioned their long-time dream of owning a resort. He advised them to make that dream a reality.

So Judy and her husband quit their jobs, sold their house, and—fulfilling their dream, and that of countless other Michigan residents—moved north. Their new home was now a house surrounded by a half dozen rental cabins on the shores of a well-known northern lake.

Judy now calls the place the "Money Pit." During a heavy thunderstorm only a week after they moved in, the kichen ceiling collapsed. When they investigated, they determined that they had to replace the entire roof. Then, while repairing the damage in the kitchen, they discovered that the studs, rafters, and joists were badly charred, evidence of a serious fire that neither the previous owners nor the realtor had considered worth bringing to their attention.

It was a classic tale of homeowners' woes: The more they tore into the house, the more they discovered wrong with it. The rental cabins, to Judy's and her husband's relief, were in much better shape than the house. They were structurally sound and neat and clean, but needed an enormous amount of routine maintenance work. In fact, there was so much work to do, and so many unexpected costs, that Judy and her husband very soon found themselves living less well off than they had been accustomed to. Winning the lottery just wasn't what they thought it would be.

"You think that if you could win the Lotto you would have so much money that you could buy a business and put people to work that were out of work," Judy says. "But it isn't like that. Maybe if you won $300,000 a year you could, maybe then you could do more good."

What advice does she have for winners who don't want to repeat her mistakes?

"You know, you always think people, winners, are going to rush out and buy, buy, buy, buy. But you should put your money in the bank awhile. Just put it away for awhile and decide what you want to do. We didn't go on a big spending spree or anything. Instead we bought the resort."

Judy still hopes the resort will prove to be a wise investment. But for now she wishes it was a job more like her old one, where she could work with people instead of toiling all day to clean and maintain empty rental cabins. "There's a lot of work to do here—a whole lot of work to do here—but it's not the same as socializing at your job. I miss that part of my old job."

But Judy thinks that eventually she and her husband would have bought a resort anyway. And there's nothing to guarantee that they wouldn't have bought into the same kind of problems they found with the Money Pit, or that it would have been any less work, or that they would have been any happier had they not won the lottery money. The only thing to do now, she admits, is proceed in the direction they've already begun and hope that hard work pays off in the long run.

Meanwhile, there's always the hope for some further lottery assistance. She still plays regularly, still buys tickets using the same sets of numbers she has always used. "My husband says he would like us to be the first ones in Michigan who win it twice," she says.

◆

Another lottery millionaire who applied his windfall to his dreams—with less than ideal consequences—is 34-year-old Kenneth Proxmire from Hazel Park. His dream had always been to own a business and be his own boss. Instead, he was tied down by financial needs and obligations to his job—a job he disliked—as a cutter/grinder at the Lear Siegler, Inc., plant in Detroit. In an August 1984 interview printed in the *Detroit News*, he explained what his life was like: "Every morning it was the same thing. Get up at 6 a.m., drive down into Detroit, and do that dirty, grimy, noisy work over and over and over. I hated it. I wanted to get out for years, but I couldn't."

He finally saw a chance to break out of that rut in January, when he was notified that he was one of 10 finalists for a Weekly Game million-dollar drawing, with a guaranteed minimum prize of $10,000. Strangely, he had been having dreams about winning the lottery for a month, ever since seeing a horoscope prediction that claimed he soon would be coming into a large sum of unexpected money. When the drawing was still two weeks away, he was so confident that he would win big—or so desperate to make a break—that he quit his $15,000-a-year factory job in Detroit and began making plans to move to California.

The morning of the drawing, February 4, 1977, Proxmire thought the signs did not bode well for him. His horoscope indicated it would be "just an ordinary luck day, nothing special about it." And the weather was oppressive. Proxmire hated Michigan winters and wanted nothing more than to escape them forever. Yet, as if taunting him, here was winter at its worst—cold and windy, with near-blizzard conditions.

By evening, the weather was the last thing on Proxmire's mind. He had survived the drawing's elimination process to become Michigan's 24th lottery millionaire. He "about jumped five feet in the air," then declared to reporters and the world that he was heading for California to find a better life.

Within a month, Proxmire, his wife, Martina, and their 10- and 12-year-old sons were on their way to Fresno, California, where they planned to buy a bowling alley. But the bowling alley they had their eye on carried a $500,000 price tag with a $100,000 down payment, far more than they could raise. Ken also faced one of the paradoxical facts of a lottery winner's life: Though he was guaranteed payments of $50,000 a year for 20 years, no bank would grant him a loan on that basis.

Undaunted, he lowered his expectations and searched for a more affordable business. He settled on a pool hall/beer bar in Fresno called "The Rack." For $100,000, with a $25,000 down payment, Ken Proxmire finally had his small business—12 pool tables and a bar.

Business was only fair at The Rack, just good enough to pay the bills and supply the Proxmires with a modest salary. Tina tended bar in the afternoons, and Ken came in to take over during the evenings, an arrangement they tired of quickly. They realized fairly soon that The Rack did not offer very bright prospects for the future.

So, sick of the drunks and the long hours, Ken began looking for a business that could earn them more money with less work. Eventually he bought a pool-supply store, with the objective of building up the business, opening more stores and hiring people to run them for him.

For a time Ken Proxmire could do no wrong. Everything he touched, it seemed, turned to gold. He opened three more stores within the first year and soon was grossing $50,000 per month. Hoping to share his good fortune, he persuaded a dozen family members from Michigan to move to Fresno and work in his stores.

His style of living was keeping pace with his new income. He and Tina bought a $100,000 house with a built-in pool, purchased half a dozen cars and trucks, and began to enter the Fresno social whirl. They held frequent parties and back-yard barbecues; Tina joined several women's clubs; they moved within circles of successful, upbeat young people like themselves.

Then, just as suddenly as their good luck had begun, it ran out. The nationwide recession of the early 1980s struck them a serious blow, as it did many small-business owners. Consumers began weeding the superfluities out of their budgets, and pool supplies were definitely not a necessity. Business dropped so drastically and cash became so scarce that Proxmire was forced to liquidate his stock at a loss. He also tried, without success, to sell some of his stores, but as he would later note, nobody seemed anxious to buy into a failing business. With plummeting sales came increasing debts.

Proxmire tried desperately to save the business. He had not only his wife and sons to consider; he also felt responsible for the dozen relatives he had convinced to move west. But, as he later said, "When the ship went down, everybody went with it."

Finally, there was no choice left. Five years after Ken had won a million-dollar lottery jackpot, the Proxmires entered a petition for Chapter 13 bankruptcy in federal court. With the help of attorney John Sirabian of Fresno, they presented a monthly budget of $2,570 for living expenses, an amount Sirabian argued was necessary to live on "in light of the standards he (Proxmire) has after receiving the $50,000 for the past (five) years." The court did not agree. It was determined that the Proxmires could live on less. Sirabian also argued that the lottery winnings were a "non-assignable obligation" and therefore could not be transferred to someone else to pay debts. It was a good argument but it, too, failed to convince the court. The court ordered the Proxmires to pay $20,000 a year to their creditors for the next five years. After taxes on their annual lottery check, the Proxmires would be left with about $20,000 a year to live on.

The bankruptcy proceedings attracted national attention. The wire services picked up the story and distributed it to newspapers all over America. The *National Enquirer* treated it in their typical lurid fashion. Proxmire was invited to appear on the "Phil Donahue" television program to discuss his misfortunes and warn future lottery millionaires how to avoid the mistakes he had made.

He did give this brief analysis of what went wrong in an interview published in the *New York Times*: "You go through an ego trip at first. If somebody says, 'Hey, you're a millionaire,' then you have to reflect that. Your lifestyle changes when you go from $15,000 to $50,000 a year. It's got to change a lot of things." He went on to say that he had learned a lot from the experience and planned to write a book detailing the pitfalls awaiting future lottery winners. Asked what his advice to those winners was, he said, "Crawl into a hole and pull the top in."

The media attention plus the pressure of money worries took their toll on the Proxmires. Soon after they had moved into a smaller, less-expensive home, Ken moved out. A few weeks later he and Tina reconciled their differences and decided to relocate to the nearby mountains where they could try to resume some kind of normal life for themselves.

For a time they lived in a modest three-bedroom home in the foothills of the Yosemite National Forest, north of Fresno. Their life was simple, "laid back," and by all indications fairly happy. Ken did not work because, as his attorney once explained, "nobody wants to hire an ex-millionaire." He spent his days restoring old autos in his driveway, walking in the hills, and fishing. At night he watched television.

But he was no recluse. He often came down from the mountains to shoot pool and drink beer with his buddies. And when, in 1984, he was interviewed for a Paramount Pictures television show called "Taking Advantage," Proxmire made it clear that he was available for other interviews because he hoped to capitalize on his hard-luck story. "If I do enough of these," he told the *Detroit News*, which also interviewed him in 1984, "maybe someone will make a movie or book about this."

His attitude about drawing attention to himself appears to have changed since then. He declined to be interviewed for this book.

But his son, Richard, who still lives in Fresno, reports that his father has moved to the Los Angeles area and has returned to factory work similar to the kind he left in Michigan. But there's a difference, Richard says, because now his father likes his job; in fact, he likes it a lot. "He's doing great," he says. "He's doing real well. And no, he hasn't written a book about his experiences, but I think it's still in the back of his mind."

In the 1984 *Detroit News* interview, Ken Proxmire said that in the future he planned to take some business classes and maybe dabble in the stock market. "I guess I'm a bit of a gambler," he said. "Of course, I wouldn't tell someone who just won the lottery to do it the same way as me. I'd tell them to be cautious. But that's not me."

◆

Charles Lynn Riddle, manager of the family-owned Long Dollar Restaurant in Detroit, was one of 30 contestants invited to the August 5, 1975, million-dollar drawing of the 50-cent Weekly Game. But the 23-year-old Trenton resident figured he would be among the first 23 semifinalists to be eliminated. He planned to gladly accept his $5,000 prize, then sit and watch the remaining seven contestants pocket checks ranging from $50,000 to $1,000,000.

But when he, in fact, survived the initial elimination process he began to get into the spirit of the event. Each time someone else was eliminated, Riddle leaped from his chair and shouted, "I love it!" In his excitement he sometimes helped to remove the chair of the departing contestant, or he often climbed onto his own chair, then jumped up and down and cheered. The 2,000 spectators loved it, and he became their favorite to win.

When only Riddle and Arthur Keedy, a steel-plant foreman from Wyandotte, remained on stage to vie for the two remaining prizes—$100,000 and $1 million—Riddle turned to Keedy and suggested that they split the prizes between them, taking $550,000 each. Keedy declined the offer, and Riddle became angry. Years later, in an interview with a *Detroit News* reporter, he recalled the incident. "I told him, 'Okay, it's an extra $450,000 for me. You're going to remember this for the rest of your life.' That's exactly what I said. I told him, 'Just for that I'm going to win.' "

When Keedy's name was drawn for the $100,000 prize, Riddle—who had just become the youngest million-dollar winner in the Michigan lottery's three-year history—leaped into the air, shouted, "I made it!" jumped from the stage, and danced across the floor of the Kalamazoo hockey arena where the drawing was held. His family charged from the audience to meet him, and they embraced in a huddle at "center ice," then all collapsed into a heap.

That night Riddle bought celebration drinks for friends at a bar near his home. But he left at a reasonable hour and was up in plenty of time the next morning to be at his $200-a-week job by 6 a.m. He assured newsmen who sought him there that the lottery money would not change his life.

Ten years later, Charles Lynn Riddle would have a radically different opinion. "I honestly wish I'd never won the damn thing. It ruined me," he would say.

When he became a lottery winner in August 1975, Riddle was already a 15-year veteran of the restaurant business and was well on his way to becoming a successful young man. He had begun working in the family restaurant, the Long Dollar, on Schaefer Highway in Detroit, as a dishwasher when he was 8 years old. At 13 he was afternoon cook; at 17 he managed 20 employees and was in charge of hiring, ordering, payroll, and all the other details required to run the busy short-order diner and truck stop. He worked hard but was paid well. When he was 16 he bought a new Volkswagen. At 22, before hitting the lottery jackpot, he bought a Jaguar.

But he also was, as he would later describe himself, a "rowdy" young man. Perhaps because of the long hours and hard work at the restaurant, he needed to apply himself equally hard to recreation. During the week, he worked 60-70 hours at the restaurant. On the weekends he relaxed, and he relaxed *hard*. Once, while at a party during his high-school days, he swallowed a quantity of drugs when a false rumor circulated that the police were about to raid the place. He was in a coma for six days. Just before winning the lottery in 1975, he wrecked his Jaguar while driving drunk. One of the first things he did with his winnings was repair the car.

The lottery win only added to Riddle's troubles. Friendships were strained when it became obvious that he was expected to pick up the tab for nights on the town, or when he was asked for loans, or when his old friends no longer knew how to approach him. He loaned $10,000 to the mother of one of his friends and learned later that she never intended to pay it back. He was bothered with calls and visits from inventors who wanted him to invest in their gadgets, or realtors who tried to sell him businesses and parcels of land. Customers at the restaurant tried to touch him or talk him into buying lottery tickets for them or accompanying them to the race tracks. His cousin's ex-wife filed a lawsuit against him, claiming that the winning ticket had actually been purchased jointly by Riddle and her ex-husband, and that they had conspired to defraud her of her share of the jackpot. The case was eventually thrown out of court, but not before Riddle had spent $5,000 on attorney's fees.

Counting on his lottery money as a "cushion," Riddle and his family invested their life's savings to open a second Long Dollar Restaurant in 1976. Riddle's brother Jim became manager, while Charles stayed at the original restaurant. There were plans to open a third establishment and even dreams of a nationwide franchise. But there were hard feelings within the family when Riddle, on his own, opened a steak-and-ale restaurant in Ypsilanti called "The Grainery." His family built the third Long Dollar without him.

Meanwhile, Riddle's appetite for the good life was growing. In the first few years after winning the lottery he bought a second Jaguar, a 1958 Bentley, a Corvette and a new Cadillac Eldorado. One day he called Pat Elliot, a girlfriend whom he had broken up with and reconciled with several times in the past few years and whom he had not seen in four months. They had dinner that evening and, on impulse, at midnight were on a plane to Nevada, where they got married. Sixteen months later a son was born.

In a December 16, 1984, story in the *Detroit* Sunday magazine of the *Detroit Free Press*, Riddle remembered those days as happy times. "My son was born and everything was fine, great. The business was doing really well. I had money. I was happy, perfectly happy. The lottery dream was working."

By late 1978 the lottery dream was falling apart. Riddle stayed away from home a great deal and drank heavily. He worked late at The Grainery and had fallen into the habit of staying after closing to drink

Scotch with the customers, often driving the drunkest ones home himself. Money was slipping through his fingers. In the *Free Press* story he said, ". . . I was living in a fantasy world. I thought I could do anything with a phone call. . . . It didn't work out that way."

His record of defeats reads like this:

—On a broker's advice he invested heavily in the commodities market. He lost $36,000 on orange juice futures, his first venture. He followed that with a $30,000 loss, then a $60,000 loss.

—He drank and used cocaine daily, and he was spending even more time away from home. One night he returned home at 4 a.m. and ended up in a fist fight with his wife, who was then pregnant with their second child. She left with their infant son, filed for divorce 10 days later, then terminated her pregnancy by having an abortion performed. The divorce trial and custody battle lasted nearly a year, and in the end, Riddle's wife won custody of their son and was awarded most of the household possessions, $48,000 alimony, and $175-a-week child support. Riddle appealed, and the case lingered another five years until the original decision was ultimately upheld. In all, he later estimated, the divorce cost him $150,000.

—In debt and suffering from depression, he moved back to his parents' home in 1981 and spent his days alone in his bedroom, using cocaine and drinking as much as a fifth of liquor a day.

—He lost interest in working at The Grainery, leaving it to employees to run, and it quickly began losing money. His debts mounted.

—Twice he was arrested for failing to pay child support.

"I really got to resent people thinking I was lucky," he told the *Free Press* reporter. "I don't think I was lucky at all. If you're lucky, you're happy. So I don't think my fortune is good fortune."

Friends suggested he get a job, anything, just to keep from sitting around all day drinking and using coke. But, as he recalled later, he could not even consider it. "I can't go work for someone else. I can't go work in a restaurant as an assistant manager, because I'm a millionaire. I couldn't stand the abuse. I can't be in a $20,000-a-year job if I'm a millionaire. I just can't make myself do it."

Things began to look up when he sold The Grainery for a $75,000 profit, then sold his share in the Long Dollar Restaurants for another $50,000. He gave his wife his $15,000 boat in lieu of $5,000 in unpaid child support, then gave her the next lottery check as alimony payment when his appeal was denied.

And for a time, unexpectedly, his prospects began to improve markedly. Always good with numbers and statistics—an interest that had attracted him to the lottery in the first place—he began to use that skill to his advantage at Northville Downs and Detroit Race Course. He did well at the races and took home as much as $2,000 a day. Suddenly he had money again. He bought a house and a Corvette and began talks with his brother about investing the 1984 lottery check in a new restaurant. They even began planning the menu.

Then Riddle's world fell apart. He had become involved with the owner of Bistro's Bourban Lounge and Restaurant in Dearborn, a man named Michael Mychajluk. Unknown to Riddle, Mychajluk was the subject of an undercover narcotics investigation, an investigation that would eventually include Riddle. Undercover agents alleged that the two men dealt cocaine from Mychajluk's restaurant, even accepting charge-card purchases. Riddle claimed innocence, but on October 26, 1984, he was indicted by a federal grand jury on one count of distributing about half a pound of cocaine and also on a charge of conspiracy to sell cocaine. The dream had crumbled.

At the time of the 1984 *Free Press* interview and story, Riddle faced trial on charges that could have resulted in a maximum 15-year prison sentence and $50,000 fine. He was, understandably, bitter and shaken when he told the reporter, "Before I won the lottery, I was 23 and I was a rowdy kid. I was partying and stuff, but I'd never spent money on attorneys. Since then I've spent over $50,000 on attorneys . . . I've got to blame the lottery for that."

Ultimately, he was found guilty of selling the cocaine to an undercover police agent. In April 1985, million-dollar lottery winner Charles Lynn Riddle was sentenced to three years in prison.

◆

One of the most tragic lottery-related incidents in Michigan occurred on March 11, 1976.

Harl Partin, a 60-year-old autoworker form Hamtramck, bought a few instant tickets each week at a neighborhood market, then took them to Will's Bar, next to his apartment, where he would rub the numbers off. On that March 11 night, Partin exposed a $10,000 winner and was understandably excited. He showed the ticket around, then had the owner of the bar—who happened also to be his landlady—lock the ticket in the bar's safe until he could return for it the next day and take it to a redemption center. Partin, a bachelor, then went home.

A few hours later, two armed bandits entered the bar, ordered the customers onto the floor, then ransacked the safe, taking cash and Partin's lottery ticket. Three days later, Police found Partin's body rolled up in a carpet in his living room. His feet and hands had been bound with electrical cords, a towel had been stuffed into his mouth, and a pillow case covered his head. He had been beaten to death, police were convinced, while being tortured to get him to tell where his winning ticket was hidden.

Meanwhile, Alfred Pomaranski, the owner of a nearby market, was approached by a regular customer he knew only as "Charlie," who offered him the chance to buy a winning $10,000 instant lottery ticket for $7,500. Charlie explained to Pomaranski that the ticket belonged to a buddy of his who was on welfare and was worried that if he redeemed it himself his welfare checks would be reduced.

"The story sounded plausible," Pomaranski later told a *Detroit News* reporter. "And listen, when you're in business, you're out to make a buck. But I told him I wouldn't pay $7,500."

Pomaranski bargained the price down to $6,500, then gave Charlie $3,000 on the spot and promised to pay him the $3,500 balance after he cashed the ticket.

"I figured I'd pay the income tax, give Charlie $6,500, and still turn a fast $1,500 for myself," Pomaranski said.

A few days later, when he and his wife went to a lottery office to cash the ticket, Pomaranski was surprised to find himself a murder suspect. "I was astonished, amazed at the story the police told me. I don't want to get messed up in murder. But, listen, I already paid Charlie $3,000. If I get it back, I'm willing to forget the whole thing. If not, I'm going to collect the $10,000."

Since an unsigned ticket is a "bearer instrument," it would seem that Pomaranski had a valid argument. A detective working on the case, however, argued that the ticket should go to the heirs of the Partin estate. Pomaranski said he would agree to that, but, "I've got $3,000 invested. Nobody's offered to return that to me. Before I give anything up, they'll have to prove to me that the man was murdered over the ticket I bought. Like I said, when you're in business, you're out to make a buck, right?"

Ultimately Pomaranski failed to make that buck. In fact, he was out three thousand of them. A circuit-court judge ruled that the entire $10,000 should go to Partin's brother and four sisters, since the ticket, according to his decision, was stolen property and should be included in the dead man's estate.

To date, the murder has not been solved. Police tracked down and questioned "Charlie" and another man, but were unable to link them to the killing. Their story was that the ticket was won in a poker game from a stranger who said that he did not want to jeopardize his welfare payments by cashing it.

Storekeeper Pomaranski was out three grand for wanting to make a quick buck. And Harl Partin, an autoworker only one year from retirement, a man who really seemed to want nothing more out of life than quiet, peaceful evenings with his friends at a favorite tavern, had died because of a moment's good fortune.

◆

Times had been tough for William Currie Sr. of Detroit. Because of heart problems, the 62-year-old man had been unable to work for eight months, and money had become so scarce that he was not able to pay his bills. His car was repossessed, his phone service cut off, and a department store he owed money to had begun garnisheeing whatever income he was able to get. He was definitely in need of a stroke of luck.

On July 12, 1987, it looked as if that stroke had come. A regular Lotto player, Currie had purchased several tickets for a $7.5 million jackpot and put them in his shirt pocket for safekeeping. Then, Sunday morning after the drawing, he took the tickets out and checked them off against the winning numbers listed in the newspaper. "The numbers (on one) matched," he was later quoted as saying. "We went crazy."

The Currie family spent the day celebrating. Their next-door neighbor, who had been saving her money to visit her son who was stationed with the Navy in Hawaii, was promised she would get her trip—compliments of the Curries. Another neighbor, a native of Brazil, was promised an all-expenses-paid homecoming to South America.

William Jr. (Billy) called the Livonia restaurant where he earned

$250 a week as manager and asked his boss, the owner, for the day off to celebrate William Sr.'s good fortune. The man expressed happiness for Billy but explained that he was short of help and needed his assistance. Eighteen-year-old Billy had an ace up his sleeve. He'd been planning to open an automotive machine shop when he had enough money. Well, now it looked as if he had enough money. He told the restaurant owner he quit.

The next morning the Curries traveled with a group of friends to the Lansing office of the lottery bureau to claim the first of the estimated $375,000 checks they expected to receive as the sole winners of the $7.5 million jackpot. Instead they received some very bad news.

As it turns out, Currie, not long after purchasing his original batch of Lotto tickets, had returned to the same store for a pack of cigarettes. While there he picked up what looked like a Lotto ticket lying on the counter. Whether he thought it was his own, or one that someone had forgotten, or whether he was simply absent-minded, nobody seems to know, but he put it into his pocket with the other tickets and forgot all about it. That ticket was the one with the winning numbers.

It was not, however, a valid Lotto ticket. Ten minutes or so after every Lotto and Super Lotto drawing, the central computer sends the winning numbers to all of the state's lottery outlets. Their terminals then print out a slip of paper with the numbers on it so that the agents can inform their customers of the winners. The slip is printed in the same style, in the same color, and on the same size and form paper as a lottery ticket. But printed clearly across the top are the words "LOTTO WINNING #'S"; across the bottom, below the date and the six numbers is printed, "NOT FOR SALE."

He later admitted that he had noticed the message on the bottom but thought it meant it was not for *resale*. "Well, hell," he explained, "I had no intention of selling it."

At the Lansing office that day, William Currie was informed that his $7.5 million salvation from debt and ill health had vanished, that he was the holder of a worthless piece of paper. He returned home to the same problems he had left.

Son Billy was not even that fortunate. His employer, angered because he would quit on such short notice, would not rehire him.

"It was a dumb mistake on my part," the senior Currie later said. But he was philosophical about his misfortune. "The Lotto giveth and the Lotto taketh away. Maybe it'll give one time for real."

◆

Valerie Kaczor was one very determined lottery player. There have been many determined players, of course, but she was in a class by herself. She wanted to win big money and was willing to spend it to get it. During one period in 1984 she was so determined to win that she spent as much as $700 a day on lottery tickets, a habit that created two major problems. One was that she was not winning as much as she was spending. The other was that she was paying the difference by altering money orders and writing bad checks—an estimated $500,000 worth.

Although she would eventually describe herself as a lottery addict, Valerie Kaczor did not always have the urge or even an inclination to gamble. In a 1985 interview, she told a *Detroit News* reporter that she did not come from a family that threw money around. The 32-year-old graduate of the Lincoln Center nursing school lived with her husband and two children in a comfortable, tri-level home in Rochester Hills and until 1983 led a normal, relatively uneventful life.

That year, the troubles began when her husband Richard's mother became ill, was hospitalized, and died, leaving them with $30,000 worth of medical bills. Mrs. Kaczor was concerned that her husband would worry about being so deeply in debt, so she concealed many of the bills, as well as the subsequent calls from creditors and collection agencies.

"The bills just started pouring in and we couldn't handle it," she told the *Detroit News.* "That was the thing that created the pressure for what I did. The impact of the bills coming in set me to thinking about the lottery. I heard my neighbors talking about it, and I figured if they could do it maybe I could, too. I figured this was my answer."

In February 1984 she purchased $100 worth of Daily 3 and Daily 4 tickets and won $1,000. Convinced that she had stumbled onto the answer to her family's problems, she increased her bets until she was spending several hundred dollars a day.

"At that point," she said, "I couldn't count a $250 winner as a winner. I had the foreknowledge that I was courting disaster, but I wouldn't admit it. In the back of my mind I kept saying, 'I'm going to hit the big one.' "

Devising a number of schemes to disguise the bad checks she was writing, Mrs. Kaczor dug herself deeper and deeper into a hole. She bought money orders for a few dollars each, then altered them to larger amounts and cashed or deposited them to cover her overdrawn checking account. To allay suspicion, she purchased the money orders in banks and post offices throughout the Detroit area and a few times crossed the river into Canada. Once, in desperation, she falsified the title to her father's leased car and sold it.

Still she was surprised when she was arrested in September 1984. "I was shocked," she said. "I thought if I could cover the bad checks, they would let me. It was very embarrassing to have all this happen."

It turned out to be much more than just embarrassing. Her trips to Canada resulted in federal charges, and in a nine-count indictment she was accused of forgery, foreign transportation of fraudulent checks, and obtaining money under false pretenses. Her husband, Richard, and her father, Henry Rust, also were arrested and charged with one count each of cashing forged checks.

Mrs. Kaczor eventually pleaded guilty to two counts of the indictment in a plea-bargained agreement that would dismiss the other seven charges. While waiting sentencing, Mrs. Kaczor checked herself into Mercywood Hospital in Ann Arbor to be treated for depression and addiction to gambling. She also began attending Gamblers Anonymous meetings and announced that she was repentant and on the road to recovery.

"I don't intend to go back to that lifestyle, no matter how broke I get," she said. "Truly, I regret everything I have done."

Her repentance seems not to have won her much favor with the court. On August 1, 1985, a judge, declaring that Valerie Kaczor had done "more damage with a pencil than most people do with a gun," sentenced her to 3-to-14 years in prison.

Oddities, Quirks, and Coincidences

"It was just a case of being at the right place at the right time."

—Janet Westover, Michigan lottery winner

W hen you take human nature, odd enough to start with, and add such volatile ingredients as random chance and vast, vast sums of money, the result can be a very strange brew indeed. While not always as sensational as "Woman, Bitten by Dog, Gives Birth to Twin Babies that Bark and Growl," many of the most unusual lottery stories are definitely in a class suited to the weekly tabloids.

Some lottery tales are simply unbelievable. And for good reason. Take, for instance, the story of the million-dollar winner and her seven Cadillacs. It's a story I have heard a number of times, before and during the research for this book. Each time the basic story was the same: A woman had lived a quiet, ordinary life until she won the lottery. She collected her prize and immediately went shopping. By the end of the day she had purchased seven brand-new Cadillacs, each a different color, each intended for use on a different day of the week.

I went searching for that woman, surely the most conspicuous spender in Michigan lottery history. But nobody seemed to know her name. One man said he heard she was from Grand Rapids or

Kalamazoo. Someone else said she was single and young, another that she was a middle-age divorcee. After 14 months of research, after talking to dozens of lottery winners, after sifting through 15 years' worth of Michigan newspapers and magazines and many more years' worth of national publications, I never found one verified piece of information about the woman or her Cadillacs. I finally came to a startling realization: She did not exist.

A noted folklore expert and professor at the University of Utah, Jan Harold Brunvand, has made a career out of tracking down and collecting stories that are widely circulated yet have no basis in fact. In his book, *The Mexican Pet: More Urban Legends and Some Old Favorites* (W. W. Norton, 1986, p. 142), Brunvand describes a frequently retold lottery tale:

> A man is sitting in a bar with his friends. He is a recent winner of the lottery, a *big* prize winner as a matter of fact—in the thousands of dollars. He passes his winning ticket around the room to show it off to everyone, but when it is returned to him it is a different ticket.

The story, although widely believed to be true, is probably apocryphal—of doubtful authenticity—and shares a number of qualities common to all "urban legends." It has been often repeated, it appears in a variety of forms, it involves people no one seems able to be able to identify with certainty, and it has logical inconsistencies. Such stories also frequently center around high-sensation subjects like murder, adultery, psychic and paranormal phenomena, and very large sums of money.

There are several commonly told lottery stories in Michigan—in addition to the one about the woman and her Cadillacs—that seem to fit Grunvand's criteria for being apocryphal. Two that are often repeated, but have never been verified, gained credibility when they appeared in media reports. In a September 9, 1984, story in the Sunday magazine of the *Detroit News*, reporter David Markiewicz, discussing the "horror stories" that have sometimes accompanied lottery wins, wrote:

> Ron Gumm of Battle Creek, a millionaire winner himself, looked into the lives of some previous winners to guard against making the same mistakes. He heard of two appalling cases.

110

One was the factory worker who used his winnings to buy a gold-plated Cadillac complete with a built-in television in the back seat. Every day at lunch time, he'd leave work and go out to that Caddy where he'd sit and eat and watch the shows. One winter day, some co-workers peered through the rolled-up windows and found him dead, a victim of carbon monoxide poisoning.

Gumm also heard about a middle-age woman who, upon winning, dumped her husband of many years for a younger boyfriend, and her job for a life of leisure. After she bought him a new car and a boat, the boyfriend split. She wound up on welfare.

Robert Wagman, a Washington D.C. journalist and author of a book about America's lottery winners, *Instant Millionaires: Cashing In On America's Lotteries*, recalls hearing those same stories many times during the research for his book. The talk of the gold-plated Cadillac came up often, he says, especially in Michigan. He spent a good deal of time trying to track it down before concluding that the incident never occurred. Another story he tried to track down is that of a Canadian lottery winner who was said to have gone out celebrating the night of his lottery victory, gotten drunk, wandered onto a road, and been struck and killed by a truck. That story, which circulated widely in western Canada, also seems to have no basis in fact.

"Lotteries are filled with such stories," Wagman says. "Why? Because they're interesting. But there's also a kind of negative wishful thinking involved, maybe because people are envious of winners but secretly pleased when they hear of their misfortunes."

It could well be that "negative wishful thinking"—plain old sour grapes—is what keeps apocryphal lottery stories circulating. After all, each is a "horror story," a miniature moral tale warning about tragedies that follow the aquisition of sudden wealth.

But there is another kind of frequently told lottery story, one that is *true*. Some of those, as we saw in the last chapter, are—like their fictional counterparts—tragic. But most are merely odd, bizarre, or inexplicable. They prove that coincidence, prophetic dreams, premonitions, and outrageously good luck are not just the raw materials of speculative fiction—they are also fairly common facts of lottery life.

◆

Considering the long odds of winning a prize of $1 million or more, it is not surprising that, even after 15 years of lottery games, there are cities and even entire counties in Michigan that have not yet had a big winner. But there is no rational explanation for why certain locations attract more than their share of lottery winnings.

Nationwide, there have been several bizarre cases of luck zeroing in on one location. One of the strangest involved the city of Florissant, Missouri, a suburb of St. Louis. Many of Florissant's 55,000 residents were in the habit of making the short drive across the Mississippi River to buy Illinois lottery tickets. Then, during a five-week period in 1984, six people from Florissant hit Illinois Lotto jackpots that ranged from $232,000 to $2,113,180. Among the winners were a man and wife who—by using numbers based on the birthdates of their three children, a combination they used independently of each other and not knowing the other was buying a ticket—*each* won a jackpot of over $1 million. By the time the Florissant spree finally ended, the city of 55,000 had scored more big winners in five weeks than the entire six million residents of Chicago had managed in several months.

Lottery luck has concentrated in a similar way on several places in Michigan. One is the town of Rockwood, south of Detroit. When you consider that the statewide ratio of lottery millionaires to general population is 1 in 33,000, it's remarkable that Rockwood, with a population of 3,400 was home to two lottery players who hit million-dollar-plus jackpots. Clean living ("per population, we've got more churches than any town in Michigan," one resident boasted), longitude and latitude, and even something in the drinking water have all been conjectured as reasons for Rockwood's lottery favor.

Rockwood's winners are:

—Matteo Galati, 49, owner of a Rockwood pizza parlor, who won $1,846,505 on December 18, 1985. Galati played the Lotto regularly and always bet the same six numbers—except once. The week of his win, he inadvertently wrote in one different number.

—Carol Ann Maloney, 40, who won $3,589,558 on November 5, 1986. Co-owner of a real-estate office in nearby Trenton, she set out immediately to buy a new car and a diamond ring, and get a manicure. After she chose the color she wanted her nails painted she was told the name of the shade was "Millionaire Red." "I'll tell you, strange things are happening to me," she said.

Rockwood is also home to a third lottery millionaire, Robert

Reese. Reese, a 65-year-old cost estimator at Chrysler's Tech Center, was living in Flat Rock when he won a one-third share of a $6,023,000 jackpot on October 9, 1985, but, soon after his win, moved to nearby Rockwood to be closer to his children

Strange things have also been happening in the tiny community of Yale, west of Port Huron. It, too, is home to three major lottery winners, including two millionaires. But with a population of only 1,800, Yale's ratio of million-dollar winners to general population (1:900) is even more remarkable than Rockwood's.

Luck first struck Yale on April 27, 1985, when 46-year-old grocery-store produce-manager John E. Harrison was the sole winner of a $2,488,636 Lotto jackpot. Next was Michael Arnold, who won a one-fourth share of a $2.46 million Lotto jackpot on February 16, 1985. Then, on October 28, 1987, Casimer Trojanowski, 59, was the sole winner of a $5,145,002 jackpot. Lottery lightning just missed striking Yale a fourth time. The very next Lotto jackpot winner after John Harrison was Constance Meyers, a 46-year-old IGA bakery manager who lived in the tiny town of Capac, about 10 miles southwest of Yale.

There are two even more concentrated examples of geographic coincidence:

—On October 16, 1985, two East Detroit residents, Margaret Ficorelli and Michael Riviello, each had a winning ticket for Lotto jackpot worth nearly $4 million. That two people from East Detroit would end up with the same six-digit numbers and share a large prize is interesting, but not extraordinary considering the large population of lottery players in that community. What *is* extraordinary is that Ficorelli, 62, and Riviello, 69, who had never met one another, lived on the same street only a few blocks apart.

—David Kuh and John Upchurch had been friends since 1980 and had, at different times, both lived in an old Victorian-style house at the corner of Washington and Henry streets in downtown Muskegon. It was after each had moved out of that house that their luck improved. First, on August 10, 1985, 23-year-old Kuh won a $1,378,430 Lotto jackpot. Fifteen months later, on November 29, 1986, his friend Upchurch followed suit, winning a $2 million jackpot.

◆

It is probably inevitable that in a game of chance involving numbers there will sometimes be numerical coincidences. One of the strangest occurred in 1977 when a Michigan lottery agent was being interviewed on a Lansing television station about the new Michigan three-digit daily game. When the interviewer asked what numbers viewers could expect to be especially lucky, the lottery agent jokingly said that 137 was a good bet since it was his favorite number at horse tracks. Hundreds of viewers took his advice and played the number. The next day the winning Daily 3 number was, incredibly, 137, and the state reportedly paid out $25,000 more than the total amount bet that day on the game.

Whenever a three- or four-digit number makes the news for any reason, it's a certainty that a disproportionate number of bets will be placed on the same number in the daily lottery games. For example, in 1981 when American hostages being held in Iran were finally released, 47,395 Michigan bets were placed on the number 444—the total number of days the 52 Americans were in captivity. Had that number come up (it didn't), the lottery bureau would have had to pay out far more than it took in.

In August 1987, when a Northwest Airlines plane crashed at Detroit Metro Airport, killing all but one of the passengers and crew members, thousands of lottery players were inspired to play a rather morbid hunch and bet on the flight number—255. Those 47,445 bets would have cost the lottery bureau $13.2 million in prizes—at least double the amount wagered for the day—had the number come up.

A similar betting frenzy took place after "Black Monday," the October 19, 1987, stock market crash that saw the Dow Jones Industrial Average plummet 508 points. On Tuesday, not surprisingly, thousands of lottery players—some perhaps trying to recoup their losses—bet the number 508 in the Daily 3 game. The winning number was 605. The next day, Wednesday, a reduced but still significant number of players were apparently counting on a delay factor and bet on 508 again. Their persistence paid off. The number came up, and the Michigan Bureau of State Lottery, for the 17th time in 1987, paid out more than it took in for the day.

◆

Sometimes a misplaced or lost ticket causes momentary good fortune to turn bad. Many winners of large lottery prizes tell how those few hours or days between the time they realize they are holding a winning ticket and the moment they can get it validated by the lottery bureau can be fraught with anxiety and fear. It is a nearly universal fear that the ticket, such a fragile slip of paper, will become lost, be stolen, blow suddenly into the fireplace, or get torn up and devoured by the family dog. There have been some unhappy stories of winners who *did* lose tickets worth thousands of dollars and spent days sifting in vain through trash at landfills.

Not all such cases, however, end unhappily. In 1976 a Massachusetts woman accidentally burned her winning ticket. When she explained to lottery officials what she had done, they naturally were dubious, but went to the trouble of having the ashes of the ticket placed inside Georgia Tech's nuclear reactor and bombarded with neutrons. Enough coded material was revealed to prove the woman's claim authentic.

There have been some happy endings of the same sort in Michigan as well. One ticket was recovered even when nobody knew it was lost. While rummaging through the garbage can in her home one day in 1973, Dorothy Lavers, a St. Clair Shores housewife, came across a batch of lottery tickets that a friend of her son's had discarded two weeks earlier. She took the trouble to inspect them and found one to be eligible for a grand-prize drawing. With it, the son's friend eventually won $10,000.

Ray Swidan of Allen Park temporarily lost a ticket under rather unhappy circumstances. In April 1986, the 31-year-old man purchased a Lotto ticket and placed it inside his car's glove compartment for safekeeping. Before he could learn whether or not he had a winner, federal drug agents, who suspected Swidan of selling nearly 53,000 tablets of LSD over a two-year period, confiscated the car.

Two weeks after the April 23, 1986, Lotto drawing, the car was returned to Swidan, who had since forgotten about his lottery ticket. His wife discovered it while cleaning the glove compartment. Her first impulse was to simply throw it away, but on second thought she decided to confirm it was a loser. It proved, ultimately, to be worth $2 million.

As of this writing, Ray Swidan is receiving annual lottery checks of $80,000. On April 14, 1988, he was arrested and charged in a

22-count federal grand-jury indictment for the sale of LSD.

Joseph Jackson of Detroit was out of town the evening of October 18, 1986, when the Super Lotto drawing was held for a $4 million jackpot. Ten months later he read in the newspaper that the lottery bureau was still looking for the winner of that and one other jackpot. He sorted through the box where he habitually kept his losing tickets and found, among them, the missing $4 million winner. Jackson claimed the money but nearly too late. Had he waited two more months, the prize would have been declared permanently unclaimed and would have gone to the state school-aid fund.

A lost ticket resulted in 40 days of "sheer hell" for a Royal Oak woman in 1978. Lorraine Joswick, a housewife and mother of four children, purchased an instant ticket at a local store and discovered she had a $5,000 winner. She and her husband bought wine and stayed up until 2:30 in the morning celebrating their good fortune. They apparently celebrated with vigor, because the next morning Mrs. Joswick could not remember where she had put the ticket for safekeeping. Her husband remembered that she had hidden it under the bedroom rug. She remembered that too, but she also remembered that, while he was in the bathroom preparing to go to bed, she had had second thoughts about the safety of that hiding place and had removed it to a less obvious one. The question was, where?

During the following days and weeks, Mrs. Joswick, her husband, and their four grown children systematically tore the house apart in a search for the missing ticket. They pried off baseboards, stripped paneling from the walls, and rented a metal detector on the chance that it might sense the foil in the ticket. They hired a hypnotist in the hope that he could dredge the memory of the hiding place out of Mrs. Joswick's subconscious. Guilt-ridden, anxious, and unable to sleep or eat, she began to take tranquilizers.

When lottery commissioner Gus Harrison decided to get involved after receiving "one of the funniest letters I've ever seen," Mrs. Joswick's luck changed. In her letter to Harrison, Mrs. Joswick explained that she and her husband "bought some good wine and partied it up." After hiding the ticket for the second time and realizing in the morning to her horror that she couldn't remember where it was, she began the search "in some sort of vague stupor with unbelievable nausea, unrelenting sleepless nights, no appetite for a solid week, and a depression coupled with mental anguish beyond description." The hardest part of it all, she explained, "was trying to explain such dumbness on my part."

Harrison and other lottery officials thought the story was plausible, so they investigated and discovered that a $5,000 ticket had indeed been sold at the store she described. They took affidavits from the store owner and informed Mrs. Joswick that they would honor her claim and pay her $5,000 if no one else appeared with the ticket before February 1979. All she had to do was be patient for a year.

Then, six weeks after she had hid her ticket so safely, Lorraine Joswick found it—pasted to the back of a mirror in her daughter's room. She had no memory of putting it there. "I don't even remember being in there that night," she said later. "I don't know how I ever lived through the experience. It was Nervous Breakdown City."

Asked what she planned to do with her hard-earned money, Mrs. Joswick said, "Let me say that I don't plan on saving the money for old age. I have a pet peeve with people who win these lottery drawings and don't know what they are going to do with the money. . . . I'm going to Las Vegas to have a good time."

◆

Winning large sums of money sometimes brings out the best in people. In April 1984, a police detective from Dobbs Ferry, New York, named Robert Cunningham made national news when he won a $6 million jackpot in the New York lottery. But it wasn't only his impressive jackpot that drew attention to him. Cunningham had filled in the lottery form while sitting in a restaurant and had asked his waitress, Phyliss Penzo, to assist him in choosing some lucky numbers. He promised that, in lieu of a tip, he would split any winnings with her. A few days later, when he learned that he was the winner of the $6 million, Cunningham proved to be as good as his word. At last report he was still splitting the $286,000 annual checks down the middle, giving half to former waitress Phyliss Penzo.

Michigan's biggest tipper is Al Urban of Lake Orion. In January 1976, Urban, 67, had several $25 winning Weekly Game tickets among those he had purchased from Richardson's Farm Dairy in Lake Orion and decided to tip the cashier who sold them to him. He gave Joy

Volant, 19, a dollar and told her to buy an instant lottery ticket. If it won, he told her, they would split the prize. A few moments later, Miss Volant suffered a painfully bruised hand, injured when she struck it on the counter while jumping up and down and screaming. The ticket was a $10,000 winner.

"I told Al he should get the entire $10,000 prize," she said. "But he insisted we share it."

Urban seemed to think that generous tipping was the key to winning at the lottery. He claimed that in 1975 he had won $25 prizes in the Weekly Game a total of 47 times, that in 1974 he had won 55 times, and in 1973 won 67 times. "I'll bet I've given away $100 in tickets to the girls who've sold me the most winners," he said. As for his $5,000 share of the winning instant ticket, he said that he would use it to purchase new equipment for his janitorial business and to maybe work a few less hours each week. Miss Volant, meanwhile, said that she would spend her share of the money on a four-wheel-drive truck.

Another generous winner was 23-year-old Mike Reardon, a teacher at Bishop Borgess High School in Redford. Reardon's luck began in 1983 when he received a $50 prize for encouraging his class to sell the most raffle tickets in a school-wide fund-raising drive. He didn't feel right about keeping the money himself, however, so he formed a lottery club with his students and told them they would split any winnings among themselves, with percentages determined by how many raffle tickets each had sold. The plan was for Reardon to buy 10 instant tickets at a time from stores in different locations—"to improve our chances"—and bring them to class on a certain day. The self-described procrastinator, however, put off buying the tickets until the last day when, on his way to school, he made a quick stop at a bar and bought all 50. At school he passed out tickets to the 14 members of his class and kept five for himself. The second ticket he scratched was a $10,000 winner.

Asked later if he still planned to share the prize with his students, he was adamant. "A deal is a deal," he said. "I have never won a thing before. In fact, this is the first time I ever bought a lottery ticket, and most likely the last."

◆

What *does* it take to win at the lottery? On that subject, there's no shortage of opinions, which range from the carefully analyzed, to the offbeat, to the absolutely bizarre.

Some players' efforts to tip the scales of chance in their favor are a bit hard to understand. In Australia, for example, where the lottery has been called a "national obsession," it is common practice for superstitious players to enter the lottery office where they purchase their tickets through the door marked "Exit," wait in the office for the clock to strike the hour, write their names upside down on the application form, pay their money, wait until the traffic light outside turns green, then leave the office through the door marked "Entrance." In France it was once common—and may still be—for lottery customers, after having clerks fan tickets across the counter, to search among them for winners using homemade divining rods. In Italy, where the Lotto is more than 400 years old, superstitions are rampant. It is, for example, bad luck to bet on a Friday. On the other hand, it is considered extremely good luck to buy tickets from a male hunchbacked clerk.

Some Michigan winners, too, have devised some rather unique techniques that have worked. Lottery Commissioner Michael Carr recalls that one winner wrote numbers on scraps of paper, spread them on the floor, then picked the ones that his cat stepped on. After his method proved effective, many people asked to borrow the cat, which, unfortunately, soon after its single act of divination, died.

Following, in no particular order, are some other techniques that have paid off for Michigan winners.

Edmund Prucnell, a 54-year-old Ford Motor Co. assembler from Roseville, won a $1.9 million jackpot on October 20, 1984, by selecting the numbers 12, 20, 31, 36, 39 and 40 from small-parts numbers stamped on pallets at the Sterling Heights plant where he worked.

Melissa Alley, 41, of Taylor used this simple method to win a $5,640,495 Lotto jackpot in September 1985: She combined the ages of her three children (15, 18, 20), the age of her husband (39), and split the digits in her own age (40, 1). Mrs. Alley later admitted that at the time she was filling out the winning ticket her oldest daughter had been about to turn 21, so she had been very tempted to change the 20 to a 21. She added that she was "real glad" she didn't.

In 1977, when Phyllis Taylor of Detroit held a $25 winning Weekly Game ticket, there wasn't as much opportunity for self-determination as there would be later when the daily numbers and Lotto games came along. Unable to have a hand in choosing her own lucky numbers, all she could do was try to influence fate by choosing the day she turned in her qualifying ticket for a grand-prize drawing. The 48-year-old mother-of-four waited several weeks for a "lucky day" to show up in her Libra horoscope. That day finally came on Saturday, February 26. A few weeks later she was informed that the ticket had earned her a place in the grand-prize drawing as a finalist, and on April 4, 1977, she won the $1 million grand-prize drawing.

Thomas LaPenna, a 45-year-old bank executive from Marquette, employed what lottery commissioner Michael Carr called "the screwiest system, the dumbest system I've heard of so far." He took the number of people in his family (5), his wife's birth date (6), his daughter's grade in school (8), his birth date added to his wife's birth date (10), the number of years he and his wife had been married (22), and the year of his birth (39). Presto! It worked. LaPenna won Michigan's first Lotto jackpot—$2,950,259—on September 1, 1984.

Elmer Fronsee, a 58-year-old retired Great Lakes seaman, knew enough to stick with a loser. When his Easy Pick numbers failed to pay off in one week's Lotto game, he marked the same numbers on a ticket form the next week and turned them into winners. His jackpot, won December 8, 1984, was worth $2,237,782.

Anna Savage won a $7.5 million jackpot in the Super Lotto game on July 11, 1987. The 58-year-old retired bookkeeper from Beaverton chose her winning numbers by taking her husband's birth date—4, 22, 30—for three numbers, then dividing them in half—2, 11, 15—for the other three.

One young couple, who preferred to remain anonymous when they were interviewed for the May 1985 issue of *Monthly Detroit* magazine, said they had been having hunches about the numbers 5 and 8. "Mike" was a member of union local #58. They had a neighbor whose address had 5s and 8s in it. When they took their car to a garage for repairs they were told to wait in line and were given ticket number 58. When they were handed a ticket stub at the theatre it had a 5 and an 8 on it. When they bought a small item at the supermarket, the price rung up on the cash register was 58 cents. Investigating further, they noticed that a lot of recent winners in the Michigan Lotto game had 5s and 8s in their winning numbers.

Times had been hard—both Mike and Carol had been out of work for awhile, and money was tight. For her husband on Valentines Day,

Carol picked out a card printed with the message, "Even though we can't afford diamonds and furs and expensive dinners, we can still afford each other." She decided she also could afford two small gifts—Lotto tickets—which she put inside the card. It was natural that one of the tickets made liberal use of the numbers 5 and 8—5, 8, 10 (5 doubled), 13 (5 plus 8), 16 (8 doubled), and 23 (5 plus 8 plus 10). A few days later those numbers were drawn, and Mike and Carol became winners of a one-quarter share of a $2.4 million jackpot.

When Vitore Vulaj of Detroit took her children shopping for clothes one day in November 1987, the bill at the first store they visited came to $57.17. Later, at another store the bill again came to $57.17. Mrs. Vulaj, a 23-year-old part-time waitress, recognized an omen when she saw one. She promptly bought a Lotto ticket using the numbers, 5, 7, 17, plus 1 and 29 (her birthdate) and 23 (her age). She forgot to watch the televised drawing for the winning numbers, but the next morning her 5-year-old child reminded her by asserting with finality that she had won. Mrs. Vulaj called the lottery hotline and discovered it was true. She was the winner of a $1.59 million jackpot.

Sometimes winners have turned a bit of misfortune into good fortune. Willie George Dooley is one of those people. In August 1981, Dooley, 47, of Detroit was ticketed for driving through a traffic light. In October, when he appeared in front of Magistrate David Harris to answer the charge, he cheerfully pleaded guilty and offered to give the police officer who arrested him a $100 reward. It seems that after he received his citation, Dooley took the first three digits of the ticket's serial number—D 057-541—and bet them heavily in the Daily 3 game. His effort to salvage the most out of a bad situation paid off—he won $3,600. Magistrate Harris, saying he had "never heard of anything like this before," suggested that police regulations would probably not allow the plaintiff to reward the arresting officer. He then gave Willie Dooley a suspended sentence, "for his honesty."

The lottery bureau couldn't have *invented* any better winners for the grand prize in their special Bicentennial Game, played in 1975 in honor of the nation's 200th birthday. The pair—brothers Sam and Thomas Randa of Fraser, who had formed the S & T Lottery Club—lived in the Concord Green Apartments, on Paul Revere Street, and purchased 13—one for each of the original 13 colonies—of the $5 instant tickets. Sam, 54, who was retired from Bendix Corporation, and Thomas, 46, a Stroh Brewing Company employee, split an initial

$500,000 cash prize and another $25,000 a year for 20 years.

What's it take to win $11.2 million? Philip Golden, who became the winner of the Michigan lottery's second-largest individually won jackpot on December 16, 1987, knows. His method is simple. Just take 44 dried lima beans, write numbers on them with a fine-tip pen, and place them in a jar. Shake well. While shaking, let six beans fall out and record their numbers. Use those numbers on a Super Lotto ticket. Place your bet. Win.

Bruce Risher, a 33-year-old assistant manager of a Holland bowling alley, selected the numbers that won him a $1,378,430 Lotto jackpot on August 10, 1985, by combining his age and birthdate with the age and birthdate of his dog.

Katharine Myatt, a 29-year-old housewife from Eau Claire, won a $7 million Super Lotto jackpot on Valentines Day 1987 by using a variation of Philip Golden's lima-beans-in-a-jar trick. She cut out 44 slips of paper, numbered them, folded them in half, placed them in an empty cigarette carton, and shook them up. The next part was easy. She simply tipped the box and used the numbers—winning numbers—on the first six slips of paper that fell out.

Nancy Zimmerman, a 57-year-old Saginaw woman, took home a one-eighth share of an August 1, 1985, Lotto jackpot by filling in five numbers absolutely at random on the Lotto form—with her eyes closed. She then took a hand in her own destiny by choosing the sixth, the number of children she had—9.

◆

If you have any doubt that superstitions and charms are important to many lottery players, remember that during a typical day a vastly disproportionate number of people place bets on numbers with lucky or mystical associations, numbers such as 777, 7171, 333, or 666 in the Daily 3 and 4 games, or 3, 6, 9, 12, 15, 18 in Super Lotto. A Friday the 13th in August 1984 inspired such heavy betting in New York state's three-digit daily game that their lottery commission halted betting on the number 813—the day's numerical date. If 813 had come up it would have cost the state about $5 million.

Such reliance on the arcane has spawned a large industry that deals in lucky charms, magic wheels, and a myriad of other devices that tap into mysterious sources for lottery luck. Shoppers' choices include, to list a few examples: "The Millionaire Lucky Number Machine," "Dimitrov's Wheel Computer Program," "Skippy's All-Purpose Magic Candle," "Old Doc's Lucky Hot Box," "Baba Mohammed's Guaranteed to Win Lucky Lottery Numbers," "Professor Zonite's Original Lucky Incense," "Professor Zonite's 'River Jordan' Botanical Roots," "Chinese 'Lucky Omen' Floor Wash," and "Wonderful Fragrance Lucky Room Spray."

So-called "dream books" have enjoyed a special and long-time popularity among lottery players. There are reports of such books being used by players of the Italian Lotto hundreds of years ago, and in this country they were used by players of illegal numbers games long before the state-run lotteries began. Their principle is simple. Dreams are divided by subject matter into categories, which are assigned numbers. If you dreamed that you rode a bicycle, for example, you would look up that subject heading, find the most specific correlative, and bet on the number indicated.

Some lottery winners take a short-cut by dreaming directly of winning. One of the most startling experiences belongs to Joseph Polachek, a 68-year-old retiree from GM's Buick plant in Flint, who won a $3.8 million Super Lotto jackpot on November 21, 1987. In a telephone interview, his wife, Marguerite, explained that five days before the drawing, his horoscope predicted that he would win a "pile of money." It was a prophecy that confirmed what he had suspected all along. He'd always had a feeling that he was going to win big in the lottery, and that week before the November 21 drawing the feeling had been growing more and more insistent. As was his habit, he did not watch the televised drawing Saturday night, preferring to wait until the next day to read the numbers in the newspaper.

The way Mrs. Polachek describes it, that night, after the drawing but before he had seen the winning numbers, he had a vivid dream in which he stood with his tickets in his hands talking to his brother. He looked down at the tickets and focused on one particular line of numbers. "I won," he said. "I've got the winning numbers. But," he added, "I'm having a hard time getting the money."

The next morning Polachek remembered which set of numbers he had dreamed were the winners. When he checked the newspaper he found that not only was he a winner, but also he had correctly dreamed which six numbers had made him one.

The dream became complete reality the next day, Monday, when the Polacheks drove to the Lansing lottery office to redeem their ticket and collect the first installment of their prize. When they got there they were met with unusual—and unexplained—difficulty. For reasons never made clear, the Polacheks were informed that they could not collect their money that day, that they would have to return the next day. They were baffled. They had called ahead and made an appointment; the ticket was confirmed as a winner; they filled out the necessary forms and applications. But, just as he had told his brother in his dream, Polachek had a hard time getting the money.

◆

Occasionally, mix-ups and miscues have had amusing—and sometimes not-so-amusing—consequences. Take John Konieczny of Detroit, for instance. The 65-year-old retired truck driver thought he was eligible for a $1,836 prize as one of 500 or so players who had matched five numbers in the January 18, 1986, Lotto drawing. When he went to the Oak Park office of the lottery to collect his winnings, he was given some bad news and some good news. The bad news was that his match-five claim was invalid. The good news was that he had matched all *six* numbers and that, instead of pocketing a check for $1,836, he would take home the first installment of a jackpot worth $3,709,932.

Konieczny wasn't the first Lotto player to make such a fortuitous error. Incredibly, just two months earlier, on November 20, 1985, a 34-year-old medical transcriptionist at Sinai Hospital in Detroit named Brunetta Blocton walked into the same Oak Park lottery office and tried to collect a $2,709 prize for matching five of six numbers in a recent drawing. Like Konieczny, she was denied the money. Also like Konieczny, she had matched six numbers and her actual prize was over $3.7 million—$3,729,619 to be exact.

There have been a few mix-ups—mechanical and human—within the lottery system itself. Some have cost the state dearly. During the Daily 3 drawing on August 10, 1979, for example, the electronic scramble board then used to pick the numbers developed a glitch. The official winning number was 039, but for just a second the number 395 also flashed on as a winner. The uproar from holders of tickets with number 395 was instantaneous and loud. The lottery bureau decided there was no alternative but to honor both numbers as winners. The malfunction ended up costing the state about $400,000.

A human error of a similar kind occurred on a live televised drawing of the Daily 3 game on May 19, 1981. The host of the program misread the number 1 when it came up on numbered balls and read it aloud as 9. Gary Barfknecht reported in his book *Michillaneous II* (Friede Publications, 1985) that although the announcer corrected himself immediately, the news media and lottery bureau were inundated with calls from viewers claiming they had seen the announcer switch balls by such varied methods as turning off the lights and falling down.

In an article in the October 1986 issue of *Lottery Player's Magazine*, Ann Arbor author Ken Wachsberger reported on a similar lottery miscue, this one with more serious results. In one of the first Super Drawings of the Weekly Game, in 1972, each of 10 finalists was given a number which would determine what prize he or she won. Betty Coleman was given the number 9. When it was determined that the top prize of $200,000 would go to the holder of number 6, Betty Coleman's 9 was read upside down and she was announced as the grand-prize winner. The actual number 6, held by a Mr. Yao, was awarded the runner-up prize, $50,000.

That same evening, however, the mistake was discovered and Coleman and Yao were informed that they must swap prizes. Mrs. Coleman felt that she had been wronged and took her claim to Court. The judge ruled in her favor, concluding that, because the money had been rescinded from Mrs. Coleman after being awarded to her, the lottery bureau was in effect guilty of breach of contract. He directed that both Coleman and Yao be awarded $200,000 prizes. But Coleman's victory was short-lived. The Court of Appeals reversed the decision, stating that she had no rightful claim to the prize "by the true facts that existed," and five years after the drawing she was forced to accept $50,000 after all.

Meanwhile, Mr. Yao had been receiving partial installments of his $200,000 prize money, and when the legal matter was settled he was owed the difference. There was a further mix-up and his payment was delayed another six or seven months. When he finally received the money owed to him, Yao decided that he also should be paid the interest it would have earned in the months he had been forced to wait for it. For the next four years he sent annual Christmas greetings to the lottery bureau saying, "Merry Christmas to everybody and, by the way, you still owe me some money."

When attorney Charles Hackney took the position of Assistant Attorney General in charge of Michigan's Agriculture and Lottery Division in 1981, he looked into the case and concluded that Yao did, indeed, have a justifiable complaint. He authorized payment of the interest and assumed that the matter was settled. Mr. Yao, however, was not satisfied. He contended that since the interest payment had been delayed four years he should be awarded interest on the interest. Hackney demurred; Yao wrote to President Ronald Reagan. That letter made its way from the president to First Lady Nancy Reagan to the Justice Department, which looked into the matter. Their conclusion was that Mr. Yao's civil rights had not been compromised. He had to be happy with what he got.

◆

Hazel Stickley, a 67-year-old housewife from Detroit who won $1 million in the Weekly Game on May 11, 1975, found it was nearly as difficult to give her money away as it was to win it. Mrs. Stickley told reporters that her husband, Joseph, was retired, and that she was already so happy with her life that the money would not make much difference to her. She wanted to use it to "help people who really need it. All I've ever wanted is good health, and I thank the Lord I've got it. I don't want to squander the money. I'm very happy with what we have." After the drawing that made her a lottery millionaire, during which she clutched a lucky stone her husband had picked up from a beach 25 years earlier, the generous Mrs. Stickley decided she would give half her prize to her brother, Melvin Smith, 54, of Ferndale.

But when she tried to get lottery officials to award half the money to Smith, Commissioner Gus Harrison informed her that her brother could not be designated co-winner unless the lottery bureau received a court order first. That policy was a "formality," lottery officials maintained, designed to protect both the winners and the bureau. Mrs. Stickley, of course, was free to give away all her money without a court order if she chose to. But the check would be made out to her alone, and she would be responsible for paying federal income taxes on the entire amount.

So Stickley and Smith filed suit in Wayne County Circuit Court to force the lottery bureau to recognize the sister and brother as "equally rightful owners of the million dollars." The court order was granted, the lottery bureau complied, and Mrs. Stickley and Mr. Smith divided the money happily and legally.

◆

When J. Elaine Baker won a $7,028,191 Super Lotto jackpot on June 27, 1987, she unknowingly complicated the lives of two other women in her home town. The problem started when Ms. Baker refused to reveal her age, address, phone number or place of employment after she had won the sizable prize. It was only natural that curious people who took the matter into their own hands would look first in the phone book. J. Elaine Baker, the winner, was not listed. Two names, however, stood out: "Jane Baker" and "Elaine Baker."

Within a few days, both of those women notified local newspapers that they were waving white flags of surrender. They wanted it made perfectly clear that they were *not* millionaires, that they never had been, and that they most probably never would be. Jane Baker said she had received about 20 calls from casual inquirers, well-wishers, and salesmen hustling cars and real estate. Her primary complaint was that the calls came not only at home, but also while she was attempting to give permanents to customers at her beauty shop. Meanwhile, Elaine Baker was busy fending off marriage proposals. The day after the announcement of the real J. Elaine Baker's good fortune, Elaine received seven calls at work and 10 at home. Two were marriage proposals, including one from a man she quoted as saying, "You don't know me, but I really love you and I want to marry you." Another caller, one with less amorous intentions, asked her if she was the lottery winner. When she explained that she was not, he said, "Too bad, I was going to ask you for a loan."

The Winning Attitude

"Somebody has to win. Why not me?"

—Any number of lottery players

J ust what are the chances of winning the lottery? More specifically, what are the chances of winning the grand prize in a 6-of-44 Super Lotto drawing? The answer—1 in 7,059,052—is thrown around so often, so carelessly, that we tend to forget just how great those odds are. In an age when our national debt is measured in trillions of dollars, seven million of something begins to sound pretty insignificant.

But consider this: If you were to begin counting at a leisurely but determined pace, you would reach 100 in a minute, 1,000 in 10 minutes, and 6,000 in an hour. At the same pace, counting to 7,059,052 would take 1,265 1/2 hours. Working at it eight hours a day, 40 hours a week, you'd better plan on devoting a little under eight months to the job.

And this: 7,059,052 automobiles placed bumper to bumper on the equator would circle more than three-quarters of the distance around the earth.

And this: 7,059,052 people stretched hand to hand, would line Highway 80 from San Francisco to New York and back, with enough left over to go from San Francisco to Portland, Oregon. That many people, gathered together to see a baseball game, would need a park with a seating capacity 130 times greater than Tiger Stadium.

It's no wonder then, that some lottery players will go to great lengths in attempts to improve their chances of winning. But, other than buying large amounts of tickets, is it really possible to improve the odds?

That question elicits two distinctly different kinds of answers. On one side are the mathematicians and statisticians, whose primary argument is that random numbers, by definition, cannot be anticipated or influenced. Their stand is that: 1) the lottery bureaus have succeeded in creating methods for choosing numbers that are absolutely random, and 2) the outcome of a random drawing is *chaotic*; it cannot be ordered, systematized or predicted. Random numbers, they say, remain random regardless of past performance—numbers do not have memories—and the odds of any six-digit set of numbers coming up always remains exactly the same.

As an example, take the numbers 1, 2, 3, 4, 5, 6. Those six numbers traditionally have been one of the most frequently played sets in any lotto game, yet as of January 1988 they had never been selected as the winning combination in the hundreds of drawings of the Michigan Lotto and Super Lotto. A mathematician will argue that the odds of 1, 2, 3, 4, 5, 6 coming up are 1 in 7,059,052, exactly the same as the odds of any other 6-of-44 combination. Furthermore, he will argue that if those numbers are picked in today's drawing, next week, in the fresh, unbiased setting of another drawing, the odds of 1, 2, 3, 4, 5, 6 winning again are still exactly 1 in 7,059,052. Chaos knows no favorites. It cannot be influenced. Numbers have no memories.

On the other side of the debate table are those who believe that chaos *can* be influenced, that it can be ordered into systems. Those systems range from the analytical to the arcane—from complex mathematical systems to those based on dreams, hunches and divinations. The common denominator in them all, however, is an opposition to the stark, logical stance of pure mathematics. Using the same example, proponents of systems either, 1) think that the numbers 1, 2, 3, 4, 5, 6 will not be drawn because they create an unlikely combination, one that contrasts too much with the scattered, more-representative distribution that seems to have appeared consistently in past drawings, or 2) they feel that 1, 2, 3, 4, 5, 6 is a good bet precisely because it is such an unusual combination, that it is a sequence with significance, whether to a personal system of hunch-betting, or because it has never been drawn and is therefore *due* to be drawn.

That latter approach is apparently quite popular, but there are a couple of problems with it. The first is that literally millions of combinations have not yet been drawn in the Michigan lotto games, and any one of them is just as likely to be drawn as 1, 2, 3, 4, 5, 6. The second problem is a more practical one. A conspicuous combination like 1, 2, 3, 4, 5, 6 attracts a large number of bets, and since the amount of the prize in Lotto and Super Lotto is determined by the number of winners, it becomes a very bad bet. In a typical week in Michigan, if you played the numbers 1, 2, 3, 4, 5, 6 and that combination won, you would share the grand prize with about 5,000 other winners. Your share of a million-dollar jackpot would be $200.

The debate eventually comes down to different modes of thought. It is very much like the classic conflict between science and religion. In the end, logic and language always collapse and each position is left with only faith to defend itself.

That faith can be an unshakable thing. Will Richey, for instance, who won $1,109,932 in a Lotto drawing on January 7, 1987, is absolutely convinced that the system he used to choose his winning numbers contributed to his win and that, furthermore, it is also going to contribute to future wins. The system Will Richey uses is a widely advertised one. In fact, he now is often pictured in full-page newspaper and magazine testimonials advertising the system, marketed by a company that will, for $12, mail a "report" detailing how to greatly increase the odds of becoming a winner. The inventor of the system, who used it herself to win 72 minor lottery prizes in 104 tests, says that she is sharing her lottery secret with the world because she wants to become the most famous woman in America.

As Will Richey describes it, the system works by analyzing trends in recent lottery drawings. It uses an arrangement of "wheels" to juxtapose favorable numbers in combinations most likely to appear again. Richey has no doubt that it works. During the first year he used it, he won, in addition to his $1.1 million jackpot, a total of $3,000 in four-digit Lotto matches and in the Daily 3 and Daily 4 games. Although he admits that he spends $25 to $100 a week on tickets, his ratio of winnings to bets remains high. "It works," he insists. "I wouldn't stand here telling you about it if it didn't."

The heart of Richey's system, and of most of the other systems commonly offered for sale, is something called "tracking." Tracking is simply any of numerous methods which use both the numbers and the patterns of numbers that have come up in the past to predict numbers that will come up in the future. At the heart of tracking is an implicit belief in the history and significance of numbers that are "hot" or "cold." By "wheeling" those hot numbers into various combinations, followers of these systems feel they can increase the odds of winning by anywhere from 100 percent to 600 percent. Statisticians scoff at the claims; people like Will Richey, who have seen results, swear by them.

But there was more than a mathematical system at work for Will Richey when he hit his jackpot. He was a winner long before that day in January 1987 when six numbers lined up for him.

Born in Geary, Oklahoma, in 1933, young Will Richey spent much of his childhood under the influence of a strong-willed and determined grandfather. That grandfather had homesteaded a parcel of Oklahoma land a mile long and a half-mile wide in the early 1900s, then settled down to "raise kids, crops and farm animals." The ambitious, hard-working man expected the same from his children and grandchildren and instilled in them a respect and belief in hard work as the way to accomplish things in life. Will watched his grandfather, through sheer hard work and unshakable self-confidence, raise himself from a poor sodbuster to a very successful farmer. By the time he died in the early 1980s at age 92, he had become a millionaire.

Dividing his childhood between country life on his grandparents' farm and urban life at his parents' home in Albuquerque, New Mexico, Will Richey grew to have a broader outlook than many people, an advantage that would later make it easier for him to step out into the world.

After high school, without plans, Will moved to Washington state. During the next 20 years he became proficient at an amazing number of occupations. At various times he was a machinist, a welder, and an inventor of tools and machinery, including a self-ventilating welding helmet that was manufactured and marketed for a time in the 1960s. He also worked as a bail-bondsman, a janitor, a sawyer in a sawmill, and a riveter on V-2 rockets at the Boeing Plant in Seattle. At one time he became an automobile mechanic and opened a shop that specialized in GM's "disaster car," the Corvair. He learned everything there was to know about that car and built such a reputation that GM hired him as a consultant to help their engineers figure out why the Corvair was prone to accidents and gas emission leaks in the cabs. Eventually he pioneered efforts to convert the Corvair's air-cooled engine to racing purposes and while racing them himself in superstock competitions, set a class record and won several trophies.

During that time, and as a benefit of his varied experiences, Richey was formulating ideas about his place in the world. He had begun to realize that there was no limit to what a person could accomplish, that the world was wide open to whatever he decided to do.

In 1971 he attended a "Dare to be Great" seminar taught by Glen W. Turner, and suddenly Richey's philosophy had found a catalyst. Turner was a man who had overcome tremendous adversity to become a multimillionaire and was using his experiences as the basis to teach others how they could do it as well. Richey was greatly impressed—so impressed, in fact, that he gave his auto shop to his father and went to work for Turner for a year, traveling with him and becoming an accomplished public speaker himself. Eventually those experiences would lead him into commission sales, where he felt he could apply the principles he had learned from Turner.

About that time, Richey found another satisfying outlet for his philosophies. While working in an organization called DECA (Distributive Education Clubs of America), he traveled to high schools to help students determine goals in their lives and set up plans to achieve them. Richey also outlined his principles in a motivational book titled, *Are You Taking the Pill?*, which he began writing in 1979. That book, he says, shows students ways to develop confidence, self-control and healthy attitudes, so that they can accomplish whatever they choose to do.

"The main thing I try to teach kids," he says, "is to reach for a destination in life. I've devised a very simple formula for doing that. That formula is kind of like a three-legged stool. If you have all three legs in a proper position, on top of the stool sits success. If you don't have all three legs, the stool will never stand up, it'll fall. That three-legged principle is simply this: one, do the thing you want to do more than anything else in the world. Two, do it to the best of your ability. Those first two go hand in hand. If you do what you like, you're going to do it better than you do anything else. Three, and foremost—if you have it you'll succeed, if you don't have it you'll fail—figure out who, and how many people you can help in the process. With those three things in place you'll have total success, undoubtedly. Success will be yours regardless of what's going against you."

Will Richey's own three-legged stool seems firmly seated. One leg is supported by his commitment to assist high school students. The other two rest on his determination to be successful in business.

In 1980, after a difficult divorce, he moved to Detroit to start a new life for himself. In 1982 he remarried and became the instant father of twin 12-year-old daughters. Although he had been very successful in Seattle as a cookware and crystal salesman (dubbed the "black Zig Ziggler of cookware"), financial rewards escaped him the first years he was in Detroit. He began a company called Miracle Performance Carpet Care, a business that did everything from cleaning, repairing, and installing carpet, to selling it. "I had a tough time putting it together," he says, "because I started building it out of my hind pocket, so to speak, and just never had the capital. When I started it I was very under-capitalized."

Yet, doubts about financial success never worried him. "I always *thought* I was a millionaire," he says, laughing. "I operated as a millionaire, I talked like one, I acted like one. There were people who thought I was a millionaire. Afterwards, when they would sometimes tell me they thought I was a millionaire all along, my quip was, 'I was, I just hadn't collected the money yet.' And I still am, though I still haven't collected the money. It didn't faze me that I wasn't a millionaire, because I always knew I would be one."

But there were days when that goal must have seemed far off and hazy. The business, although holding steady, was not making the progress he was hoping for.

One thing that had never figured much in his plans was the lottery. The odds seemed too long to make it a serious possibility. He played only occasionally, and if he spent $5 at a time on tickets, that seemed exorbitant. But in December 1986 that attitude changed. Suddenly, Richey says, "I saw it as a way, not just to become a millionaire, but as a way to get the things done I had to get done."

Two incidents changed his mind about the lottery. First, he took a close look at a packet of advertisements that he received unsolicited in the mail. The literature promoted a system that promised to increase the odds of winning lotteries by 500 percent. "I thought that was phenomenal," he recalls. "I just had to see how it worked." So he invested $12 and sent away for a report that outlined how the system operated. After reading it, he says, he knew right away that it was the way to win.

But he may never have used it, had a second incident not occurred. Early one morning while coming out of a store, he spotted an envelope laying directly in his path on the sidewalk. His first inclination was to kick it out of the way, but he caught a glimpse of green through the envelope's window and picked it up instead. Inside was $221 in cash.

When efforts to find the owner of the money failed, he decided to use the cash to test his new lottery system. Starting with $12-15 bets, he increased the number of tickets he purchased for each Lotto drawing until he was spending up to $46. By his fourth attempt—for a Saturday drawing in early January 1987—he thought he had a lock on the jackpot. All the evidence pointed to a win. The numbers he was tracking had aligned in such a way that he was confident—no, *positive*—that he would win. But he did not.

"I felt like somebody had stolen something from me," he says. "I mean I was literally upset, and I don't get upset. I take everything on the chin and just keep rolling. But I just internally felt like somebody had stolen something from me because I'd missed it. I knew that I should have hit it. I just felt so confident, based on the material in that book, that those numbers should have come out."

Then a strange thing happened. His wife, Juanita, who Richey says has often had premonitions that proved correct, told him not to worry because they were going to win the following Wednesday's jackpot. She began to jump up and down, saying, "We're going to win the Lotto! We're going to win the Lotto!"

"The kids were kind of looking at her cross-eyed," Richey says, "like they were thinking, 'Oh-oh, Mama's slipped.' But I knew better than to think that, because she's very psychic. She's seen things and told me about enough things, that I've learned to really respect everything she says. I said, 'Well, all right, we're going to win.' And sure enough, Wednesday night, I was sitting on the sofa, and she was in the kitchen, and the Lotto came on. The first number popped out there and I could see it. I said, 'I got that one.' So then the next one came out, and I said, 'I got that one, too!' Juanita came in real quick and said, 'Are they together?' And I said, 'I got the third one too!' And she said, 'Are they together?' and she started getting excited, and I said, 'I got the fourth one, too!' And then I said, 'I got the fifth one!' And when I said, 'I got the sixth one!' she was leaping and jumping and saying, 'ARE THEY TOGETHER? ARE THEY TOGETHER? ARE THEY

TOGETHER?' And I was looking at my tickets and the third ticket had all six numbers. It was spooky. It was absolutely spooky. Now her and the two girls were leaping and jumping all over, and I was just sitting there looking at those numbers. I looked at them, and I looked at the numbers on the ticket, and I looked at the numbers I had written down, and I looked at the ticket, and I looked at them a dozen different ways to make sure I was not seeing things. Of course she did the same thing, and consequently we didn't sleep much that night, and the next morning we were still checking those two tickets—the ticket and the numbers I had written down—to make sure that we had the numbers. From then until the time we found out, we prayed we were the only winners."

As it turned out, the Richeys shared the $3.3 million jackpot with two other winners, making their win worth $1,109,932.

For Will Richey, the lottery checks of more than $40,000 a year are just another step toward the destination he had decided on years earlier. After winning, he considered dropping the carpet business "for about 10 or 15 seconds." But he says he has seen too much of life to be influenced by matters of very good or very bad luck. "I've always been taught not to look at the peaks and valleys, but to have a goal set far in the distance, so when you go down in the valleys you don't let that affect the goal, and when you go high on the peaks, you don't let that affect the goal either."

Instead of abandoning his goal and settling, at 53, into early retirement, he decided to push ahead full steam to build the kind of business he had always dreamed of. Since then he has purchased six lots on a city block near Detroit City Airport and has plans to build an office complex, a retail carpet outlet, a quick-change oil and lubrication garage, and an auto-rental agency there. He also hopes to organize other lottery winners in the Detroit area so that they can leverage their winnings into significant investments rather than watch time and inflation dwindle them away to nothing.

But just as important as the march toward millionaire status are his plans to continue the work of helping teenagers find purpose in their lives. He has begun a second book aimed at young people and has plans to develop his company to the point where it can be run by competent, trustworthy managers, freeing him to spend even more time with youths. And that, according to Will Richey's personal philosophy, is the third leg vital to his concept of success.

"Money is merely a tool," he wrote in his first book in 1979. "I plan to become a millionaire so that I may cause this to be a better world in which to live."

.

Multiple Winners

"Oh no, not all over again."

—Layton Willis, Michigan lottery winner

rank Gorske was on a hot streak. The 73-year-old retiree had the time to indulge his fondness for bingo, poker and lotteries, and lately he'd been winning. A lot. He could almost taste a major prize coming. Certain numbers had been winning for him so often, especially in bingo, that he was starting to suspect that mysterious forces were at work.

A few days before the November 7, 1987, Super Lotto drawing, he purchased 25 tickets, choosing sets of numbers he considered lucky. One of them—7, 8, 9, 12, 13, 14—was such an oddball combination that it stuck in his mind. He chose it, he would later say, because 7, 8 and 9 had been lucky for him all year in bingo, and by combining those numbers with 12, 13 and 14 it was unlikely that he would have to share the prize with anyone else if he won. But all six numbers, he said, "were famous winning numbers in all my gambling days."

That Saturday, he and his wife were playing bingo at the Chippewa reservation near Mount Pleasant. During the evening, as was customary, the bingo announcer stood up to give the night's recently drawn Super Lotto numbers.

"He's a real joker," Gorske recalls of the announcer. "I didn't know if he was kidding around or not. I heard him say something about 'real weird numbers,' then he read off 7, 8, 9, 12, 13 and 14. I didn't have to check my tickets. I *knew* I had that one. I turned a hundred-thousand colors! The guy next to me, he looked at me funny, like I was sick or something, so I told him I had the winner. He stood right up and shouted it to everybody in the whole room. Well, everybody there just cheered and gave me a standing ovation. It was really something." Gorske's jackpot, won with the most unusual set of numbers yet to be drawn in Michigan's Lotto games, was worth $5.4 million.

But that's just the beginning, says Gorske, who lives in the town of Linwood, on the shore of Saginaw Bay. "I've had uncanny luck this year," he says. "Uncanny. I'm not stopping with this. You watch. I'll win again."

Frank Gorske is not alone in his determination. Joe Swierczynski, a young lottery millionaire from Roseville, is convinced that *he* will be the first to win two million-dollar jackpots. So is Will Richey, who won $1.1 million in January 1987. And so is William McCarthy of Plymouth, who—after winning five third-place Lotto jackpots by matching four of six numbers, and narrowly missing a five-number winner (the one week he neglected to purchase a ticket with his usual numbers)—won a $2.3 million jackpot in April 1985. "I want to be known as the only person to have won the Lotto twice," he said.

A 1987 survey of 128 lottery millionaires by the Michigan Lottery Bureau indicated that 98 percent of them continued to play the Lotto games, where the chances of winning the largest prizes exist. Clearly, the thought of winning again is on almost all of their minds.

But does lottery lightning ever strike the same spot twice? The odds of winning a 6-of-44 Super Lotto jackpot are 1 in 7,059,052. The odds of Frank Gorske or any other previous winner again hitting a six-number jackpot are also 1 in 7,059,052; they have just as good a chance as anyone else. It's not likely to happen, of course, but then neither was it likely to happen the first time. Random chance dispenses favors with an unbiased hand and is as capable of making a double winner of Frank Gorske as it is of making a first-time winner of his hapless neighbor who has never won as much as a fruit basket at a church bingo game. The only observation that is safe to make on the subject is that the longer the lottery continues and the more winners that are created, the more likely it becomes that a lottery millionaire will repeat.

That has yet to happen in Michigan. Elsewhere, however, it has—several times. A 33-year-old Canadian, Pierre Casault of Montreal, won Quebec's Super Lotto for $1 million—lump sum, tax free—twice, in July 1980 and February 1983. Then there are the employees of the Shuttle Meadow Country Club in Berlin, New Jersey. Twenty-three workers at the club joined together to form a lottery club in September 1985. The very first week that they pooled their money to buy tickets they became the sole winners of a $4.2 million jackpot, worth $9,000 per year for 20 years to each of the 23 members. After that, they played haphazardly, placing bets only when the jackpots were swollen to sizable proportions. They almost didn't bother with a $2.1 million prize in January 1987. At the last minute they bought tickets and again were the sole winners.

A New Jersey woman is the only U.S. lottery player to date who has been the sole winner of more than one million-dollar jackpot. Evelyn Adams, who was 33 and single, worked as a cashier at a Point Pleasant Beach, New Jersey, party store that was an outlet for the state lottery. In October 1986 she sold herself a lotto ticket that won a $3.9 million jackpot. Four months later, with another ticket bought at the party store where she worked, she hit again, this time for $1.4 million. "Shocking, definitely shocking," she was quoted as saying. "They say good things come in threes, so . . ."

Although no Michigan lottery player has yet struck million-dollar jackpots twice, there have been a number of winners who have collected multiple prizes of lesser amounts.

◆

In August 1977, 74-year-old Rusty Bradfield purchased an instant ticket at the corner grocery near his home in Elk Rapids, north of Traverse City, scratched it off and revealed a $5,000 winner. Exactly one week later, Bradfield returned—same time, same place—again bought just one ticket, and again won an instant $5,000.

◆

Instant tickets also figured in the multiple jackpots won by George LaBoube of Adrian in March 1981. The 61-year-old man, who was disabled and collecting Social Security payments, had won $50 with an instant ticket earlier in the year. That ticket also qualified him to be in a special million-dollar drawing. When a representative of the lottery bureau contacted him by phone to inform him that he was one of six finalists for that drawing—and therefore assured of a minimum prize of $10,000—he simply did not believe it.

Unsure what to do, he returned to the store where he had purchased the original ticket to ask how he could verify the phone call he had just received. While waiting at the store, he dug into his pocket for a dollar, purchased an instant ticket, and won an instant $25,000.

◆

Edward Telesz certainly earned his new nickname, "Lucky." In 1973 the 59-year-old tool-and-die maker from Detroit won $10,000 in a 50-cent game's Super Drawing. That day on the stage, he vowed that he would be back.

He made good on his promise. Four years later he was selected as a finalist in a Super Drawing held July 7, 1977. Telesz, who said that he spent $10, $20, or more each week in the Michigan and Canadian lotteries, told officials before the drawing that he fully expected to win the grand prize this time around. He did. It was worth $109,000.

◆

Larry Hannah, a 29-year-old grocery-store owner from Detroit, beat 10,000-to-1 odds on November 1, 1982, by hitting a four-digit straight bet in the Daily Four game. That feat, and his $5,000 prize, were noteworthy but hardly big news. What set him apart from the hundreds of other winners of Daily 4 straight bets was that the next day, November 2, he did it again.

"I've never had any luck in my life. I swear," he was quoted as saying later.

Hannah almost didn't make his second wager. "I wasn't even going to play the second day," he said. "Whoever heard of anyone hitting two days in a row?" But he placed his usual $1 bet and chose the serial number on the lottery machine in his grocery store—0177. The number came up, and for the second time in two days he beat 10,000-to-1 odds and won $5,000.

◆

A multiple winner who beat even longer odds—and came away with considerably larger prizes—was Layton Willis, a 50-year-old bachelor and truck driver from Dearborn Heights. In September 1974 he won $20,000 a year for life as the grand-prize finalist in a Weekly Game's Super Jackpot drawing. Four months later, on January 14, 1975, Willis was again among five finalists in an elimination drawing, this time for a million-dollar jackpot. After the $5,000, $10,000, and $50,000 prizes had been awarded, Willis, who had cut short a vacation in England to attend the drawing, stood on stage as one of the two remaining finalists. He admitted later that he had been thinking, "Oh no, not all over again." In the end, the $1 million went to the other contestant, 53-year-old Edward Kulis of Swartz Creek, and Willis received the second-place prize of $200,000.

"It was nice winning (so much)," he said afterwards, "but I was ready to accept the $5,000 check."

◆

In October 1975, Kenneth Fox of Rapid River rubbed the covering from an instant ticket and exposed a $10,000 winner. Fox, however, may not have been as excited as some people. Two years earlier he had been a finalist in a Super Drawing and went home the winner of the grand prize of $200,000.

◆

Janet Westover, a 39-year-old nurse's aid from Wyoming, near Grand Rapids, won a second-place jackpot in an April 22, 1983, drawing held as the conclusion to the Surprise Package instant game.

The $50,000 prize came at a good time for the mother of three. In an interview in the July 1985 issue of *Grand Rapids Magazine*, she explained that before the win she had worked at two jobs to make ends meet and to pay the bills that had accumulated after her husband, James, was injured in an accident.

Two years after her win, after paying taxes and outstanding bills, the frugal Mrs. Westover still had $24,000 in the bank. "If you keep spending it you ain't going to have any left," she said. "You can't play easy come, easy go. You have to be practical in this world."

But her practical attitude did not preclude buying more lottery tickets, and on April 23, 1985, while playing the Michigan Fortune instant game, she collected all six letters to spell "Fortune," which qualified her to spin a special "Wheel of Fortune" for prizes of $10,000 to $100,000. She spun and won the top prize, $100,000.

"I was shocked when I won, just shocked," she said in the magazine interview. "It was just a case of being at the right place at the right time."

After the second win, the Westovers evidently felt they could afford some luxuries. They added a garage to their home and bought a pickup truck and camper. But that was the extent of their extravagance. When someone tried to sell them a condominium they said they just weren't interested.

◆

The A. C. Six Lottery Club probably had no trouble soliciting new members after an incredible run of good luck in 1977. Their streak began in June that year when they were selected as finalists in a Michigame grand-prize drawing. They won the top prize of $100,000 that night, which qualified them to return the following week for a chance at another jackpot. They won that jackpot as well, worth $105,000, for a two-week total of $205,000.

And that wasn't the end of their luck. In November they were selected as finalists in another Michigame grand-prize drawing and again walked away with the top prizes of $100,000 and $105,000 in consecutive weeks.

The club members, six employees of A. C. Spark Plug in Flint, attributed their good luck to the "precise" way they purchased tickets each week. Club spokesman William Palacios said he thought it would be appropriate for them to return a few more times so that everybody in the club could get a nice round total of $100,000.

◆

Lottery clubs proved to be more than a little lucky for Jim Chesney of South Lyon and John L. Sharrow of Romulus. Both men belonged to a 10-member lottery club called the "Lotto Engineers" that was the sole winner of a $3,289,814 jackpot on November 19, 1986. Both later joined another club—"Lot A Noah," composed of six co-workers at CEC Products in Center Line—that then won a $2 million Super Lotto jackpot on March 21, 1987. As a result of their shares, Chesney and Sharrow each receive a total of more than $13,000 annually. Since checks are issued on the anniversary dates of their wins, they receive that amount in two installments, and Chesney reportedly joked that he was only two wins away from receiving quarterly payments.

◆

One multiple win, of sorts, occurred due to a winner's mix-up. On October 13, 1984, Steve Glesner, 31, of Midland shared a $7,795,896 Lotto jackpot with a 28-year-old unemployed pipefitter named Thomas Horney.

But Glesner and Horney did not share the prize 50-50 as you would expect. Glesner, who worked as a production cameraman at the printing plant of Central Michigan Newspapers in Alma, took home two-thirds of the prize because he had *two* tickets with the winning numbers; Horney had only the more-usual single ticket. One of Glesner's winning tickets came from his lottery subscription, which each week automatically entered a set of numbers that he had distilled from his birthday, driver's license number, and Social Security number. Each week before he had bought the subscription, he had played those numbers by taking the same computer card into a local drugstore and buying a ticket. The week of his double win he again ran that well-worn card through the terminal.

So why did he play the numbers again, even after they were automatically covered by his subscription? "I guess I was just too lazy to fill out a new card," Glesner said in a post-win news conference.

◆

Another mix-up involving a lottery subscription took place on May 21, 1986. Melvin Hutchinson, 67-year-old owner of Gittleman's Stores in Alma, had given his 43-year-old daughter Sally a Lotto subscription as a gift. He thought, however, that it had expired before the May 21 drawing, so he stopped at Wilhelm's Grocery in Alma and purchased a ticket using the same numbers. It turned out to be a winning ticket, but not the only one. Hutchinson shared the $8,117,713 jackpot with three other winners—including his daughter, whose subscription had *not* expired.

From Rags to Riches

"You need a poor man's appetite to enjoy a rich man's fortune . . ."

—Rivarol

I t's a sweet kind of justice when the winner of a major lottery prize turns out to be someone desperately in need of it. Too often it seems the opposite is true; a winner picks up the first of 20 checks for $50,000 and admits that he really doesn't have any plans for the money, other than to put it away somewhere safe with the rest of his investments. It's much more satisfying when winners are people who are in debt—even destitute—people like Hermus Millsaps, whose car tires were "bare as a bone," and couldn't be trusted for the ride to Lansing; or Norman Fletcher, whose shoes flopped; or Ronnie Jonason, who said, "I was broke. I mean, man I was *broke.* I would have been tickled pink just to win a few hundred dollars, because that would have been a pretty big chunk to me."

◆

There have been many winners who would have considered a few hundred dollars quite a chunk. One is Ray Clincher.

Clincher's problems began when he slipped and badly twisted both knees while walking between factory lines at his job as a quality-control inspector for the Chrysler Corporation. What at first appeared to be a routine industrial accident developed into a permanent disability. After seven years and several operations, Clincher was left with an artificial left knee and a right knee fused so that it would not bend at all. He could walk only with the aid of crutches and lived on $182 a week in workers' compensation and Social Security disability payments. And, he admits, his misfortunes also caused him to drink a great deal.

On January 29, 1988, 49-year-old Ray Clincher's seven years of bad luck ended when, as the lone survivor of the Fall Fiesta instant-ticket elimination drawing, he went away the winner of $1,000 a week for life. His prize, guaranteed to be worth at least $1 million, brought instant relief to the Detroit resident.

"It's a godsend," was his reaction at a press conference following his lottery win. Clincher, who described himself as a recovering alcoholic, then added, "I haven't had a drink in five years. Maybe God rewarded me for that."

But he said that the lottery windfall was most valuable for what it meant to his entire family. "It's a tremendous burden off my shoulders," he said. "If anything happens to me, now I'll know my wife and children (a 23-year-old daughter and a 17-year-old son) will be taken care of. That means an awful lot to me."

◆

In 1973, after 23 years of employment at Federal Mogul Corporation in Detroit, John Ranusch was permanently laid off and forced to begin taking a succession of odd jobs to make ends meet. Eventually he became a security guard at Samaritan Health Center in Detroit. That job lasted six years until he was again laid off and, at 63, faced the unpleasant fact that a man his age would find it difficult to get work of any kind. He and his wife, Anna Mae, were accustomed to getting by on an income of about $12,000 a year, but now it looked like they would have to live, somehow, on even less.

Then on November 24, 1984, nearly two months after the lay-off, John Ranusch bought a Lotto ticket, only the seventh one he had purchased since Lotto had begun the previous August. His wife chose the numbers by using her relatives' birthdates. That evening Mr. Ranusch fell asleep on the couch and slept through the televised Lotto drawing. Mrs. Ranusch watched it but wasn't able to write down the numbers fast enough. She woke her husband, and he made some phone calls to confirm what she suspected: They had hit all six numbers. That night they went to a neighborhood bar to celebrate.

The following Monday they drove to Lansing and picked up a check for $91,284, the first installment of a jackpot worth $2,255,405.

"I only got 13 bucks in my pocket, so this check feels pretty good," Ranusch said. "The first thing I'm going to do is head straight for the bank. It will be non-stop."

The second thing he would do was buy a new Pontiac, giving his 1973 Plymouth to his nephew. Meanwhile, he made it clear that he would not return to his job. "I was second on the list to be called back, but they can keep the job. I won't go back."

Eventually the Ranuschs moved out of the East Detroit home that John had lived in nearly all his life and into a new ranch-style house they bought in a "nice suburb." They would buy all new furniture, giving the old away, then settled down to begin enjoying a very relaxing, and worry-free retirement.

◆

Another winner who saw his life change drastically was David Angell, a 28-year-old self-employed electronics technician from Grosse Pointe Park. After he had come forward as the only winner of a $2.5 million Lotto jackpot on August 17, 1985, he made it clear that his Grosse Pointe Park address was misleading. His income had never met the standards associated with that well-to-do Detroit suburb. In fact, he said, his average annual income in the several years preceding his lottery win was only about $5,000. The week before winning, he earned $60, enough to pay just one overdue bill.

Angell played the Lotto regularly—at least one number every week—and estimated that he had spent about $100 on lottery tickets during the previous year. Before he purchased his winning ticket, he had noticed that the Lotto numbers had recently been "running close together," so he randomly chose the numbers 3, 4, 9, 19, 21, and 24. He spent that Saturday night "losing miserably" playing poker with friends and went home despondent. On Sunday morning he walked to a party store near his apartment, bought a newspaper to check the lottery numbers, but avoided looking at them until he got home. There, he took his ticket out of his wallet and compared the numbers. Later he would say that he could not believe his eyes.

Angell's immediate plans, after driving his beat-up Ford Granada to Lansing to pick up the first installment check, for $123,401, were to hide at a friend's house until the excitement wore off, then go shopping to buy a home in the Metro Detroit area. The bachelor also planned to buy a Pontiac STE 6000 and further his education.

Angell said that he had studied electronics since he was eight years old and had taught himself "everything from house wiring to computer technology." He would not let the money change him, he said, because "electronics is not just my job, it's my life."

◆

Merton Lee Hanna and his wife had grown discouraged as they watched their family lose ground in the struggle to create a good life for themselves. Merton, a machine operator at a Detroit manufacturing plant, had to work hard to support five children, but their problem wasn't just lack of money. Their inner-city neighborhood had deteriorated so badly that the house they had purchased 17 years earlier for $9,000, would bring only $7,000 when they sold it in 1986. Even more distressing was the effect their situation was having on their children. Their son, for example, hated and feared high school and was getting grades of D's and E's.

Early in 1986, Hanna purchased several $1 Winds of Fortune instant-game tickets, one of which won him a free ticket. Hanna wrote his name and address on the back of the free-ticket winner, then mailed it to lottery headquarters in Lansing where it—along with about 3.5 million others—was entered in a special grand drawing. From that pool, 115 semifinalists were selected randomly and awarded one-year Lotto subscriptions. Six of those semifinalists were then designated, again randomly, as finalists. Five received prizes ranging from $11,000 to $25,000. One, the grand-prize winner—Merton Lee Hanna—went home on July 11, 1986, the winner of $1,000 a week for life, with a guaranteed minimum of $1 million.

That good fortune brought immediate changes to the Hanna family. They sold their Detroit home and moved into a new house on a country road near Milford. And they found they had less to worry about—"fewer headaches," as Mrs. Hanna says. But most important, the children became happier. Their son, for instance, earned A's and B's at his new school and planned to go to college and work toward a degree in electronics.

Mr. Hanna still works as a machinist/repairman because—while his monthly lottery checks provide enough money to pay the bills and "put some away for retirement in a couple years"—it is not, he says, as much money as most people assume, certainly not enough to allow him to retire immediately.

◆

Anne Sigsbee says she never felt poor, not even when times were the hardest. She and her husband were raising two teen-age children on a total income of $700-$800 a month, but she didn't feel poor. She didn't feel poor when the doctor bills piled up and there wasn't enough money to pay them. And she didn't feel poor even when she had to plug the holes in her husband's shoes with cardboard.

"Poor is a state of mind," she says. "We had no money, but we were not poor."

Yet misfortunes kept piling up. They had begun seven years earlier when her husband, Dan, had unexpectedly disappeared from their home in Clare. Pressures and frustrations at his job as a crew chief for a cabinet-building company finally proved too much for him to bear; he suffered a severe nervous breakdown. When he was found, after several weeks during which he "just disappeared off the face of the earth," there was no choice but to hospitalize him.

They had always lived on what Dan earned, first from his job in a machine shop, then as service manager of a small-engine repair dealer, then at the cabinet shop. From the day they were first married they agreed that Dan would work and Anne would stay home to take care of the children.

Now she was forced to take care of him too. Stripped of Dan's income, they had to rely entirely on Social Security disability payments for their living expenses, payments that proved hopelessly inadequate. Medicare covered some of the medical bills for Dan's treatment, but he needed so much and the expenses were so varied that more and more of the bills started coming back to them for payment.

It was a losing battle, and by November 1984 it got to be too much for Anne. "It was a nightmare," she says. "There was just no money. Dan was making progress, but he still needed so much medical attention. One day he had to go in for some special tests, and we found out afterwards that Medicare wouldn't pay for them. We were suddenly faced with a $1,000 doctor bill that we had absolutely no way to pay. I didn't know what to do."

Anne was not a lottery player. She had never purchased a ticket, did not know how to play, and had no idea what was at stake. Never before had she shown even the slightest interest in it or, for that matter, in the subject of money at all. Her interest was in the spiritual world, not the financial. The devout Roman Catholic turned to prayer.

And, in desperation, the lottery figured in her prayers. "I made a barter with the Holy Spirit," she says. "I asked God to enter the computer and choose numbers for me, and I would buy tickets whenever I could. I promised that if I won enough to pay that doctor bill I would never forget where it came from and would share with the church and people who were less fortunate."

From November through January, whenever she felt she could spare a dollar, she bought an Easy Pick Lotto ticket. Some weeks, spending that dollar meant that she could not afford to buy milk for the family. But she persevered.

On February 2, 1985, Anne Sigsbee's faith was rewarded.

"We were sitting watching the 11 o'clock news that Saturday night, and the announcer said the winning Lotto numbers. My brother-in-law was there, and he wrote the numbers down. But I knew right away they were mine. My husband argued with me and said it couldn't be, and my brother-in-law finally asked where the ticket was. It was in the pocket of my husband's shirt, which was hanging on the banister. So my brother-in-law went and got it, and read the numbers and looked up and said, 'I don't know what you're arguing about, you've got 'em all.' My husband still didn't believe it, he said we must have written the numbers down wrong. So we called the lottery hotline, and sure enough, they were the same. Then we called a friend who plays the lottery a lot, and he told us the same thing.

"My husband was so excited that he stayed up all night. Not me. I wanted to sleep. I had to teach Sunday school to a bunch of kindergartners the next morning and wanted to get my rest. I wasn't excited. I've never been very excited about money."

The Sigsbees learned the following Monday that their ticket was one of three that had matched that week's winning numbers. Their one-third share of the $2,756,086 jackpot came to $918,695, or nearly $46,000, before taxes, every year for 20 years.

"I was not surprised when it happened," Mrs. Sigsbee says. "God has always provided for me. I knew he would again."

Now, three years after winning, she says that she has not failed to keep her end of the bargain. Ten percent or more of her income goes to churches and charity organizations. One of her favorite churches, St. Anne's in Detroit, benefited soon after the win.

"St. Anne's has always been special to me. I was named for Saint Anne, I was married in the cathedral, my mother was buried there and my father will be. So when we went to Detroit to visit Dan's parents I made a call on the cathedral. There was no one there but one young priest, and when he saw me he said that he had been expecting me. A week earlier, during Mass, it had come to him that someone was going to visit soon and give a large sum of money. St. Anne's is a very poor parish, and that Sunday there was a woman in attendance who was in serious financial need. The priest said that it was all he could do to keep from shouting out during Mass that the woman's problems would be over within a week. I wrote them out a check right on the spot."

Life is not all roses now, of course; no amount of money guarantees that. There is a certain amount of pressure from the outside world—something Anne's husband does not need—especially from people who consider the Sigsbees millionaires and treat them differently. Also, their increased income has meant increased taxes and the elimination of all assistance in meeting medical expenses. There have been a few friends who proved not to be such good friends.

And though some of the worries are gone, there is still very little extra money. "I have to watch what I spend," Anne says. "We can't be frivolous. But it did make life easier. We don't worry about buying new shoes now. And it's been good for the children, because now they don't feel poor anymore and we can afford to buy them nice clothes and things for special occasions. We've also set up funds for them so when they retire they won't have to worry about where the next meal is coming from."

The Sigsbees did make one major purchase, a house in Clare that they eventually plan to live in but have temporarily rented to someone else. For now, they live in a rented house with Anne's 86-year-old father. "Every once in awhile it hits me that we're doing fine," she says. "It's still not easy, because we still have a lot of obligations and doctor bills, but I am very glad I won. The thing to remember is it was a gift. I never forget that."

Lottery Millionaires: The First 15 Years

1. **Hermus Millsaps**, 53, Taylor (February 22, 1973)

Millsaps, a sawman at a Chrysler plant, won Michigan's first million-dollar jackpot in the 50-cent Weekly Game's first grand-prize drawing, held February 22, 1973, at the Lansing Civic Center. Because he didn't trust the bald tires on his automobile, Millsaps and his wife, Ann, carried sack lunches onto a Greyhound bus and rode to Lansing. After winning, he retired from his job, bought a new car, and made improvements to his home. (Further details, pgs. 1, 7, 19 & 147.)

2. **Christeen Ferizis**, 46, Detroit (April 5, 1973)

Ferizis, a Greek immigrant, was able to speak only a minimal amount of English, so she relied on a friend to act as interpreter during the 50-cent Weekly Game's second grand-prize drawing. After Ferizis had collected the first installment of her $1 million prize, she, her two sons, and her husband, Elias, a tool-and-die worker, returned to Greece for an extended vacation. (Further details, p. 15.)

3. **Mary A. O'Dell**, 30, Sterling Heights (May 10, 1973)

The housewife and mother of two, who won a grand-prize drawing of the 50-cent Weekly Game, held the "title" of youngest Michigan lottery winner for more than two years. Her husband, Lee, made immediate plans to retire from his job as a draftsman for Chrysler and become a "gentleman farmer."

4. **James D. Fisher**, 55, St. Johns (June 21, 1973)

The father of five children—three of whom were grown and on their own—retired from his job at Motor Wheel in Lansing after winning $1 million in the 50-cent Weekly Game. He and his wife, Doris, also built a new home and traveled after their lottery win.

5. **Frank G. Kaminski**, 57, Toledo, Ohio (August 2, 1973)

Kaminski became the first out-of-state lottery millionaire when he won a grand-prize drawing for the 50-cent Weekly Game. A few years earlier, he had lost his career job and pension and had not been looking forward to retirement. After winning, he continued to work for several years at his most-recent job as a water reclamation engineer for the city of Toledo. (Further details, p. 16.)

6. **Victor Robinson**, 59, Toledo (September 25, 1973)

Robinson—who with his wife, Jenna, owned and operated a grocery store in Toledo—promised that the $1 million he had won in the 50-cent Weekly Game would not affect his life and that he would keep working.

7. **Lotta Four Lottery Club** (November 12, 1973)

Members of this lottery club, the first to win $1 million, were: Carl Guiseppe, 59, of Mount Clemens; Michael Parda, 50, of Mt. Clemens; Thomas McClure, 29, of Fraser; and Philip Malo, 42, of St. Clair Shores. In April 1974 the four co-workers won again, that time a new car in a bonus drawing. (Further details, p. 18.)

8. **Paul D. Wedell**, 34, Gladstone (December 18, 1973)

After winning a $1 million jackpot in the 50-cent Weekly Game, Wedell, his wife, Carole, and their two children moved into a new home. The first lottery millionaire from the Upper Peninsula also sold his furnace-and-appliance installation business and took some time off to remodel that new house. Later, he took a job and worked as a union plumber for a number of years. (Further details, p. 19.)

9. **Ruth E. Cotter**, 54, West Unity, Ohio (February 5, 1974)

After winning $1 million in the 50-cent Weekly Game, the mother of six grown children and grandmother of three quit her jobs as bus driver and Avon saleslady to devote more time to volunteer activities and community work. Her husband, Vincent, continued at his job as street superintendent of West Unity. (Further details, p. 20.)

10. **Kathryn Brosch**, 66, Allen Park (March 26, 1974)

Brosch, a widow who won $1 million in the 50-cent Weekly Game, planned to share her winnings with her two children and to make contributions to her church.

11. **Elmer E. Neal**, 62, Grayling (April 30, 1974)

At the time of his $1 million win in the 50-cent Weekly Game, Neal was commuting several hundred miles each week between his home in Grayling and his job as a timekeeper for a Highland construction company. His wife, Frances, expressed interest in retiring from her job at Grayling Mercantile, where she had worked for 30 years, but Neal was reluctant to quit his own job, fearing that he would miss his co-workers.

12. **Felix L. Cayemberg**, 75, Isabella (June 11, 1974)

The retired commercial fisherman became Michigan's oldest lottery millionaire, an honor he held for more than five years. Because he had recently suffered a serious illness, Cayemberg was unable to attend a 50-cent Weekly Game's $1 million grand-prize drawing and was represented by his son Laverne of Kalamazoo. Cayemberg and his wife, Mata, had seven children and 32 grandchildren.(Further details, p. 22.)

13. **William Costello**, 44, Kinde (July 22, 1974)

Because one of their five teen-age children was ill, Elaine Costello had to stay home the night her husband won the $1 million jackpot in a 50-cent Weekly Game drawing. William, who had lost his right hand in a railroad accident 19 years earlier, thought he might continue working for the C & O Railway in Sebewaing, "at least for awhile." His only immediate plans were to use the money to put his five sons through college.

14. **Norman P. Fletcher**, 44, Detroit (September 17, 1974)

The mechanic for the Wayne County Road Commission announced that he would split his $1 million prize, won in the 50-cent Weekly Game, with his best friend, James Lewis, who lived rent-free on a farm in Deckerville that Fletcher had purchased before his win. The arrangement ended unhappily, however. Fletcher reneged on his promise to share the money, Lewis left town, and Fletcher moved onto the farm. (Further details, pgs. 23 & 147.)

15. **Lottie Romanowski**, 58, Hamtramck (November 4, 1974)

Romanowski, an electrologist and hair dresser at a St. Clair Shores beauty parlor, repeatedly told the audience before the Weekly Game's grand prize drawing at which she was a finalist that she would win "the big one." She did, for $1 million.

16. **Edward Kulis**, 53, Swartz Creek (January 13, 1975)

Kulis, an inspector for Fisher Body in Flint, won $1 million in the 50-cent Weekly Game. He and his wife, Caroline, who worked in the sanitation department at the Fisher Coldwater Plant in Flint, had six children.

17. **Betty Parker**, 46, Plymouth (March 18, 1975)

Betty Parker was represented at a 50-cent Weekly Game grand-prize drawing by her husband, Harold, who accused her of being too "chicken" to attend herself. Betty, an assistant manager at an elementary-school cafeteria in Plymouth, and Harold, a metallurgist at G.M. Hydromatic in Willow Run, were the parents of a son and daughter.

18. **Hazel Stickley**, 67, Detroit (May 11, 1975)

During a 50-cent Weekly Game grand-prize drawing, Mrs. Stickley clutched a purse full of lucky charms given to her by friends and relatives. After she won the $1 million grand prize, she announced she would share it with her brother. Stickley and her husband, Joseph, were both retired when she won. (Further details, p. 126.)

19. **Charles L. Riddle**, 23, Trenton (August 5, 1975)

At the time he won a 50-cent Weekly Game drawing, Riddle, who managed a family-owned restaurant in Detroit, was Michigan's youngest lottery millionaire. A few years later, he was arrested and convicted for selling cocaine. Winning the lottery, he said, "ruined my life." (Further details, p. 98.)

20. **The S & T Lottery Club** (October 14, 1975)

The two brothers, Sam and Thomas Randa of Fraser, who formed this club waited nearly four months to turn in their winning ticket for the grand prize in a special $5 Bicentennial Game. Sam, 54, a retiree from the Bendix Corporation, and Tom, 46, an employee of the Stroh Brewing Company, split the initial $500,000 payment, plus $25,000 a year for 20 years. (Further details, p. 121.)

21. **Edward A. Bringleson**, 68, Lansing, Illinois (November 12, 1975)

Bringleson, a retiree from Inland Steel Company in Chicago, was the fourth non-Michigan resident—and the first from Illinois—to win $1 million in the 50-cent Weekly Game. He and his wife, Ruth, had three children.

22. **Carolyn Jones**, 35, Detroit (January 12, 1976)

Jones, who was employed by the Chrysler Corporation in Dearborn, was the winner of a drawing for a $1 million jackpot in the

Michigan lottery's first instant-ticket game, called, simply, The Instant Game. (Further details, p. 27.)

23. Rose D'Amico, 57, Grand Rapids (February 3, 1976)

The owner and operator of D'Amico Supermarket in Grand Rapids, who won $1 million in the 50-cent Weekly Game, became Kent County's first lottery millionaire.

24. Alfred W. Bennett, 74, Troy (April 21, 1976)

The retired National Cash Register Company sales manager won his $1 million in the Antique Auto instant-game drawing. Bennett, who was married and had one grown son, said his plans were to travel.

25. Fred Molitor, 66, Royal Oak (May 27, 1976)

Molitor, who had recently retired from a career as a plumbing-supply salesman, was vacationing in Colorado with his wife when he was selected as one of 50 finalists in the first of two $1 million grand-prize drawings in the Michigan Landmarks instant game. His neighbors contacted a park ranger in the campground where he and his wife were staying, and the ranger left a note on their windshield that said: "Contact me immediately. I have wonderful news." The Molitors left their camper, flew home to attend the drawing, then, after winning the grand prize, returned to Colorado and resumed their vacation. (Further details, p. 58.)

26. Donna Griffin, 45, Leonard (June 8, 1976)

After Donna had won $1 million in the 50-cent Weekly Game, she and her husband, Rhueben, a supervisor for a home-construction company, invited their friends to the "biggest party Leonard (Oakland County) has ever seen." The Griffins were the parents of five children.

27. Charles S. Bevier Jr., 53, Jackson (September 9, 1976)

Saying that his job should go to "someone who needs it," Bevier— the second Michigan Landmarks instant-game $1 million prize winner— announced immediate retirement from his janitorial job. He and his wife had four children and seven grandchildren.

28. The 73-21 Lottery Club (September 30, 1976)

This Jackson lottery club, consisting of 20 co-workers at LaPaul Tool and Die Company, won $1 million in the 50-cent Weekly Game. Spokesman John Kistka explained that the name came from the fact that the club was formed in 1973 with 21 members. (At the time of the win, one unidentified member had dropped out.)

29. **David Shepherd**, 29, Onsted (January 17, 1977)

The self-employed carpenter won a $1,893,742 jackpot in The Presidents instant game. The prize—at the time, the largest ever awarded in a U.S. lottery—was determined by tallying $1 for every Michigan vote cast for the presidential candidate who carried the state in the previous November's election. Gerald Ford carried the state of Michigan but lost the election. (Further details, p. 40.)

30. **Kenneth P. Proxmire**, 34, Hazel Park (February 4, 1977)

Shortly after Proxmire, a tool worker at Lear-Siegler in Detroit, won $1 million in the 50-cent Weekly Game, he, his wife, and their two sons moved to California. There, they bought a pool hall, then opened a string of pool-supply stores. When those businesses failed, he made national news as the lottery millionaire who filed for bankruptcy. (Further details, p. 94.)

31. **Alvin Hurry**, 54, Detroit (March 14, 1977)

After winning $1 million in the 50-cent Weekly Game, Hurry said only that he planned to continue working as a machine operator at a Chrysler plant and "spend, spend, spend."

32. **Phyllis Taylor**, 48, Detroit (May 3, 1977)

Taylor, a housewife, waited to claim the $50 prize that entered her into a finalist drawing for the Bingo instant game until her horoscope indicated that it was a good day to do so. After her $1 million grand-prize win, Taylor said that she and her husband, Arthur, a truck driver for a steel company, planned to take their four children on a ferry-boat cruise. (Further details, p. 119.)

33. **Paul Jusovsky**, 57, Detroit (June 29, 1977)

Jusovsky had been disabled for several years and was in the hospital the night his $1 million was awarded in a 50-cent Weekly Game drawing.

34. **Joseph Barinka**, 64, Kalamazoo (July 20, 1977)

The retired milling-machine operator, who won $1 million in the Horoscope instant-game drawing, said his immediate plan was to take his wife, Emma, on a fishing trip.

35. **Ocell Louis**, 52, Flint (January 10, 1978)

Louis, who worked at Grand Blanc Fisher Body, won the $1

million grand prize in the Three-of-a-Kind instant game. He and his wife, Maggie, a teacher's aide at Jefferson School, were the parents of 11 children.

36. **Barbara Papler**, 35, Livonia (January 18, 1978)

The mother of three won $1 million in an elimination drawing of Michigame. Her husband, Gordon, was a financial analyst with Blue Cross-Blue Shield in Detroit.

37. **Jay Hite**, 56, East Jordan (June 13, 1978)

The registered pharmacist, who won $1 million in a Michigame drawing, said he had no plans to let the money change his life much, and, in fact he did continue to work in his pharmacy until 1983, when he sold it. He and his wife, a former reporter for the Lansing *State Journal*, were the parents of a daughter. (Further details, p. 57.)

38. **Evelyn Ransom**, 69, Detroit (June 27, 1978)

The retired nurse, who won the $1 million jackpot in the Tic-Tac-Dough instant game, said her immediate plans included a vacation to Hawaii.

39. **Eva Ewalt**, 50, Imlay City (September 12, 1978)

The grandmother of eight, who worked as an attendant nurse, won $1 million in the 7-11-21 instant game. She and her retired husband made immediate plans to visit relatives in Virginia.

40. **Gladis J. DiAngelo**, 61, St. Clair Shores (November 29, 1978)

After she had won $1 million in a 50-cent Weekly Game grand-prize drawing, DiAngelo, a homemaker and mother of five children, said that from the moment she had learned she was a finalist, she knew she would win the top prize. Her immediate plans were to vacation in Florida, then begin shopping for a larger house.

41. **Martin Scully**, 52, Taylor (April 11, 1979)

Scully, a sales manager at a Highland Appliance store in Taylor, won the $1 million grand prize in the Michigan Jackpot instant-game drawing. He and his wife, Catherine, were the parents of four children and grandparents to six.

42. **Robert L. Robbins** (June 12, 1979)

Robbins was employed as a building inspector for the state of Michigan when he won $1,000 a week for life in the Royal Bingo instant game. Robbins said he planned to use his jackpot, a guaranteed $1 million minimum, to assist his family—which included four children and six grandchildren—and close friends.

43. Joseph James Frolich, 75, Taylor (November 1, 1979)

The retiree, who won $1 million in the Michigan 1000 instant-game drawing, had two children and four grandchildren.

44. Chelsey J. Tebo, 67, Mt. Clemens (January 8, 1980)

After winning $1 million in the Instant 3 game, Chelsey, who had retired from Jamestown China, said he planned to enjoy his hobbies, gardening and wine making. Chelsey was the father of four and grandfather of six.

45. Anthony Kopcik, 65, Dearborn (May 15, 1980)

The carpenter for the Bob-Lo Company in Detroit said that he and his wife, Mary, planned to use part of the $1 million he won in a Michigame drawing to travel. The couple had two children and four grandchildren.

46. Erma Woodman, 70, Rochester (June 3, 1980)

After she won $50,000 a year for life, with a guaranteed minimum of $1 million, in the Michigan Double instant-game drawing, the mother of three and grandmother of seven said her only immediate plans were to take a vacation.

47. Kathryn Boyle, 73, Westland (August 28, 1980)

The homemaker—who was active in a number of clubs, including the Wayne-Ford Civic League, the Westgate Tower Club, and St. Theodore's Over-50 Club—made plans for investments and travel after she won $1 million in the Michigan Baseball instant game.

48. Ronald H. Gumm, 37, Holt (January 20, 1981)

After he won $1 million in the Michigan Football instant game, Gumm said that he and his wife, Linda, planned to invest wisely and continue working until they could afford to purchase a resort on a Caribbean island. He was the general manager of Long's Restaurant and Convention Center in Lansing, and she was employed by Michigan Bell Telephone. (Further details, p. 110.)

49. Gale J. Houchen, 26, Litchfield (August 21, 1981)

The homemaker won $1 million in the Big Deal instant game. Her husband, Gerald, worked for Robert's Construction in Jonesville.

50. Alice Jo Zdebski, 35, Irons (September 22, 1981)

Zdebski, a college student and mother of three, won the $1 million grand prize in the Crystal Ball instant game. She and her husband, James, planned to make home improvements and investments.

51. **John William Hall**, 20, Waterford (January 14, 1982)
After winning $1 million in the Aces 3 instant game, Hall, an avid hunter, said he planned to spend part of his initial prize installment on a new truck. Hall was employed as a maintenance worker at Community Activities, Inc. in Waterford.

52. **Terry Larsen**, 29, Greenville (May 20, 1982)
At the time he won $1 million in the Match 2 instant-game drawing, Larsen worked at Greenville Products and ran the family farm with his wife, Ethel, and their two daughters. After his win he quit his job and farmed full time.

53. **Margaret M. Bernard**, 75, Clarkston (July 15, 1982)
The widow and mother of four children won $1 million in the Double Feature instant game.

54. **Monica M. Berkowski**, 78, Dearborn Heights (January 13, 1983)
When she won $1 million in the Good Life instant-game drawing, Berkowski became Michigan's oldest lottery millionaire to date. Berkowski was very active in the Red Cross, church organizations, and senior citizens groups.

55. **Tibor Kerti**, 49, Sterling Heights (April 22, 1983)
Fearing that it would affect his luck, Kerti did not inform his family that he was a finalist in the Surprise Package instant-ticket drawing until after he had won the $1 million grand prize. Kerti, a barber, and his wife, Margaret, a cosmetologist, planned to start their own business after a family vacation to visit relatives in Hungary.

56. **Millicent Gallup**, 58, Traverse City (June 3, 1983)
At the time, Gallup's $2 million Tic-Tac-Two grand-drawing jackpot was the largest single prize ever awarded in the Michigan lottery. The widow, who was employed as a directory-assistance operator for Michigan Bell, planned to donate to her favorite charities, buy gifts for her family and a new house and car for herself, and travel. (Further details, p. 41.)

57. **Louis Morgando**, 65, Giles, Wisconsin (June 27, 1983)
Confident that he would win a major prize, Morgando and his wife, Elizabeth, purchased a new car to make the drive from their home to the Superplay grand drawing in Flint. After he won the $1 million

grand prize, Morgando, a retiree, said his plans included "lots of travel."

58. **Jan Ery**, 47, Morenci (July 29, 1983)

The mother of two and grandmother of two was employed as a shipping clerk at Tecumseh Products in Tecumseh when she won $1 million in the Michigan Baseball instant-game drawing.

59. **Claudia Susalla**, 32, Novi (November 10, 1983)

Susalla's husband, Gary, an engineer for the Jervis B. Webb Co. in Farmington Hills, represented her at the grand-prize drawing for the Loose Change instant game. Their immediate plans after winning $1,000 a week for life, with a guaranteed minimum of $1 million, were to pay bills, buy a new car, and set up an education fund for their three children.

60. **Douglas Simpson**, 24, Marquette (March 9, 1984)

The unemployed, part-time Northern Michigan University student said he planned to share the $2 million he won in the Instant Lotto instant-ticket drawing with family members. (Further details, p. 41.)

61. **Stanley Karol**, 70, Detroit (July 19, 1984)

Karol, who had retired from American Motors, planned to buy a new boat with part of the $1 million he won in the Joker Plus instant-game drawing.

62. **Thomas G. LaPenna**, 45, Marquette (September 1, 1984)

The banking executive for Detroit & Northern Savings and Loan won $2,950,259 in Michigan's first Lotto jackpot. After building a new home and establishing education funds for his three children, he planned to invest the remainder of his winnings, $146,500 a year through 2003. (Further details, pgs. 42 & 120.)

63. **Grace Bommarito**, Detroit (September 15, 1984)

Reportedly because she and her husband were in poor health and afraid that publicity would aggravate their conditions, the state's second Lotto millionaire sent a representative to Lansing to claim the first installment check, $57,858, of her $1,432,722 jackpot.

64. **Steve Glesner**, 31, Midland (October 13, 1984)

The production cameraman at a printing plant won two-thirds of a $7,795,896 Lotto jackpot because, out of "laziness," he had purchased two tickets with identical sets of numbers. (Further details, pgs. 42 & 145.)

65. **Thomas Horney**, 28, Monroe (October 13, 1984)

The unemployed man won the remaining third, $2,598,632, of the October 13, 1984, Lotto jackpot. (Further details, pgs. 42 & 145.)

66. **Edmund Prucnell**, 54, Roseville (October 20, 1984)

After discovering on Saturday that he held the winning Lotto ticket, Prucnell and his wife, Florence, found it very difficult to sleep until they could get the ticket safely validated on Monday morning. Prucnell, an assembler at the Ford plant in Sterling Heights, planned to pay off his house mortgage, then invest much of the rest of his winnings toward retirement. (Further details, p. 119.)

67. **Carol Furay**, 22, Detroit (November 17, 1984)

After winning $1,000 a week for life, with a guaranteed minimum of $1 million, in the 7-11-21 instant-game grand drawing, Furay said she planned to buy a new car—"a small one, an economical one"—and to continue studying computer operations at night school.

68. **Patricia Parker**, Kalamazoo (November 17, 1984)

Asked what she planned to do with her $10,397,771 Lotto jackpot, the largest Michigan lottery prize to date, Parker made national news by announcing that she intended to buy actor Tom Selleck. (Further details, p. 42.)

69. **John Ranusch**, 63, Detroit (November 24, 1984)

The laid-off security guard described his $2,255,405 Lotto jackpot as a "godsend." After winning, he and his wife bought a new car and moved to a home in St. Clair Shores. (Further details, p. 148.)

70. **William P. Walker**, Clarkston (December 1, 1984)

Perhaps for tax reasons, Walker delayed claiming his $2,362,498 Lotto jackpot for over a month. After discussions with his family, an attorney, and a financial advisor, he finally picked up the first install-ment of his prize on January 4, 1985. At that time, he stated flatly that he wanted to avoid all publicity, then disappeared from public view.

71. **Elmer L. Fronsee**, 58, Kingsford (December 8, 1984)

Fronsee and his wife, Beverly, a retired beauty-shop owner, said that they were undecided how to spend their windfall, a $2,237,738 Lotto jackpot. Fronsee, a retired seaman from the Cleveland-Cliffs Iron Co., joked that, after 30 years of sailing the Great Lakes, the last thing he wanted to buy was a boat. (Further details, p. 120.)

72. Lynda Libey, 37, Munith (December 15, 1984)

The systems analyst for Consumers Power was playing bingo when she learned she had matched all six winning numbers for a Lotto prize worth $2,171,574.

73. The Family Four Lottery Club, Westland (December 22, 1984)

Members of this lottery club that won a $2,085,029 Lotto jackpot were: Kenneth O. Ottinger, 66; his wife, Netti, 61; their son, Kenneth, 43; and their daughter, Joyce A. Kozub, 40.

74.-79. On January 19, 1985, six winners split a record $13,300,931 Lotto jackpot. The winners of $2,216,821 each were: (Further details, p. 43.)

—**John D. Macon**, 43, an auto mechanic from Houghton Lake.

—**Russell W. Lansford**, 28, Millington. He immediately took a 30-day leave from his job as a set-up man for an automotive parts supplier to decide what to do with his future.

—**Casimir W. Kliza**, 48, of Livonia, a toolmaker at the General Motors Hydramatic Transmission Plant in Ypsilanti.

—**Martha L. Slavik**, 32, a hair stylist from Ann Arbor.

—**Bernard Betke**, 52, Plainwell. After his win, the part-owner of an industrial boiler-repair firm told an interviewer that, "What you have to do is make sure you don't go hog wild. It's real exciting at first, but then you have to use your head."

—**Antonio P. Galan**, 69, a retired Pontiac Motors employee from Romeo.

80. Geraldine Reinert, Sebewaing (February 2, 1985)

The mother of two grown children planned to buy a new car and pay off bills with the first installment of the $1 million she won in the 3 For the Money instant-game drawing. She and her husband were the owners and operators of Duffies Tavern in Sebewaing.

81. John E. Kearbey, Pleasant Lake (February 9, 1985)

Kearbey had once jokingly told his fiancee that he would be a millionaire before he reached the age of 40. After winning a $2,604,722 Lotto jackpot, Kearbey said he planned to continue working as an auto mechanic at Favor's Auto Body in Jackson, buy a new home, and carry out plans to get married.

82. **Arnold Priebe**, Roscommon (March 2, 1985)

The retired postal worker was in Florida for the winter when he was notified that his Lotto subscription had won him $2,438,702. Priebe said he planned to get a new car, make investments, and buy a new wardrobe for his wife, Helen.

83. **John Felosak**, 72, Flint (March 9, 1985)

The retired Buick employee said he would use his $2,395,125 Lotto jackpot to purchase securities and make other investments. Felosak had two grandchildren and one great-grandchild.

84. **Detroit Diesel Lottery Club** (March 23, 1985)

Members of the club, who won a $2,695,955 Lotto jackpot, were: Colin McCarter of Novi; Armando Fallone, Detroit; and William Pendycraft, Westland.

85. **Janice Morris**, 40, Wyandotte (March 23, 1985)

The homemaker had won three third-place prizes in the first seven months of the Michigan Lotto before finally hitting all six numbers for a jackpot of $2,695,955. She used her winnings to buy a house next door to her ailing mother.

86. **Judy Pfoutz**, 34, Barton City (March 23, 1985)

The homemaker won the $1 million grand prize in the Holiday Bonus instant-game drawing.

87. **William McCarthy**, 55, Plymouth (March 30, 1985)

When McCarthy, a building superintendent, told his boss not to go on vacation the week of March 30, 1985, because he, McCarthy, was going to win the Lotto jackpot, the boss thought he was kidding. He wasn't; he won $2,384,704. (Further details, p. 140.)

88. **Richard Berdeski**, 41, Utica (April 20, 1985)

Saying, "I always knew I would be one of the early Lotto jackpot winners," the machinist at a Sterling Heights manufacturing plant walked away from a Lansing press conference with the first installment of a $9,194,911 prize, the second-largest individual Michigan lottery prize to date. (Further details, p. 43.)

89. **John E. Harrison**, 46, Yale (April 27, 1985)

The grocery-store produce manager matched all six numbers for a Lotto jackpot of $2,488,636. (Further details, p. 113.)

90.-94. On May 18, 1985, five winners shared a $5.1 million Lotto jackpot. Those winners, each of whom received $1,029,434, were:

—**Constance Meyers**, 46, Capac. Meyers said she planned to quit her job as bakery manager at the Capac IGA store and join her husband, Norman, in retirement. She also said that portions of her prize would go toward travel and leisure and to help her two children.

—**Gussie Malone**, 52, Detroit. After picking up the first installment of her share of the jackpot, she quit her job as a small-parts packer at General Motors' Willow Run Warehouse. She and her husband, Henry, planned to build a new house and share the wealth with their four daughters.

—**Carol Wrobel**, 38, Warren, who discovered she was a winner while watching the drawing on television at a local restaurant. Wrobel, an office worker at K mart in Warren, planned to use the money for her son's college education and to buy a new Corvette for herself.

—**Joy Joseph**, Lansing, who said she cried for half an hour after learning that she had matched all six numbers. Joseph, a checker at General Motors Warehouse in Lansing, said she planned to pay for college for her daughter and purchase land near the Upper Peninsula town of St. Ignace, where she grew up.

—**Linda Deckard**, 31, Detroit. After watching the televised Lotto drawing and realizing she had matched all six winning numbers, she said she remained in a state of shock for days.

95. **Edward Stein**, 57, Prudenville (May 25, 1985)

The owner of the Lakeside Party Store in Prudenville won $1,000 a week for life, with a guaranteed $1 million, in the grand drawing for the Lifetime Deal instant game. He said he planned to take a highway tour of the Pacific Northwest.

96. **Lucky Eleven Lottery Club** (June 1, 1985)

The club, composed of 11 co-workers at the Wayne County Risk Management Office, hit a Lotto jackpot for $2,222,030. Club president Oneida Atkins said she chose the winning numbers using a system based on her dreams.

97. **Virginia Lee Rodziczak**, 36, Detroit (June 8, 1985)

The checker at Chrysler Corporation's Warren Stamping Plant said she planned to use some of her $2,222,258 Lotto prize for home improvements and investments.

98. Mark Gieseking, 27, Grosse Pointe Park (June 15, 1985)

The electronics technician, who won a $2,259,592 Lotto jackpot, said he planned to buy a few "toys," invest, and continue working. (Further details, p. 59.)

99.-101. On July 13, 1985, three winners—all from the Detroit area—shared a record $15.2 million Lotto jackpot. They were: (Further details, p. 44.)

—**Terry W. Showalter**, 28, East Detroit. Showalter claimed the first installment of his $5,055,996 share without informing his wife, whom he planned to surprise by showing up in a limousine at her parents' home in Tennessee, where she was visiting.

—**Harry Fryckland Sr.**, Detroit. Fryckland represented 10 family members who had been pooling $5 a week for Lotto tickets and who planned to divide the winnings among themselves. When asked his age after he had picked up the first installment check, Fryckland would say only, "too old."

—**Gerald Rickrode Sr.**, Detroit, who said he planned to share his $5,055,996 with his five children and four grandchildren.

102. Robert J. White, 40, Detroit (July 20, 1985)

After a winning streak that included matching five numbers in a previous Lotto drawing and winning in the Daily 4 game, White felt he was due to hit a major jackpot. He did, for $2,644,285. White, who had worked as a laborer at Borman's Food Warehouse for 16 years, planned to share his winnings with his family.

103. Norbert Brohl, Utica (July 26, 1985)

The self-employed carpenter, who won $1 million in the Michigan Fortune instant game's grand drawing, said he planned to travel and invest money in his own business. Brohl was the father of seven children.

104-107. Four winners split an August 10, 1985, Lotto jackpot worth $5.5 million. They were:

—**David A. Kuh**, 23, Whitehall. Kuh had been laid off from his job with the Bennett Pump Co. in Whitehall when he matched the six numbers in the Lotto drawing. He and his wife, Jill, planned to invest much of their $1,378,430 share of the jackpot. (Further details, p. 113.

—**James H. Bullock**, 49, Belleville. After picking up the first installment of his share of the jackpot, Bullock said he intended to keep his Ford Motor Co. job. His wife, Martha, however, said she planned to immediately retire from her job at University Hospital in Ann Arbor.

—**Fred Shortsle**, 33, Lowell. Shortsle's wife and children chose the numbers that won his $1.4 million share, which he said he planned to set aside for retirement.

—**Bruce W. Risher**, 33, Holland. The assistant manager of a Holland bowling alley said he would follow the advice of relatives—a family of accountants—as to how best invest his winnings. (Further details, 122.

108. **David S. Angell**, 28, Grosse Pointe Park (August 17, 1985)

The self-employed electronics technician, who admitted he had had serious financial troubles before winning a $2,456,601 Lotto jackpot, planned to buy a new house, a car and a personal computer. (Further details, p. 149.)

109. **Reino Pesola**, 59, Champion (August 24, 1985)

The Cleveland Cliffs Iron Company employee said he planned to use the $1 million he won in the Celebration instant game's drawing for travel and retirement income. He and his wife, Carol, had two children and one grandchild.

110. **R. Zuliani**, 43, Farmington Hills (August 24, 1985)

The partner in an accounting firm said he planned to use his $2,539,823 Lotto jackpot to put his two children through college and for investments.

111. **Melissa Alley**, 41, Taylor (September 11, 1985)

The nursing-desk secretary won $5,640,495 in the Michigan lottery's first Wednesday Lotto drawing. She and her husband, Gary, a truckdriver, both immediately retired from their jobs "to create openings for others." Mrs. Alley, who commented that she had often been accused of being a dreamer, said that her lottery win "proves that dreams come true." (Further details, p. 119.)

112. **Janett Wynn**, 30, River Rouge (September 21, 1985)

The mother of two planned to start a business and share some of her $2,121,691 Lotto jackpot with both her and her boyfriend's parents.

113. **Herman C. Key**, 59, Detroit (September 28, 1985)

Key had just retired from his job as warehouseman for a federal-government tank plant in Detroit when he won half of a $3.6 million

Lotto jackpot. He and his wife, Barbara, planned to travel and invest their $1,801,526 share.

114. **Mary J. Ling**, 53, Plymouth (September 28, 1985)

Ling did not have to check her ticket; she *knew* she had matched the six winning Lotto numbers. She and her husband, John, planned to use their $1,801,526, half of the jackpot, to buy a new car and "enjoy life."

115.-117. On October 9, 1985, two individuals and a lottery club shared an $8 million Lotto jackpot. The winners were:

—**Helen McIvor**, 54, Kaleva. The nurse's aid at Manistee Medical Care planned to share her $2,007,733 prize with her daughter and granddaughter, to keep working, and to "take one day at a time."

—**Mike Mammo**, 33, and **Harry Mammo**, 39, Southfield. The two brothers, who had formed a lottery club, bought their winning ticket at the Food Basket Food Center in River Rouge, a store that they co-owned.

—**Robert E. Reese**, 64, Flat Rock. It wasn't until two days after the winning numbers had been announced that Reese, while standing in line to purchase tickets for the next Lotto drawing, discovered he was a winner. The cost estimator for Chrysler Corporation's Tech Center, who was only one year away from retirement, said that he and his wife intended to "invest wisely." (Further details, p. 113.)

118. **Michael Riviello**, 69, East Detroit (October 16, 1985)

Riviello said he was "shocked" to discover that he held one of two winning tickets for a $3.9 million Lotto jackpot. He and his wife, Anna, said they had no definite plans for their share, $1,972,277. (Further details, p. 113.)

119. **Margaret Ficorelli**, 62, East Detroit (October 16, 1985)

Ficorelli lived on the same street only a few blocks away from Michael Riviello, with whom she split a $3.9 million Lotto jackpot. She claimed that her $1,972,277 share would not change her or her husband, Peter's, lives much. "We'll just live a little more comfortably," she said. (Further details, p. 113.)

120. **Kay L. Beasley**, 42, Harrison (October 19, 1985)

The library aide at Amble Elementary School in Harrison was one of two winners of a $2.1 million Lotto jackpot. She and her husband,

Ron, planned to use their $1,043,365 share to take the honeymoon they'd never had, pay for college for their two sons, buy a new car, and redecorate their house.

121. **Anna V. Adams**, 72, Houghton Lake (October 19, 1985)

Adams planned to share her half of the Lotto jackpot with her children and grandchildren but thought, too, that she might use some of the $1,043,365 to trade in her 10-year-old car and buy a new one.

122.-124. Three winners shared an October 26, 1985, Lotto jackpot worth $3.6 million. They were:

—**Lester R. Bovia**, 61, Auburn. Bovia, who had already retired from his job with the Northern Die Company in Bay City, said he was determined to begin enjoying life with his $1,200,518 share.

—**Patricia A. Pinchot**, 26, Detroit. After winning one-third of the jackpot with numbers chosen from "special dates," Pinchot immediately quit her job as a mail sorter with Adcom in Detroit. She said she planned to share her $1,200,518 with family members.

—**Anthony Beavers**, 26, Montrose, As part of a sales promotion offered by the three IGA grocery stores owned by his family, Beavers had won a Lotto subscription, a prize which turned out to be worth $1,200,518. He planned to continue working, set up college funds for his four children, remodel his home, and make investments.

125. **Stanley R. Bojanowski**, 45, Sylvania, Ohio (November 2, 1985)

Bojanowski planned to use his $2,069,828 Lotto winnings to buy a new car and give assistance to his wife's parents.

126. **Derek D. Looman**, 29, Allegan (November 6, 1985)

Looman and his wife, Denise, had only been playing the Lotto for a month when their numbers came up for a jackpot worth $1,421,707. They planned to buy a new house, purchase land, and set up a trust fund for their 7-year-old son.

127. **Larry James**, 41, Lansing (November 9, 1985)

The General Motors worker won the Michigan Summer instant-game grand drawing. After collecting the first installment of a $1,000-a-week-for-life prize, with a guaranteed minimum of $1 million, he planned to take a vacation to Paris, France.

128. **Robert J. Smith**, 28, Northville (November 9, 1985)

Even though he watched the televised Saturday night Lotto drawing, Smith didn't realize that he had a winning ticket until he read the numbers in the paper the next morning. The Ford auto-parts manager and his wife, who was expecting their third child, planned to use their half of the $2,010,995 jackpot for investments.

129. **William Tillman**, 64, Detroit (November 9, 1985)

The auto worker, who had already planned to retire in one year, said he would make improvements to his home, then purchase a new one with his share, $1,005,497, of the Lotto jackpot he split with Robert Smith.

130. **Raymond Reed**, 50, Canton (November 13, 1985)

The aerospace supervisor for Ford combined his and his wife's birthdates to come up with the winning numbers for a Lotto jackpot worth $1,374,307. Reed said he would buy a car for his daughter and make investments.

131. **Brunetta Blocton**, 34, Detroit (November 29, 1985)

Blocton, a medical transcriptionist at Sinai Hospital, went to the Oak Park office of the lottery bureau to claim, she thought, a several-thousand-dollar prize for matching five numbers in the Lotto drawing. She was informed, instead, that she had matched all six numbers and would receive $3,729,619. The mother of two planned to take a vacation, buy a car, and invest in real estate. (Further details, p. 124.)

132. **Rosemary Moore**, 44, Gaylord (November 30, 1985)

After winning a $6,554,711 Lotto jackpot, the waitress said she planned to quit her job and do some traveling.

133. **James Renfro**, 46, Taylor (December 18, 1985)

Renfro, who split a $3.7 million Lotto jackpot, said he planned to use his $1,846,505 for travel and investments. Renfro, who worked as a factory set-up man for Kelsey Hayes in Romulus, was married and had two children.

134. **Matteo Galati**, 48, Rockwood (December 18, 1985)

The self-employed pizza-parlor owner realized he had matched six numbers in the Lotto game while watching the televised drawing in his pizzeria. He planned to invest his $1,846,505 jackpot in his business and help his four children. His wife, Dolores, planned to quit both of her part-time jobs. (Further details, p. 112.)

135. **Ron Northey**, 32, Madison Heights (December 21, 1985)

At the time Northey hit six numbers in the Lotto drawing, the computer-graphics company he worked for as a production supervisor was two weeks away from closing down. Northey planned to buy a new house and make investments with his half of a $2 million jackpot. (Further details, p. 53.)

136. **Harold Oertel**, 55, Drayton Plains (December 21, 1985)

The father of two realized he had won a grand prize in the Lotto game while watching the 11 p.m. news. He planned to continue at his job as a printer for Division Printing, and to use portions of his $1 million prize, half of a jackpot he shared with Ron Northey, to build a sauna in his cottage at Alger, share with his children, and give to his church.

137.-139. Three winners shared a January 4, 1986, Lotto jackpot worth $6.5 million. They were:

—**Barbara Stefko**, 31, Monroe. The mother of two, who worked as a waitress, planned to use her $2,173,504 share to build a log home on acreage she had purchased in the Monroe area.

—**Ronnie Jonason**, 70, Bangor. Jonason, who worked part time in a neighbor's fruit farm, planned to donate to his church, update his own farm equipment, and help out his four children.   (Further details, pgs. 81 & 147.)

—**Wil and Lil Enterprises**, Frankenmuth. Wilbert and Lillian Keinath, who had formed a husband-and-wife lottery club, lived up to the pact they had made with each other before winning: Both quit their jobs to spend more time with each other. (Further details, p. 60.)

140. **Nancy Justice**, 33, Clarksville (January 11, 1986)

The mother of four, who won $1,000 a week for life with a guaranteed minimum of $1 million, purchased her winning ticket for the Joker Plus instant game at Cobb's Corner, the store where she worked as manager. She said she might "splurge" and build a new home and buy a new truck for her husband.

141.-143. Two individuals and a lottery club split a January 18, 1986, Lotto jackpot worth more than $11 million. The winners were:

R & E Lotto Club, Brooklyn, Michigan. Robert L. and Emerson Parks, the father-and-son team who formed this lottery club, hired a limousine to drive them to the Lansing office of the lottery commission to claim the first installment of their share, $3,709,932. Robert, 53, planned to invest toward retirement. Emerson, 33, thought he might quit his job and go to college.

—**John Konieczny**, 65, Detroit. Like Brunetta Blocton (#131), Konieczny went to the Oak Park office of the lottery bureau to collect a prize for what he thought was a ticket that matched five of six winning Lotto numbers. Instead, he learned he had matched all six numbers and had won a one-third share of the $11.1 million Lotto jackpot. The retired truck driver said his only plans were to "live a little better" and to be worry-free for the rest of his life. (Further details, p. 124.)

—**Catherine Span**, 66, Detroit. After claiming her $3,709,932 share, Span said she planned to retire from her job as an apartment-building manager, share the money with her two sons, and buy a dog.

144.-147. Four people won $1,005,132 each in a January 26, 1986, Lotto drawing. They were:

—**James Laguire**, 56, Freeland, who said he planned to spend his prize—part of it on a new house—so that it wouldn't be left for his children "to fight over" when he died.

—**Daniel Yesko**, 27, Ann Arbor. The father of two, who worked as a salesman, said he would spend part of his $1,005,132 on a new house.

—**Henry Buffa**, 22, Detroit. Buffa, employed as a dispatcher, said he wanted to use his winnings to take a vacation from the cold.

—**James Israel**, 49, Milan. The father of three, who worked as a millwright for Ford Motor Co., said he planned to give 10 percent of his winnings to his church.

148. **Milton Bloom**, Southfield (January 29, 1986)
Bloom had purchased two identical tickets, the only two winners in a Lotto drawing worth $1,498,217.

149. **Harry Greene**, 81, Bellaire (February 1, 1986)
Greene had been retired from his job as an electrician for the Ford Motor Co. for exactly 25 years when he hit a Lotto jackpot for $2,091,663. He set out immediately to buy a new car and a new house. He and his wife, Julia, were the parents of three children, grandparents of 12, and great-grandparents of five. (Further details, p. 80.)

150. Robert E. Krauser, 62, South Bend, Indiana (February 12, 1986)

After winning half of a $6.3 million Lotto jackpot, Krauser said he was going to follow through with plans for a fishing trip to a lake near Ludington, and then spend some time figuring out what to do with his winnings. Krauser, who was employed as an engineer for the University of Notre Dame, was married and had two children.

151. Richard L. Monteith, 63, Birmingham (February 12, 1986)

The engineer for Randall Associates in Royal Oak was nearing retirement when he split a Lotto jackpot with Robert Krauser. Monteith, married and the father of two sons, said that the unexpected $3,176,649 would go a long way toward making his retirement more pleasant.

152. Martin E. Jones, 27, Charlotte (February 19, 1986)

Jones, married and the father of a son, picked up his final unemployment check the day before he discovered he was one of two winners of a Lotto jackpot worth $4,134,098. Jones said he might use his $2,067,049 share to start a business.

153. Jerome & Gail Trembath Partnership, Rochester (February 19, 1986)

The married couple—Jerome, a dentist in Rochester, and Gail, his office secretary—who formed this lottery club, planned to buy new cars with their half, $2,067,049, of the Lotto jackpot.

154. Jerome AuClair, 49, Marine City (February 26, 1986)

After he realized that his Lotto subscription had won him half of a $4.1 million jackpot, the father of two, who worked as a tool maker, made plans to go to the Bahamas, then buy a new house.

155. The Les & Debbie Beare Family Club, Union Lake (February 26, 1986)

This family club—composed of Les Beare; his wife, Debbie; their children, Megan and Adam; and Les' mother, Roslyn—planned to purchase a new house and put money toward college educations for the children with their half, $2,065,305, of the Lotto jackpot.

156.-158. On March 12, 1986, two lottery clubs and an individual winner split a $6.6 million Lotto jackpot. The winners were:

—**Freddie Nelson**, 54, Detroit. Nelson, a utility man for Ford Motor Co., said he planned to use his one-third share, $2,194,668, to travel. He was married and the father of four children.

—**The NVM Lottery Club**. This club—composed of two sisters, Jean Vaughn of Howell and Sharon Monette of Redford Township, and their brother Patrick Norton of Farmington—had previously matched four of six Lotto numbers a total of four times before finally hitting all six. Plans for their $2,194,688 included college educations for Monette's and Norton's children, new cars, and the paying of outstanding bills.

—**Mared Trust**, Allen Park. Each member of this club—sister and brother Marilyn and Ed Bianco and their father, Pete Bianco—had selected two of the six winning numbers. Like the NVM Lottery Club, the Mared Trust had matched four of six numbers on several occasions. The Biancos said they planned to invest most of their $2,194,688 prize.

159. **Doris Mida**, 50, Ypsilanti (March 15, 1986)

The mother of three won $1,000 a week for life, with a guaranteed minimum of $1 million, in the Winter Windfall instant-game drawing. Mida said she planned to share her prize money with people and organizations that had helped her and her family through the years.

160.-162. A March 22, 1986, Lotto jackpot worth $3.8 million was shared by three winners, each of whom won $1,271,724. They were:

—**Vitina Laudicina**, 69, Novi. Laudicina said that after she had discovered she was a winner, she and her husband laid awake all night listening to their grandfather clock chime every quarter hour. She and her husband, a retired custodian for Dearborn Schools, planned to take a long-overdue honeymoon and buy cars for their two grown children.

—**Jerry B. Orlowski**, 31, Warren. The truck driver for DPD, Inc., said he planned to make sure his family members were taken care of, then he might buy a new car.

—**John A. Orzel**, 71, Dearborn. The retired Chrysler Corporation foreman announced that his wife, Helen, could now buy "anything she wants," and that the rest of the prize money, "if there was any left," would go toward making retirement more comfortable.

163. **Robert E. Latty**, 52, Baroda (March 26, 1986)

When Latty's wife, Ruby, invited him to watch the March 26, 1986, Lotto drawing on television, he declined, saying, "I never win anything." He later discovered that he had, indeed, won—$1,521,354. The toolmaker with Bendix Allied Automotive in St. Joseph planned to share his winnings with his five children and 11 grandchildren.

164. **Christopher M. Belza**, 47, Southfield (March 29, 1986)

The U.S. Postal Service letter carrier combined family birthdates for the Lotto subscription numbers that won him $2 million. He planned to take a trip to the Philippines to visit family members, with whom he said he would share his winnings.

165. **Nellie Woolfolk**, Detroit (April 2, 1986)

Woolfolk used Easy Pick to select the numbers that won his $1,451,451 Lotto jackpot.

166. **Robert W. Gray**, 68, Auburn Hills (April 5, 1986)

The retired skilled tradesman for General Motors said he was unable to sleep all night after seeing his six numbers selected in the televised Lotto drawing. He and his wife, Frances, planned to make home improvements, buy a new car, and take life easy with their $1 million, half of a jackpot they split with Richard Miller.

167. **Richard D. Miller**, 48, Grand Rapids (April 5, 1986)

In March 1986, Miller's youngest daughter had a dream that her father won a million dollars in the lottery. A week and a half later, Miller opened the Sunday newspaper and let out a holler the whole neighborhood could hear. He had matched all six numbers in the April 5 Lotto drawing and had won half of the $2 million jackpot. He and his wife, Shirley, planned to buy a new car and begin looking for a cottage on a lake.

168. **The Clarence W. Scott Lotto Club** (April 19, 1986)

The four co-workers from Blue Cross Blue Shield who made up this lottery club won the Michigan lottery's first Super Lotto jackpot. The four planned a variety of ways—retiring, making investments, buying new houses—to spend their $2 million prize.

169.-173. Five ticket holders split an April 23, 1986, Lotto jackpot worth $10 million. They were:

—**Rodriquez Family Lotto Club**, Flint. The family members who made up this lottery club planned to make investments and buy automobiles with their $2 million share.

—**Ray J. Swidan**, 31, Allen Park. Two weeks after the drawing, Swidan's wife checked a ticket she found while cleaning the glove compartment of his car and discovered it was a winner. Swidan, who owned two party stores and a gas station, planned to take his wife and two children on a vacation to the Bahamas. (Further details, p. 115.)

C. Paul Otto, 21, Dexter. Otto, a heating and cooling repairman, purchased his winning ticket at the Dexter IGA, whose owner rented a limousine to drive him to Lansing to claim his prize. (Further details, p. 71.)

—**Gaylen K. Wallis**, 34, Utica. When Wallis, a manufacturing supervisor, informed his wife that he had all six winning numbers—a stunt he had pulled many times before, including the previous week—she did not believe him.

—**Wilbert Brashears**, 61, Belleville. Brashears' wife had to remind him three times to buy Lotto tickets, one of which proved to be the winner of a $2 million share. Brashears, a machine operator for the Ford Motor Co., said he planned to retire early.

174. **Anita B. Hall**, 24, Olivet (May 3, 1986)
Hall, who worked for Form Rite in Charlotte, matched six numbers to win the second jackpot in the new Super Lotto game. She planned to use her $4 million prize to build a house, buy herself a car, and buy her boyfriend a stock car.

175.-178. On May 21, 1986, four people shared an $8.1 million Lotto jackpot. They were:

—**John Matteis**, 67, Westland. The laundromat owner planned to use his one-quarter share, $2,029,428, to pay off mortgages. Matteis was married and had two children.

—**Melvin J. Hutchinson**, 67, Alma. Hutchinson purchased a Lotto ticket using the same numbers as those on a gift subscription to his daughter, because he was unsure whether or not the subscription had expired. It hadn't, so he and his daughter both held winning tickets, each worth $2,029,428. Hutchinson, who owned Gittleman's Stores in Alma, planned to invest his winnings. (Further details, p. 146.)

—**Sally A. Hutchinson**, 43, Alma. Hutchinson announced no plans for the $2,029,428 she had won with a subscription given to her by her father. But her 6-year-old son said he wanted a "limousine he could sit in while waiting for the school bus." (Further details, p. 146.)

—**Phyllis M. Long**, 44, Spring Arbor. The mother of five rented a luxury bus and brought her husband and 19 friends with her to Lansing to claim the first installment of her $2,029,428 share of the jackpot. Long was vice president of Happy Housing Manufacturing, and said she planned to invest her winnings in that family-owned business.

179. **Clyde E. Mitchell**, 37, Detroit (May 31, 1986)

Mitchell, a Technical Sergeant with the Air Force, was commuting every weekend between Wurtsmith Air Force Base in Oscoda and his home when he hit for half of a $10 million Super Lotto jackpot. The father of six planned to apply his $5 million toward early retirement.

180. **Anne Salem**, 35, Southfield (May 31, 1986)

The married mother of three said she would enjoy her half of the $10 million Super Lotto jackpot with the "best of health."

181. **Janene Budnik**, 54, Grand Rapids (June 11, 1986)

Just half an hour before sales closed, Budnik had to be reminded to purchase a Lotto ticket, a ticket that made her the sole winner of $5,160,207. She said she planned to share the money with her two daughters and set up trust funds for her grandchildren.

182. **Lucky 6 Club**, Posen (June 25, 1986)

The two members of this club, Thomas and Loretta Olson, won a $3,271,286 Lotto jackpot with a ticket purchased at Mr. Ed's IGA in Rogers City.

183. **Rose Marie Lajoie**, 43, Livonia (June 28, 1986)

Lajoie's $10 million Super Lotto jackpot was the second-largest Michigan lottery prize to date to go to an individual. The single woman planned to take an indefinite leave of absence from her job at Chrysler, buy a new house, and engage in volunteer work. (Further details, p. 44.)

184. **Mary Frances Conry**, 36, Westland (July 2, 1986)

Conry said she thought she would "have a heart attack" when she realized she was a winner of a Lotto jackpot worth $1,522,682. The mother of a 9-year-old daughter said she planned to continue at her job as a party store cashier.

185. **Walter Schwochow**, 42, Lincoln Park (July 5, 1986)

Schwochow, married with two children, was employed at a paper mill in Port Huron when he hit for a Super Lotto jackpot worth $2 million. He planned to buy a new house, a car and furniture.

186. **S. Joseph Swierczynski**, 21, Roseville (July 9, 1986)

As the owner of Daybreak Lawn Maintenance, Swierczynski was mowing lawns for a living when he learned he was the winner of a $1,476,650 Lotto jackpot. He planned to take a break from his business, tend bar part time, and buy a house. The new Corvette he coveted, however, proved to be too expensive; he settled, instead, for a Ford Escort. (Further details, p. 66.)

187. **Merton Lee Hanna**, Detroit (July 11, 1986)

The father of five children won $1,000 a week for life, with a guaranteed minimum of $1 million, in the Winds of Fortune instant-game drawing. He planned to buy a house in the suburban Detroit area, buy land in the Upper Peninsula, and keep working at his job as a machine operator for a Detroit firm. (Further details, p. 150.)

188. **Thomas D. VanAcker**, 37, Detroit (July 12, 1986)

The Detroit police officer, married and the father of three, planned to buy a new car and take a vacation to Mississippi and Florida with part of his $2 million Super Lotto jackpot.

189. **Eileane M. Clary**, 42, Leslie (July 16, 1986)

The mother of two was playing bingo when the winning Lotto numbers were announced and she realized she was the winner of $1,437,460. She planned to buy a new mobile home and a camping trailer and also, while vacationing in Hawaii, search for television-actor Tom Selleck.

190. **Maie Allison**, 40, Muskegon (July 19, 1986)

Allison, who was employed at Shaw-Walker, a manufacturer of office equipment, said she would use her $1 million windfall, half of a Super Lotto jackpot, to retire young—or at least take a trip to Hawaii. Allison was the mother of one child.

191. **Frederick James**, 61, Detroit (July 19, 1986)

The retired detective from the Hamtramck Police Department, who was married and had four children, said he would use his $1 million half of a Super Lotto jackpot to shop for a home on the West Coast, where he could get away from Michigan winters.

192. **Romil Matti Georges**, 32, Warren (July 23, 1986)

The butcher planned to use his $1,398,746 Lotto jackpot for a vacation to Hawaii and, possibly, business ventures.

193. **Robert W. Calhoun Jr.**, 36, Royal Oak (July 26, 1986)

Calhoun purchased his $2 million winning Super Lotto ticket at the Little Professor Book Center in Oak Park.

194. **Raymond A. Christel**, 50, Roseville (August 9, 1986)

Christel, a retired grinder, rented two limousines to bring family and friends to Lansing to pick up the first installment of his $4 million Super Lotto jackpot. The father of five said he planned to buy a new house on the water, buy a new boat, and share the money with his children.

195. **Pamela Van Dyke**, 31, Grant (August 13, 1986)

Van Dyke, who was employed as a retail clerk when she won half of a $5 million Lotto jackpot, said she planned to use some of her $2.5 million prize to pay off her home mortgage, catch up on her bills, and buy toys for her three children.

196. **Margie Lowry**, 51, Lowell (August 13, 1986)

After winning half of a $5 million Lotto jackpot, the mother of six said she planned to retire immediately from her job as a factory worker for Root-Lowell Manufacturing.

197. **William Albert Olger**, 57, Lansing (August 16, 1986)

Olger, a machine repairman for Motor Wheel, said he would use his $2 million Super Lotto jackpot to retire early and travel extensively around the United States. Olger was the father of two children.

198. **Catherine Draine**, 57, Saginaw (August 27, 1986)

Draine, who worked at a private child-care agency and had five children of her own, said she would use her $1,493,317 Lotto jackpot to pay off bills, make home improvements and buy a new car.

199. **Bruce J. Elwart**, 62, Ferndale (September 3, 1986)

The General Motors retiree, who earned extra money by working as a model maker for the Terrol Tool Company, supplemented his income in a big way when he won a $1,468,211 Lotto jackpot. Elwart was married and had two children.

200. **Martha Kemp**, 42, Grand Rapids (September 6, 1986)

With a Michigan Payday instant-game ticket she purchased at the Grand Rapids bus station, Kemp won $1,000 a week for life, with a guaranteed minimum of $1 million. The mother of two planned to take a cruise, buy a house, and help pay off the mortgage on her sister's house.

201. **The Windfall Seven Partnership**, West Bloomfield (September 6, 1986)

Two club members, David Rosenmann and Karen Marx, claimed the first installment of the $3.5 million half of the Super Lotto jackpot their club had won with a ticket purchased at the Bloomfield Wine Rack.

202. Rowena M. Rudnianin, 62, Dearborn Heights (September 6, 1986)

The retired nurse's aid planned to use part of her half of a $7 million Super Lotto jackpot to buy a recreational vehicle and to travel to Las Vegas and Hawaii. Rudnianin was married and had three children.

203. Milton R. Broeders, 50, Perkins (September 20, 1986)

The laborer for Subservice Pipeline claimed that he'd had a premonition that he would win. He had no immediate plans for his $2 million prize, half of a Super Lotto jackpot.

204. Steven's Partnership, Mancelona (September 20, 1986)

Steven McLellan, 20, purchased a ticket that won half of a $4 million Super Lotto jackpot. But before claiming the prize, he formed a lottery club so that he could share his good fortune with five family members. He had no immediate plans other than to continue his job running a press at Alken-Ziegler Inc. in Kalkaska.

205.-207. Four winners held tickets that matched six numbers in a September 24, 1986, Lotto jackpot worth $5 million. Two individuals and a lottery club collected the first installment of their $1.25 million prizes. But the fourth share was never claimed, and after one year it reverted to the state School Aid Fund. The three winners were:

—**The Paintbusters**, Detroit. The club was made up of 10 co-workers from the BASF Inmont Division of Detroit, manufacturers of automotive paints.

—**Arthur Roberts**, Lansing.

—**Harold E. Liebetreau**, 68, Rockford. The retired die-setter from Wolverine Fabricating announced no specific plans for his winnings other than to "invest and spend." Liebetreau was married with two children.

208. Peggy Meyers, 33, Spring Lake (October 4, 1986)

Meyers, who won half of a $4 million Super Lotto jackpot, said she would throw a big party for her friends, "the biggest party Spring Lake has ever seen." She also planned to visit her brother, who was stationed with the Navy in Hawaii. Meyers, who worked as an inspector for Wayburn and Bartel, manufacturers of camshafts, was married and the mother of four children.

209. **Robert Pakulak**, 48, Warren (October 4, 1986)

The salesman for Kowalski Sausage rented a limousine to drive him to Lansing to claim the first installment of his $2 million half of a Super Lotto jackpot. Pakulak, the father of three, said he planned to buy a new house.

210. **Joseph Jackson**, Detroit (October 18, 1986)

Jackson didn't discover he was the winner of a $4 million Super Lotto jackpot until he read a newspaper article about the unclaimed prize 10 months later. He explained that he'd been out of town at the time of the drawing and forgot entirely about the ticket he had purchased. (Further details, p. 116.)

211. **Vivian Bennington**, 51, Drayton Plains (November 1, 1986)

Bennington, manager of a gift and furniture store in Southfield, planned to use her $2 million prize, half of a Super Lotto jackpot, to buy a house in Florida.

212. **James L. Ware**, 45, Detroit (November 1, 1986)

Ware split a $4 million Super Lotto jackpot with Vivian Bennington.

213.-215. On November 5, 1986, three winners split a $10,768,674 Lotto jackpot. They were:

—**Carolann F. Maloney**, 40, Rockwood. Maloney said plans for her $3,589,558 included a family cruise to Alaska or Hawaii, and a new home on the water. Maloney, married with three children, was the co-owner of Southern Wayne Realty in Trenton. (Further details, p. 112.

—**Ghanim Y. Shaba**, 51, Southfield.

—**Ronald E. Batts**, 42, Southfield. Batts, a registered nurse who worked at the Hutzel Emergency Room in Detroit, said he planned to share part of his $3,589,558 winnings with a friend.

216. **Sahira Younan**, 25, Sterling Heights (November 15, 1986)

Younan won $1,000 a week for life, with a guaranteed minimum of $1 million, in the Michigan 150 instant game's grand drawing. The homemaker and mother of three was unsure what she would do with her winnings.

217. The Lotto Engineers (November 19, 1986)

Heavy-equipment operators and members of the International Union of Operating Engineers made up this Detroit-area club, which won a Lotto jackpot worth $3,289,814. (Further details, p. 145.)

218. Robert M. Allen, 41, Jenison (November 22, 1986)

Allen, a salesman for Michigan Homes in Wyoming, said he planned to use his $7 million Super Lotto jackpot to buy a new house and establish trust funds for his three children.

219. Jean E. Brown, Bellevue (November 26, 1986)

Brown said she planned to share her $1,535,690 Lotto jackpot with her family and set up trust funds for her grandchildren.

220. John Upchurch, 29, Muskegon (November 29, 1986)

The Howmet Company employee planned to use his $2 million Super Lotto jackpot to pay off bills, buy a house, and, possibly, buy a new sailboat. (Further details, p. 113.)

221. Maher A. Jabero, 33, Northville (December 10, 1986)

Jabero, married with three children, planned to buy a new house with part of his $3,076,155 Lotto jackpot.

222. George M. Webster, 56, Taylor (December 13, 1986)

Webster, who said he was already semi-retired, planned to buy a used car with the first installment of his $4 million Super Lotto jackpot. Webster was married and had two children.

223. Josephine Pelot, 49, Redford Township (December 17, 1986)

The Sweden House cook said plans for her $1,430,931 Lotto jackpot included a Las Vegas vacation and, perhaps, a cruise. Pelot was married and had two children.

224. Sin-J Lotto Club, Cheboygan (December 24, 1986)

Members of the club, four co-workers at the Citizen's National Bank in Cheboygan, won a $1,544,494 Lotto jackpot.

225.-227. Three winners split a January 7, 1987, Lotto jackpot worth $3,329,796. Those ticket-holders, each of whom won $1,109,932, were:

—**Will Richey**, 53, Detroit. Richey's plans included expansion of his business, self-publication of an inspirational book, and a continued commitment to helping high-school-age students. Richey, married and the father of twin girls, was the owner/manager of Miracle Performance Carpet Care Company. (Further details, p. 131.)

—**Lawrence J. Saladin**, 49, Dearborn. Saladin, a millwright for the Ford Motor Company, planned to buy a new car and take a vacation to Hawaii. Saladin was the father of one child.

—**Loretta Dunec**, 62, Harper Woods. The retired school teacher planned to visit her two children, one in California and one in Alaska.

228. Fred L. Goodson, 59, Pontiac (January 10, 1987)

The General Motors retiree made it clear that he did not intend to let winning a $10 million Super Lotto jackpot change him much. "I like cornbread and beans rather than fancy dinners. I want to be myself," he said. (Further details, p. 46.)

229. Byron C. Fiedler, 55, Sterling Heights (January 21, 1987)

The father of three planned to travel to Hawaii. He also said he would share some of his $3,146,787 Lotto jackpot with his favorite charities.

230. Rodney C. Kniebbe, 42, Marshall (January 24, 1987)

The father of two planned to use his half of a $4 million Super Lotto jackpot to purchase a new car and do some traveling.

231. Evelyn Miller, Taylor (January 24, 1987)

Miller won $2 million, half of a Super Lotto jackpot, with a ticket she purchased at Arbor Drugs in Taylor.

232. David N. Miller, 34, Benton Harbor (January 28, 1987)

Miller, a district manager for Pepsi Cola, said he would use his $1,474,987 Lotto jackpot to pay off bills and make investments. Miller had three children.

233. Nicholas R. Klein, 59, St. Clair Shores (February 4, 1987)

Klein, who worked in the shipping department of a graphics distributing company, said that plans for his $1,499,583 Lotto jackpot included fixing up his home, taking a vacation, and making investments.

234. Katherine Myatt, 29, Eau Claire (February 14, 1987)

Myatt, who worked at the Plaza Zephyr gas station in Benton Harbor, won her $7 million Super Lotto jackpot on Valentines Day. The mother of one planned to buy a new house and car. (Further details, p. 122.)

235.-237. Three people held winning tickets for a February 18, 1987, Lotto jackpot worth $3.1 million. They were:

—**Wanda J. Capers**, 35, Detroit. After winning her $1,037,815 share, Capers, who was married and the mother of one son, kept her job as a janitor at Great Lakes Steel Company.

—**Charles W. Craig**, 59, Indian River. The General Motors retiree and father of two children said he planned to use his share of the jackpot to make home improvements and investments.

—**Darlene Pruneau**, Brighton. Prunea, a part-time waitress for the Nugget Restaurant in Brighton, planned to use her $1,037,815 to pay off bills, make investments, and help her four children and four grandchildren.

238. **Daniel F. Grabowski**, 36, Dearborn (March 7, 1987)

Grabowski, a construction superintendent for the General Development Company, said he would use part of his $7 million Super Lotto jackpot to set up college funds for his two children.

239. **Lucky 4 Painters Club**, Troy (March 11, 1987)

The club, composed of journeyman painters, won a $3,039,653 Lotto jackpot.

240. **Natalie L. Armendariz**, Detroit (March 14, 1987)

Armendariz was the sole winner of a Super Lotto jackpot worth $2 million.

241. **Lot A Noah** (March 21, 1987)

The workers at CEC Products in Center Line who made up this lottery club won a $2 million Super Lotto jackpot. Two of them, James L. Chesney of South Lyon and John L. Sharrow of Romulus, had also been members of the Lotto Engineers, a club that won a November 19, 1986, jackpot worth $3,289,814. (Further details, p. 145.)

242. **Kerilee McCarthy**, 22, Mt. Clemens (March 25, 1987)

The Macomb Community College student planned to share her $1,357,089 Lotto jackpot with her father, who had paid for the winning ticket.

243. **Craig E. Bruder**, 24, Taylor (April 4, 1987)

Bruder, who was employed as a dispatcher, planned to apply his half of a $2 million Super Lotto jackpot toward investments.

244. **The Mooahesh and Dibartolomeo Lotto Club**, Center Line (April 4, 1987)

Members of this lottery club that won half of a $2 million Super

Lotto jackpot were Kamel Mooahesh and Edward Dibartolomeo.

245.-247. On April 8, 1987, a lottery club and two individuals split a $3 million Lotto jackpot. The winners of $1 million each were:

—Louis Blessman Sr., Detroit.

—William E. Hogan Sr., St. Helen. The retired General Motors employee planned to use the first installment of his prize to buy a new home and take a vacation to Arkansas.

—Double 3 Lotto Club, which was composed of workers from Standard Automotive in Muskegon.

248. Jane A. Lasiewicki, 44, Saginaw (April 18, 1987)
   The secretary for a security company planned to use portions of her $4 million Super Lotto jackpot to buy a new house and car, and make arrangements for her three children's education.

249.-251. Three people held winning tickets, worth $1 million each, that matched the Lotto numbers drawn April 22, 1987. The jackpot winners were:

—Jack Brockway, 62, Quincy. Brockway, married with three children, planned immediate retirement from his job as a car salesman.

—James W. Collier, Williamston. The plant superintendent at R. N. Fink Manufacturing planned to purchase a fishing boat and take a vacation to Hawaii. Collier had eight children.

—Donna Rogers, Saginaw. The data processor for Car Quest Auto Parts planned to purchase a ranch where she could raise her 11 Arabian horses. Rogers was married and the mother of one daughter.

252. Karen Brown, 40, Addison (April 25, 1987)
   The housekeeper for Addison Community Hospital said she would use her half of a $2 million Super Lotto jackpot to buy a new car and make investments. Brown was married and the mother of four children.

253. Raymond A. Lehtinen, 65, Livonia (April 25, 1987)
   The Ford Motor Co. retiree said he planned to use his $1 million prize, half of a Super Lotto jackpot, to make home improvements.

254. Elma I. Nurmela, 76, Watton (May 6, 1987)
   The widowed mother of three won $3 million in the final Lotto

6-of-40 game, which was discontinued. The Baraga County woman, who won her jackpot with a subscription, announced that she would do "good things" with her money.

255. **7 Million To One Club**, Grosse Pointe Woods (May 20, 1987)
Members of this club, Mary Derany and Robert and JoAnn Barto shared a $9,348,754 Super Lotto jackpot.

256. **George F. Shaffer**, 92, Grand Rapids (May 27, 1987)
The retired steamfitter and welder, who was living with his wife, Glenna, at the Veteran's Facility in Grand Rapids, became the nation's oldest lottery millionaire to date when he won a $3,032,863 Super Lotto jackpot. His plans included moving into a new home and hiring someone to care for him and his wife. (Further details, p. 79.)

257. **Ollie McKinney Jr.**, 55, Detroit (June 3, 1987)
McKinney, who was the Director of Employment and Training for the city of Detroit, won a Super Lotto jackpot worth $3,024,313. He and his wife, Carole, a Michigan Bell employee, had two children.

258. **J. Elaine Baker**, Battle Creek (June 27, 1987)
Baker, who was employed as an auditor, won half of a $14,056,382 Super Lotto jackpot. She planned to use a portion of her $7,028,191 share to purchase a new home. (Further details, p. 127.)

259. **Albert J. Fuciarelli**, 40, Westland (June 27, 1987)
Fuciarelli, who worked as a head grocery clerk, said he planned to use his half of a $14 million Super Lotto jackpot to start a business of his own. He was the father of two children.

260. **Anna J. Savage**, 58, Beaverton (July 11, 1987)
When the retired bookkeeper realized she had a winning ticket—which turned out to be the sole winner of a $7.5 million Super Lotto jackpot—she videotaped it, "just to be safe," then locked it in a fireproof safe until she could redeem it. She and her husband, Marlin, had three children. (Further details, p. 120.)

261. **Frances L. Dinkel**, 49, Pinckney (July 18, 1987)
The mother of three won a $3,242,412 Super Lotto jackpot.

262. **Arthur J. Banaszak**, 58, Lincoln Park (July 25, 1987)
The bachelor, who won a $1,554,304 Super Lotto jackpot, retired immediately from his job as an appliance repairman.

263. Our Gang Lotto Club, St. Johns (July 29, 1987)

The nine friends who formed this club divided a $1.5 million Super Lotto jackpot among themselves.

264. Clifford A. Nutto, 48, St. Joseph (August 15, 1987)

Nutto won the largest individual lottery prize in Michigan to date, a $13 million Super Lotto jackpot. Plans for his winnings included buying a fishing boat and a new truck and taking a vacation. Nutto, who was married and had three children, worked in a sheet-metal shop and also as a part-time farmer. (Further details, p. 47.)

265. Charles E. Johnson, 37, Oak Park (September 5, 1987)

Johnson, one of two winners who shared a $12 million Super Lotto jackpot, retired immediately from his job as an assemblyman for General Motors.

266. Anna E. Michalski, 69, Traverse City (September 5, 1987)

Michalski, who won half of a Super Lotto jackpot, planned to share her $6 million with her three children, set up a trust fund for her granddaughter, and travel, possibly to Spain. (Further details, p. 57.)

267. Lydia Frizzell, 57, St. Joseph (September 9, 1987)

After winning a $1.5 million Super Lotto jackpot, Frizzell and her husband planned immediate retirement. The couple had six children.

268. Delbert Whitney, 60, Midland (September 19, 1987)

The self-employed realtor, who won a $5,722,390 Super Lotto jackpot, planned to share the money with his wife and three children and take a cruise.

269. Patricia A. Bloess, 72, Dearborn (September 23, 1987)

The married mother of three planned to invest her $1.5 million Super Lotto jackpot and possibly take a vacation to Hawaii.

270. Gary Moore, 43, Harrison (September 30, 1987)

Moore, who was married and had two children, planned to retire from his job as an account manager for Oven Fresh Bread. Other plans for his $3,262,779 Super Lotto jackpot included the purchase of a new mobile home and travel.

271. Emory L. Smith, Taylor (October 17, 1987)

Smith was one of two winners who split a $7.5 million Super Lotto jackpot.

272. **Kelley Choate**, 70, Adrian (October 17, 1987)

Choate, part-owner of a janitorial service, planned to purchase a new house with his $3.75 million prize, half of a Super Lotto jackpot. Choate was married and had two children.

273. **Casimer S. Trojanowski**, 59, Yale (October 28, 1987)

Trojanowski, who worked for GM's Chevrolet Division, said he would use his $5,145,002 Super Lotto jackpot to build his "dream house." Trojanowski was married and had two children. (Further details, p. 113.)

274. **Frank Gorske**, 73, Linwood (November 7, 1987)

Following a "hot streak" during which he had won numerous small lottery, bingo, and poker jackpots, the retired bait-and-tackle shop owner said he knew he was due to win something big. While playing bingo, he learned he was a winner—the sole winner, it turned out—of a $5,444,898 Super Lotto jackpot. (Further details, p. 139.)

275. **Joseph A. Polachek**, 68, Owosso (November 21, 1987)

After he had picked up the first installment of his $3,814,733 prize, half of a Super Lotto jackpot, the retiree from the Flint Buick plant, admitted that his horoscope had predicted he would win money soon, and that, the night of the drawing, he had dreamed he would win the lottery jackpot. (Further details, p. 123.)

276. **Brenda S. Jarvis**, 38, Milan (November 21, 1987)

After learning that she had matched all six winning numbers in a Super Lotto drawing, Jarvis and her husband, Gary, sat up all night drinking coffee and talking. Jarvis won half of a $7,629,466 jackpot, and neither she, a manager of administrative services for an Ann Arbor company, nor her husband, a plumber, were sure whether they would keep working.

277. **Ronald N. Rosen**, 46, Lansing (November 28, 1987)

The manager of Leonard's Luggage, in Lansing, combined the birthdates of three friends to win half of a $3.2 million Super Lotto jackpot. He said he planned to keep working and live essentially the way he always had, but would replace the car he called "Dog Meat," and repay debts to his parents.

278. **Vitore Vulaj**, 23, Detroit (November 28, 1987)

After playing the lottery only four times, the part-time waitress won $1,591,875, half of a Super Lotto jackpot. She planned to use the money for her children's future education. (Further details, p. 121.)

279. Phil J. Golden, 55, Grand Rapids (December 16, 1987)

The former professional hockey player won an $11,196,667 Super Lotto jackpot, the second-largest individual prize awarded to date in the Michigan lottery. Golden, who worked as a press operator, planned to share the money with his five sons, purchase land in the U.P., and build a log cabin. (Further details, p. 122.)

280. Gerald N. Henshaw, 57, Suttons Bay (December 26, 1987)

The commercial loan officer at a Traverse City bank planned to use his $5,305,206 Super Lotto jackpot to provide for his five children's and three grandchildren's educations.

Important Dates in the Michigan Lottery

May 16, 1972:   Voters approve Public Act 239 by two-to-one margin, establishing the Michigan Bureau of State Lottery.

November 13, 1972:   Lottery tickets go on sale in Michigan for the first time in 143 years.

November 24, 1972:   The first winning numbers are drawn in the Michigan lottery.

November 30, 1972:   The first Super Prize drawing is held, awarding nine prizes ranging from $10,000 to $200,000.

February 22, 1973:   The first millionaire drawing is held, making Hermus Millsaps, of Taylor, Michigan's first million-dollar winner.

July 24, 1975:	First televised weekly drawing.
October 7, 1975:	First instant-game tickets on sale.
January 12, 1976:	First instant-game millionaire, Carolyn Jones, of Detroit, is selected in a special drawing.
October 7, 1976:	Michigame sales begin.
June 6, 1977:	The Daily 3 game begins.
May 7, 1981:	Michigame sales end.
May 13, 1981:	Public Act 40 is signed by the governor, earmarking lottery profits to go to the state School Aid Fund.
May 14, 1981:	Superplay sales begin.
October 4, 1981:	The Daily 4 game begins.
August 28, 1982:	Card Game sales begin.
June 21, 1984:	Superplay sales end.
August 14, 1984:	Lotto 6/40 sales begin.
September 1, 1984:	Thomas LaPenna, of Marquette, wins first Lotto jackpot of $2,950,259.
November 17, 1984:	Patricia Parker, of Kalamazoo, wins Lotto jackpot of $10,397,771.
July 13, 1985:	Three winners share jackpot of $15.2 million.
August 12, 1985:	Card Game sales end.
April 19, 1986:	Super Lotto 6/44 sales begin.
May 6, 1987:	Lotto 6/40 sales end.
August 15, 1987:	Clifford Nutto, of St. Joseph, wins Super Lotto jackpot of $13,000,000.
January 20, 1988:	A $28.9 million Super Lotto jackpot—the largest Michigan lottery prize to date—is shared by five winners.

Famous
Winning Numbers

First winning numbers in first Michigan Weekly
    Game, November 24, 1972   130   544

First Daily 3 winners,
    June 6, 1977   420

First Daily 4 winners,
    October 5, 1981   3870

First Lotto numbers drawn,
    August 25, 1984   4,5,18,21,32,40

First Lotto jackpot won,
    September 1, 1984   5,6,8,10,22,39

$10,397,771 Lotto jackpot,
    November 17, 1984   5,6,8,12,19,39

$13,300,931 Lotto jackpot,
    January 9, 1985   2,9,14,18,30,36

$15,167,989 Lotto jackpot,
July 13, 1985   11,16,21,24,25,33

$11,129,797 Lotto jackpot,
January 1, 1986   11,16,19,22,33,35

First Super Lotto drawing,
April 19, 1986   6,9,29,30,35,44

$10,000,000 Lotto jackpot,
April 23, 1986   1,12,15,26,36,40

$10,000,000 Super Lotto jackpot,
May 31, 1986   1,7,10,15,34,37

$10,000,000 Super Lotto jackpot,
June 28, 1986   2,13,14,25,28,42

$10,768,674 Lotto jackpot,
November 5, 1986   4,9,16,18,19,20

$10,000,000 Super Lotto jackpot,
January 10, 1987   1,10,13,17,27,43

$14,056,382 Super Lotto jackpot,
June 27,1987   10,13,20,25,40,41

$13,000,000 Super Lotto jackpot,
August 15, 1987   1,11,18,27,39,44

$12,000,000 Super Lotto jackpot,
September 5, 1987   4,10,11,23,25,29

$11,196,667 Super Lotto jackpot,
December 16, 1987   8,22,26,38,39,44

$28,914,801 Super Lotto jackpot,
January 20, 1988   2,26,29,31,35,41

The Odds of Winning

Game	Prize	Odds
Weekly Game	$25	1:250
Weekly Game	Super Prize finalist	1:500,000
Weekly Game	Million-Dollar Drawing semi-finalist	1:250,000
Weekly Game	$1,000,000	1:29,969,999
Instant Tickets*	Free Ticket	1:6
	$2	1:12
	$5	1:75
	$10	1:300
	$20	1:600
	$50	1:1001
	$1000	1:33,690
Daily 3	Straight	1:1,000
Daily 3	Boxed	1:166
Daily 4	Straight	1:10,000
Daily 4	4-Way Box	1:2,500
Daily 4	6-Way Box	1:1,666
Daily 4	12-Way Box	1:833
Daily 4	24-Way Box	1:416
Lotto (6/40)	Six Numbers	1:3,838,380
Lotto	Five Numbers	1:18,816
Lotto	Four Numbers	1:456
Super Lotto (6/44)	Six Numbers	1:7,059,052
Super Lotto	Five Numbers	1:30,961
Super Lotto	Four Numbers	1:669

*"Three Cards Up" game January - March, 1988

Million Dollar Jackpots By Game*

Year	Weekly (50 Cent)	Instant	Michi-Game	Super-Play	Lotto	Super Lotto	Total
1973	8						8
1974	7						7
1975	5						5
1976	3	5					8
1977	3	3					6
1978	1	3	2				6
1979		3	1				4
1980		4					4
1981		3					3
1982		3					3
1983		5		1			6
1984		3			11		14
1985		6			57		63
1986		5			59	24	88
1987					18	37	55
Total	27	43	3	1	145	61	280

*Includes jackpots won by individuals and lottery clubs.

How Large Jackpots Are Funded and Paid

From the very first million-dollar drawing in 1972, large jackpots in all Michigan lottery games have been funded and paid in installments rather than in a lump sum. Following is an analysis of that funding and payout structure using a typical Super Lotto game as an example.

In this example, ticket sales for the week have totaled $3,181,080. Legislation requires that the lottery return, "as nearly as is practicable," 45 percent of those gross proceeds as payment to winners.* In this example, the grand prize for matching all six numbers is $1.5 million (the minimum prize in Super Lotto). Since that jackpot by itself exceeds the 45-percent limit, if the lottery bureau paid it in a lump sum, it would be the only prize. There would be no money left to reward ticket holders who matched four or five numbers.

So instead of a lump-sum payment the bureau places 25 percent of the tickets sales—$795,270 in this case—into an annuity fund administered by the Michigan Department of Treasury. The $1.5 million prize for a match-six winner is then paid in 20 annual $75,000 in-

---

*Actual jackpots paid are 48% of gross *earnings*, which include ticket sales, interest on investments, unclaimed prizes, license fees, and other sources of income.

stallments out of that account. From the principal plus interest, at the end of the 20 years the winner has been paid a total of $1,500,000, and the account is exhausted. (See chart below)

The remaining 21 percent of the sales amount earmarked for prizes—the amount that is *not* invested—is immediately paid out as lesser prizes. In our example, 8 percent ($254,486) is divided among ticket holders who matched five numbers, and 13 percent ($413,540) is divided among winners who matched four numbers.

By paying the large jackpot in installments, then, it has become possible to hand out an additional $668,026 in prizes to winners who otherwise would have received nothing for their near-misses.

Year	Investment Balance	Interest Earned	Payments to Winner	End Balance
1987	$795,270.00		$75,000	$720,270.00
1988	720,270.00	$57,621.60	$75,000	$702,891.60
1989	$702,891.60	$56,231.33	$75,000	$684,122.93
1990	$684,122.93	$54,729.83	$75,000	$663,852.76
1991	$663,852.76	$53,108.22	$75,000	$641,960.98
1992	$641,960.98	$51,356.88	$75,000	$618,317.86
1993	$618,317.86	$49,465.43	$75,000	$592,783.29
1994	$592,783.29	$47,422.66	$75,000	$565,205.95
1995	$565,205.95	$45,216.48	$75,000	$535,422.43
1996	$535,422.43	$42,833.79	$75,000	$503,256.22
1997	$503,256.22	$40,260.50	$75,000	$468,516.72
1998	$468,516.72	$37,481.34	$75,000	$430,998.06
1999	$430,998.06	$34,479.84	$75,000	$390,477.91
2000	$390,477.91	$31,238.23	$75,000	$346,716.14
2001	$346,716.14	$27,737.29	$75,000	$299,453.43
2002	$299,453.43	$23,956.27	$75,000	$248,409.70
2003	$248,409.70	$19,872.78	$75,000	$193,282.48
2004	$193,282.48	$15,462.60	$75,000	$133,745.08
2005	$133,745.08	$10,699.61	$75,000	$ 69,444.68
2006	$ 69,444.68	$ 5,555.57	$75,000	$ .26
TOTALS		$704,730.26	$1,500,00	

County Distribution of Million-Dollar Lottery Winners

(Through 1987)

(Includes members of million-dollar-winning lottery clubs when known)

County	Number of Winners	Winners Per 100,000 Population
Alcona	1	10.3
Alger	0	0
Allegan	3	3.7
Alpena	0	0
Antrim	2	12.4
Arenac	0	0
Baraga	1	11.8
Barry	0	0
Bay	3	2.5
Benzie	0	0
Berrien	5	2.9
Branch	1	2.5
Calhoun	2	1.4
Cass	0	0
Charlevoix	1	5.0
Cheboygan	2	9.7
Chippewa	0	0
Clare	2	8.4

Clinton	2	3.6
Crawford	1	10.6
Delta	3	7.7
Dickinson	1	3.9
Eaton	3	3.4
Emmet	0	0
Genesee	5	1.1
Gladwin	1	5.0
Gogebic	0	0
Grand Traverse	2	3.6
Gratiot	2	4.9
Hillsdale	1	2.4
Houghton	0	0
Huron	2	5.5
Ingham	8	2.9
Ionia	1	1.9
Iosco	0	0
Iron	0	0
Isabella	0	0
Jackson	7	4.6
Kalamazoo	2	0.9
Kalkaska	0	0
Kent	8	1.8
Keweenaw	0	0
Lake	1	13.0
Lapeer	1	1.4
Leelanau	1	7.1
Lenawee	4	4.4
Livingston	3	3.0
Luce	0	0
Mackinac	0	0
Macomb	22	3.2
Manistee	1	4.3
Marquette	3	4.0
Mason	0	0
Mecosta	0	0
Menominee	0	0

(Continued on p. 206)

COUNTY DISTRIBUTION
OF MILLION-DOLLAR LOTTERY WINNERS
(Continued from p. 205)

County	Number of Winners	Winners Per 100,000 Population
Midland	2	2.7
Missaukee	0	0
Monroe	4	3.0
Montcalm	1	2.1
Montmorency	0	0
Muskegon	3	1.9
Newaygo	1	2.9
Oakland	36	3.6
Oceana	0	0
Oge·naw	0	0
Ontonagon	0	0
Osceola	0	0
Oscoda	0	0
Otsego	1	6.7
Ottawa	2	1.3
Presque Isle	1	7.0
Roscommon	5	30.5
Saginaw	4	1.8
St. Clair	4	2.9
St. Joseph	0	0
Sanilac	0	0
Schoolcraft	0	0
Shiawassee	1	1.4
Tuscola	1	1.8
Van Buren	1	1.5
Washtenaw	4	1.5
Wayne	103	4.4
Wexford	0	0

City Distribution of Million-Dollar Lottery Winners

(Through 1987)

(Includes members of million-dollar-winning lottery clubs when known)

City-Number of Winners

Addison-1
Adrian-1
Allegan-1
Allen Park-3
Alma-2
Ann Arbor-2
Auburn-1
Auburn Hills-1
Bangor-1
Baroda-1
Barton City-1
Battle Creek-1
Beaverton-1
Bellaire-1
Belleville-2
Bellevue-1
Benton Harbor
Birmingham-1
Brighton-1

Brooklyn-2
Canton-1
Capac-1
Center Line-2
Champion-1
Charlotte-1
Cheboygan-1
Clarkston-2
Clarksville
Dearborn-6
Dearborn Heights-1
Detroit-43
Dexter-1
Drayton Plains-2
East Detroit-3
East Jordan-1
Eau Claire-1
Farmington-1

(Continued on p. 208)

CITY DISTRIBUTION OF MILLION-DOLLAR LOTTERY WINNERS
(Continued from p. 207)

City-Number of Winners

Farmington Hills-1
Ferndale-1
Flat Rock-1
Flint-3
Frankenmuth-1
Fraser-3
Freeland-1
Gaylord-1
Gladstone-1
Grand Rapids-6
Grant-1
Grayling-1
Greenville-1
Grosse Pointe Woods-1
Grosse Pointe Park-2
Hamtramck-1
Harper Woods-1
Harrison-2
Hazel Park-1
Holland-1
Holt-1
Houghton Lake-2
Howell-1
Imlay City-1
Indian River-1
Irons-1
Isabella-1
Jackson-2
Jenison-1
Kalamazoo-2
Kaleva-1
Kinde-1
Kingsford-1
Lansing-5

Leonard-1
Leslie-1
Lincoln Park-2
Linwood-1
Litchfield-1
Livonia-4
Lowell-2
Madison Heights-1
Mancelona-1
Marine City-1
Marquette-2
Marshall-1
Midland-2
Milan-2
Millington-1
Monroe-2
Montrose-1
Morenci-1
Mt. Clemens-4
Munith-1
Muskegon-2
Northville-2
Novi-3
Oak Park-1
Olivet-1
Onsted-1
Owosso-1
Perkins-1
Pinckney-1
Plainwell-1
Pleasant Lake-1
Plymouth-3
Pontiac-1
Posen-1
Prudenville-1

Quincy-1
Redford Township-2
River Rouge-1
Rochester-2
Rockwood-2
Romeo-1
Roscommon-1
Roseville-3
Royal Oak-2
Saginaw-3
St. Clair Shores-3
St. Helen-1
St. Johns-2
St. Joseph-2
Sebewaing-1
Spring Arbor-1
Spring Lake-1
Sterling Heights-3
Suttons Bay-1
Swartz Creek-1
Taylor-9
Traverse City-2
Trenton-1
Troy-2
Union Lake-1
Utica-3
Warren-4
Waterford-1
Watton-1
West Bloomfield-1
Westland-9
Whitehall-1
Williamston-1
Wyandotte-1
Yale-2
Ypsilanti-1
Unknown-1

Out-of-State Winners

Giles, Wisconsin-1
Lansing, Illinois-1
South Bend, Indiana-1
Sylvania, Ohio-1
Toledo, Ohio-2
West Unity, Ohio-1

Age-Group Distribution of Million-Dollar Lottery Winners

(Through 1987)

(Includes members of million-dollar-winning lottery clubs when known)

Age Group	Number of Winners	Percent of Total
20-24	13	4.7
25-29	17	6.2
30-34	25	9.1
35-39	17	6.2
40-44	29	10.5
45-49	26	9.5
50-54	27	9.8
55-59	30	10.9
60-64	18	6.5
65-69	20	7.3
70-74	11	4.0
75 and older	7	2.5
Unknown	35	12.7

Where the Money Goes

B y legislative mandate, the Michigan Bureau of State Lottery must distribute gross lottery earnings (ticket sales plus investments, unclaimed prizes, license fees, and other miscellaneous income) according to this schedule:

> 48% —Prizes.
> 41% —State School Aid Fund.
> 6.6% —Commissions to lottery ticket sales agents.
> 4.4% —Operating costs.

Prizes: See Appendix VI, p. 202.

School Aid: Lottery funds earmarked for the School Aid Fund are turned over to the Michigan Department of Education for distribution to individual school districts, according to the Michigan School Aid Formula. Those funds support K-12 education.

Sales Agent Commissions: Michigan lottery ticket vendors (about 8,000 in 1986) collect a commission of 6 percent on their lottery sales. In addition, they receive a commission of 2 percent of the dollar value of the prize for redeeming winning tickets up to $600. (Larger prizes can only be redeemed at lottery offices). In 1986 the average vendor earned about $8,380 in lottery commissions.

Operating Costs: The lottery bureau's operating costs include salaries, wages, and fringe benefits for its employees, plus such expenses as advertising, printing costs for instant tickets, paper stock for on-line game tickets, and the leasing of dedicated telephone lines for on-line game terminals.

About the Author

J erry Dennis is a full-time freelance writer whose articles, essays, and short fiction have appeared in such publications as *Michigan Natural Resources Magazine*, *Great Lakes Quarterly*, the *Detroit News*, *Canoe*, *Sports Afield*, *River Runner*, *Flyfisher*, and *Gray's Sporting Journal*. He is coauthor (with Craig Date) of *Canoeing Michigan Rivers: A Comprehensive Guide to 45 Rivers* (Friede Publications, 1986).

Dennis, 33, lives in Traverse City with his wife, Gail, a freelance graphic artist, and their two sons, Aaron and Nicholas.

OTHER TITLES BY FRIEDE PUBLICATIONS

Michillaneous
Murder, Michigan
Mich-Again's Day
Michillaneous II
Fish Michigan — Great Lakes
Canoeing Michigan Rivers
Natural Michigan
A Guide to 199 Michigan Waterfalls